MW01069529

HELEN
TAFT

MODERN FIRST LADIES

Lewis L. Gould, Editor

TITLES IN THE SERIES

First Lady Florence Harding: Behind the Tragedy and Controversy, Katherine A. S. Sibley

Grace Coolidge: The People's Lady in Silent Cal's White House, Robert H. Ferrell

Lou Henry Hoover: Activist First Lady, Nancy Beck Young

Mamie Doud Eisenhower: The General's First Lady, Marilyn Irvin Holt

Jacqueline Kennedy: First Lady of the New Frontier, Barbara A. Perry

Lady Bird Johnson: Our Environmental First Lady, Lewis L. Gould

Betty Ford: Candor and Courage in the White House, John Robert Greene

Rosalynn Carter: Equal Partner in the White House, Scott Kaufman

Nancy Reagan: On the White House Stage, James G. Benze Jr.

Barbara Bush: Presidential Matriarch, Myra G. Gutin

Hillary Rodham Clinton: Polarizing First Lady, Gil Troy

HELEN TAFT

OUR MUSICAL FIRST LADY

LEWIS L. GOULD

UNIVERSITY PRESS OF KANSAS

© 2010 by the University Press of Kansas
All rights reserved
Published by the University Press of Kansas (Lawrence, Kansas 66045),
which was organized by the Kansas Board of Regents and is operated
and funded by Emporia State University, Fort Hays State University,
Kansas State University, Pittsburg State University, the University
of Kansas, and Wichita State University
Library of Congress Cataloging-in-Publication Data

Gould, Lewis L.
Helen Taft : our musical first lady / Lewis L. Gould.
    p. cm. — (Modern first ladies)
Includes bibliographical references and index.
ISBN 978-0-7006-1731-9 (cloth : alk. paper)
1. Taft, Helen Herron, 1861–1943. 2. Presidents' spouses—United
States—Biography. 3. Taft, William H. (William Howard),
1857–1930. I. Title.
E762.1.T12G68 2010
973.91'2092—dc22
[B]
2010005703

British Library Cataloguing-in-Publication Data is available.
Printed in the United States of America
10 9 8 7 6 5 4 3 2 1
The paper used in this publication is recycled and contains 30 percent
postconsumer waste. It is acid free and meets the minimum requirements of
the American National Standard for Permanence of Paper for Printed Library
Materials Z39.48–1992.

CONTENTS

Notes

ACKNOWLEDGMENTS

This book could not have been written without the assistance of many individuals and libraries across the country. My greatest debt is to two dedicated scholars, Stacy Cordery and Kristie Miller. During the 1990s, Cordery provided copies of documents from the papers of Mabel Boardman and Charles Phelps Taft, long before I even contemplated working on Helen Taft. These letters supplied a foundation for further research when I did turn to Mrs. Taft's tenure in the White House.

During the actual research and writing of the book, Kristie Miller made copies of key letters in the papers of Robert A. Taft, Helen Taft Manning, and the Grosvenor family at the Library of Congress that I could not have done on my own. Her thoughtful work enabled me to understand Mrs. Taft's interest in music, for example, in ways that papers of William Howard Taft, available on microfilm, did not reveal. Without the unselfish cooperation of Stacy and Kristie, this book would have been less thorough and less complete about what Helen Taft achieved as first lady.

Anne Bogaev of Austin, Texas, kindly put me in touch with Mrs. Helen Manning Hunter. Mrs. Hunter was a rich source of information about her grandmother during the 1920s. I am indebted to Mrs. Hunter for her generosity in sharing these details of the Tafts and their lifestyle with me.

For timely assistance in locating documents and illustrations, I owe thanks to Kevin Proffitt at the American Jewish Archives in Cincinnati, Martha Sachs of the Penn State Harrisburg Library, Mary Linnemann at the Hargrett Library of the University of Georgia, Anne Shepherd at the Cincinnati Historical Society, and Karen Smith at the Dalhousie University Archives and Special Collections. Jeni Dahmus at the Library of the Julliard School provided timely information about the Kneisel Quartet.

Jason dePreaux did invaluable research for me in the microfilmed edition of the William Howard Taft Papers at the University of Texas at Austin. I also owe thanks for research ideas and leads to other sources to Gregor Benko, Jennifer Ferrone, David Hudson, Mary Talusan Lacanlale, Dall Wilson, and Jeremy Young.

Stacy Cordery provided an incisive and thorough critique of the book. Jonathan Lurie read the entire manuscript and supplied many thoughtful suggestions and insights. The reader for the University Press of Kansas showed me some lines of research that proved fruitful. Karen Gould encouraged me to emphasize Mrs. Taft's musical interests, compiled much of the factual information about the artists who appeared at the White House, and saved me from the countless errors that might befall a neophyte in the world of classical music. None of these generous friends and colleagues are responsible for any errors that might remain in this book. Those are the result of my mistakes in writing and research.

Lewis L. Gould
Austin, Texas

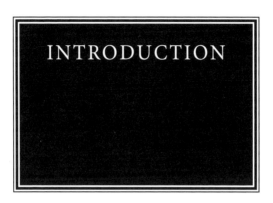

INTRODUCTION

Of all the twentieth-century first ladies, Helen Herron Taft remains the most obscure and least understood. To the degree that her White House career is examined at all, coverage consists of her desire to see her husband as president, the effects of her stroke in May 1909, and the authorship of the first true first lady memoir in 1914. Although she served longer than Ellen Wilson, Florence Harding, Jacqueline Kennedy, and Betty Ford, Taft did not attract a biographer until 2005. And even though her time in the White House equaled the tenures of Lou Henry Hoover, Rosalynn Carter, and Barbara Bush, she has never seemed as important as those three modern successors.

Helen Taft deserves better from history. When she came to the White House in March 1909, she brought with her ambitious goals to make Washington, D.C., the social and cultural center of the nation. The breadth of her design for the national capital, though it was scarcely begun, warrants more careful analysis than it has received. To implement that vision, Nellie Taft was prepared to exert her will within her husband's administration. The assertion of her influence contributed in a direct way to the development of William Howard Taft's break with his one-time patron and close friend, Theodore Roosevelt.

This book argues that Helen Taft did succeed in two areas, despite her physical disability. She secured cherry trees from Japan that, after an initial setback, transformed the look of monumental Washington in a manner that did not occur again until Lady Bird Johnson during the 1960s. Important as the cherry trees were, they were secondary to Helen Taft's main campaign: to fill the White House with the finest serious music and musicians that her country afforded. In that endeavor, she achieved a record of bringing excellent performers to the executive mansion that can stand comparison with any of her successors as first lady.

Among the famous musicians who came to play for Mrs. Taft and her guests were the violinists Fritz Kreisler and Efrem Zimbalist, the pianists Fannie Bloomfield-Zeisler and Olga Samaroff, and the singers Ernestine Schumann-Heink and Leo Slezak—all performers with enduring musical reputations. Less known now than they were in Mrs. Taft's time were singers Frances Alda, Johanna Gadski, and Loraine Wyman. Women pianists such as Yolanda Mero, Ellen Ballon, and Alma Stenzel were featured artists, as were male pianists including Ernest Schelling and Arthur Shattuck. The Kneisel Quartet played for Nellie Taft, and Julia Culp, Otto Goritz, Karl Jorn, and Paul Reimers sang for her.

Two chapters of this book trace how this array of musical talent was persuaded to come to the White House, how these appearances before the president and first lady influenced subsequent careers, and the impact of Mrs. Taft's campaign on the musical world of early twentieth-century society. The exploration of these events shows a much richer cultural impact from Nellie Taft on American society. An inveterate theatergoer as well, she brought an outdoor Shakespeare performance to the White House in 1910, provided a venue for the dramatic monologist Ruth Draper, and even entertained Lady Augusta Gregory of the Irish Players in 1911. It is time that Nellie Taft's significant contributions to the cultural life of her era are brought out of the historical shadows.

Because there is only one other biography of Helen Taft, it is important to point out where this book diverges from Carl Anthony's *Nellie Taft: The Unconventional First Lady of the Ragtime Era* (New York: William Morrow, 2005). Although Anthony's book is well researched and contains much interesting information about Mrs. Taft, the emphasis on her place in the ragtime era misses the significance of her intense patronage of classical artists throughout her four years. Moreover, this book examines the full range of musicians and choral groups who came to the White House, discusses for the first time the role of Joseph Burr Tiffany of the Steinway Piano Company, and recaptures from the memoirs of the musicians themselves the experience of entertaining Nellie Taft and her guests. The treatment of such figures as Fritz Kreisler, Josef Hofmann, and Leo Slezak, for example, provides important new information on the musical life of the United States during this period.

Beyond the musical side of Nellie Taft, this narrative treats the ouster of Henry White as ambassador to France as part of the efforts of Nellie Taft to eclipse the administration of Theodore Roosevelt. It also restores the third of Mrs. Taft's social secretaries, Katherine Letterman, to her proper place in the story of Mrs. Taft as first lady. There is new information about the writing of Mrs. Taft's memoirs and the role of journalist Eleanor Egan in that endeavor. The important appearance of Charles Coburn and the Coburn Players at the White House in June 1910 with their performances out of doors of two Shakespeare plays is given full attention for the first time as part of Mrs. Taft's cultural agenda. Finally, the story of her stroke and the work of medical specialists on her case is told in more detail than in any previous account. When her cultural contributions are properly assessed, Helen Taft becomes a far more interesting and consequential first lady than Anthony and other authors have perceived.

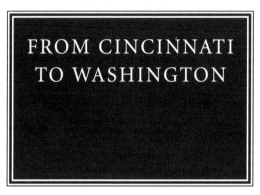

CHAPTER 1

FROM CINCINNATI
TO WASHINGTON

For Nellie Taft, it all began with Cincinnati. She grew up in the cosmopolitan atmosphere of the "Queen City of the West," where the presence of German Americans fostered a spirit of cultural tolerance, good music, and public-spirited citizens. Recalling her girlhood for her daughter and their friend Eleanor Egan in 1913–1914 as they wrote her memoirs, Helen Taft remembered the Conservatory of Music, the conducting of noted musician Theodore Thomas, and the widespread interest "in every kind of intellectual activity." For a bright young woman, it was a stimulating environment in which to find her place in post–Civil War Ohio.[1]

Helen Herron "Nellie" Taft was born in Cincinnati, Ohio, on 2 January 1861, one of six daughters among the eleven children of John Williamson Herron and Harriet Collins Herron. The Herrons had close ties to the leadership of the Ohio Republican Party. Her father was a college classmate of Benjamin Harrison and served a term as a United States attorney in Ohio during Harrison's presidency. Her mother's father, Ela Collins, had been a Democratic-Republican member of Congress from New York during the 1820s. The family tradition of politics disposed young Nellie to a lifelong interest in cultural and public affairs.

Whatever political ambitions John Herron may have had, the need to support his growing family consumed most of his time and energy during Nellie's youth. The Herrons lived in reasonable comfort on Pike Street in Cincinnati, but they could not match the affluence of Larz Anderson and Charles P. Taft, whose mansions also stood in the same thoroughfare. The Herron girls attended Miss Nourse's school, where Nellie spent her youth "quite placidly." From an early age, she found pleasure in music, "the absorbing interest of my life in those days, the inspiration of all my dreams and ambitions."[2]

Her teacher was George Schneider, a German immigrant who had come to the United States in 1866 after studying piano with some of the finest teachers in Europe, including Ignaz Moscheles (1794–1870). Schneider established the Cincinnati Music School in 1880 and became an active figure in the newly formed Music Teachers' National Association. Accounts from that period said that "his artistic work has placed him in the front rank of pianists and teachers." When he played at the association's convention in 1882, a reviewer labeled him "a remarkably fine technical player, but is lacking in sympathetic quality."[3]

Nellie Herron mentioned in her memoirs that "Much of the time, outside of that taken up in regular school work, I devoted to the study of music, and I practised my scales on the family piano with such persistence that I wonder the whole neighborhood did not rebel." With Schneider's Germanic heritage and technical expertise, it is likely that he instructed Helen Herron in the intricacies of the Klavier Schule of piano teaching, which involved extensive daily practice and the belief that "the piano was a steed to be conquered by the most forceful means." Although many piano students rebelled, Helen Herron seems to have reveled in the process of playing scales and mastering her chosen instrument.[4]

From her childhood onward, Nellie Herron displayed a facility for the piano that made her a capable amateur musician. During the years when her husband was in Theodore Roosevelt's Cabinet and in the early months of the Taft presidency, she found "time for daily practice as well as daily recreation at the piano." Contemporary newspaper reporters called her "something of a musician herself" and an "expert" on the instrument. Music and its practitioners were part of Nellie Herron's world from childhood.[5]

The Herrons were family friends of President Rutherford B.

Hayes and his wife, Lucy. During the Hayes presidency in 1878, Nellie was invited to accompany her newly married sister, Jennie, and her husband, Charles Anderson, on a Christmas visit to the White House. Nellie had not yet made her debut and so could not join the parties and other activities. President Hayes did mention her in his diary for 28 December 1878 as part of "a fine company, who make the house alive with laughter, fun, and music." By 1908 newspapers, writing about Helen Taft as a prospective first lady, expanded on this occasion to conclude that Nellie "spent the greater part of each year at the White House." According to Taft family lore, she did decide on the occasion of that first visit that she wanted to return to the executive mansion one day as the wife of a president.[6]

After graduation from Miss Nourse's school, she took courses in German and chemistry at the University of Cincinnati during 1882. Thereafter, Nellie taught at two private schools in the Cincinnati area. At this time she wrote in her diary, "to one who feels, as I do, that I will probably never marry, this leaving school seems like settling down in life." Her energy and drive soon made her a force among the young adults of Cincinnati. She and her friends formed a salon where they discussed important books of the day and staged amateur theatricals. She hoped the group would "engage in what we considered brilliant discussion of topics intellectual and economic" for especially invited guests."[7] She read Darwin, Goethe, and Schiller, as well as other serious writers of the time, and seems to have been an advocate of broader rights for African Americans. A lifelong habit of attending concerts and musicales emerged in this period as well. A taste for cigarettes in private and an enjoyment of the German beers of Cincinnati in public were other characteristic Nellie Herron traits. Not the most beautiful of the Herron women, she despaired of marrying and resigned herself to a spinster life of good works and family duties. "I am very exacting," she wrote in June 1881 about her choices in suitors, "and at the same time unwilling to make the least advance, so what wonder that I am not always satisfied."[8]

Among the young men who participated in the salon were Horace and William Howard Taft, brothers out on their own who were then rooming together as young aspiring attorneys. By 1882, Will Taft, as everyone called him, was writing to his father that "you may travel to Constantinople or Jerusalem but nowhere I venture to say will you find girls as pretty, as interesting, as stylish, and as fresh as our American girls." He had known Nellie Herron since her late teens, but they were no more than casual acquaintances until the early 1880s. At about this time, Will asked Nellie to go out with him to one of the German dances at neighboring Clifton. "The pleasure of a dance," he wrote her, "in that beautiful Clifton Hall we ought not to forgo."[9]

Taft was twenty-five in 1882. He had graduated from high school in Cincinnati and then attended Yale College, from which he graduated in 1878. After studying at the Cincinnati Law School, he began his professional career as an assistant prosecutor in Hamilton County. A year later, he accepted a federal patronage position as collector of internal revenue for the Ohio and Kentucky district. Will Taft was marked out for political and legal prominence—a destiny that caught the eye of the shrewd and intelligent Nellie Herron. Taft was a large man but unusually light on his feet and a superb dancer. The two began seeing each other, though Will was more smitten than Nellie was at this stage of their lives. Their friends hoped that the couple would marry; one companion expressed the sentiment in verse:

> St. Valentine the good!
> Now cheer & cheer him still
> For giving Will to Nellie
> And giving Nellie to Will.[10]

In her midtwenties, Helen Herron knew that she was approaching an age when spinsterhood would be a reasonable expectation if she did not marry soon. Will Taft had much to offer as a promising attorney with a positive future in Ohio politics and government ahead of him. Will Taft first proposed and was rejected in April 1885. Although it was customary in the late nineteenth century for the woman to turn down the first proposal, Nellie did so with some vehemence. She instructed her suitor that he should not even write to her about the subject. Taft persisted and Nellie accepted with the caveat that no one be told about their engagement. Not until the fall of 1885 did the news become more generally known. The prospective groom told his father, "Her eagerness for knowledge of all kinds puts me to shame. Her capacity for work is just wonderful."[11]

Years later, when her husband was running for president, Mrs. Taft scoffed at rumors that she and Will had a "school romance." At the same time, she engaged in some positive historical revision of her own to make it seem that their relationship dated back to her late teens. She told the reporter that "the engagement, however, was not announced until Mr. Taft graduated from Yale, though it had been a tentative one from our earliest years."[12]

The wedding took place on 19 June 1886, concluding, as a newspaper's column wrote, "a week notable in the local annals of society." The couple then left "on the City of Berlin for a summer tour of the Continent." In London, a small incident occurred for the honeymooners that would have consequences in the future. The new Mrs. Taft wanted to attend a session of the House of Commons, which required admission tickets. She and her husband approached the secretary of the American legation, a young diplomat named Henry White. White claimed that he could not get them the tickets that they needed for the Commons. Instead, he obtained for them entry to the Royal Stables. Nellie Taft was miffed at the apparent snub. Years later, when Helen took her revenge, a British diplomat said of White "what a mistake he made in treating Taft and Mrs. Taft as travelers of no importance."[13]

Upon their return from the honeymoon, they settled into life in a house on McMillan Street in Cincinnati. A few months later, Governor Joseph B. Foraker appointed Will Taft to a vacancy on the Ohio Superior Court. Nellie was not thrilled with a judicial position for her husband, which would take him away from elective politics. To earn money and to pursue her own interests, Mrs. Taft taught at a kindergarten that Edith Nourse launched as part of her larger school. In September 1889, their first child was born, a boy named Robert Alphonso Taft. Will Taft was reelected to the Superior Court in 1888; he seemed headed for a life on the bench—and, he hoped, in time an appointment to the United States Supreme Court.

Their marriage was by most accounts a happy one. Will Taft was in love, remained faithful, and admired his wife's foibles. He could, however, be difficult to live with. As a judge, colonial governor, secretary of war, and president, he enjoyed travel and was often away from his wife and family. These separations were more of an emotional trial for Nellie Taft than she allowed her husband to know, especially when he became more famous. Yet Will never abated his journeying ways. Managing her three children alone put a strain on Nellie Taft's health, especially during the time when her husband was in the War Department. Like other men of that era, Will Taft assumed that his professional needs came first, and it was up to his wife to adjust to his demands and obligations.

On her side, Nellie Taft insisted that her husband conform to her personal standards of ambition and drive. She wanted him to control his weight, both for health reasons and for esthetic considerations. Will Taft struggled all his life with his eating habits and excess pounds. There were periodic diets and intense campaigns to get weight off and keep it off. A binge eater when he was nervous, Will tried his best to please his wife, but when she was not around, his nerves and appetite took over.

Although he was never close to being a feminist, Will Taft treated Nellie as his intellectual equal in their discussions of politics and his various career choices. He did not comment about the law and its complexities to her. He came to regard her as an astute adviser who often pointed him in the direction he wished to go anyway. She became the center of his emotional life. In 1893, he told her: "My love for you, dear, grows each year and you become more and more indispensable to my life and happiness. This is not the enthusiasm of the wedding journey, but it is the truth deliberately arrived at after full opportunity for me to know."[14]

Nellie Taft's affection for her husband was not as passionate as his devotion to her. "I know that I am very cross with you," she informed him in 1890, "but I love you just the same." Over the course of their life together, her feelings for him became warmer as she learned of his positive qualities in detail. She wanted to mold him in the image of what she thought he should be. She prodded him to dress better, present himself with more effectiveness in public appearances, and pursue his goals in a more open manner. She developed ways around his stubbornness and insistence on doing things his way. At the same time, she knew there were boundaries as to how far he could be moved once his mind was made up to do something. The pressures of managing the temperamental and often stubborn Will Taft took their toll on her during the first decade of the new century.[15]

The family faced monetary demands that shaped how Nellie Taft viewed the world. From 1891 onward through his election to the presidency, Will Taft was a salaried employee of the federal government. Although his incomes as a federal judge, governor of the Philippines, and secretary of war were ample by the standards of what an industrial worker or subsistence farmer earned, the amounts were not large enough to sustain the lifestyle that someone of his stature had to maintain. Frequent monetary gifts from his rich half brother, Charles, publisher of the Cincinnati *Times-Star* and other newspapers, helped Will and Nellie make ends meet, but she chafed at being dependent on the largesse of a relative. She scrimped and saved to carry the family through the rough times. "Do you wonder," she said of her husband's spending habits when they were in the White House, "that we have only saved in all this time five thousand dollars?—and we should not have that now, had I not worried over every expenditure."[16]

Later in life, Will Taft would say that like any good Ohio politician, he had his bowl turned up when offices were being passed out. The next step in his upward climb came in early 1890, when President Benjamin Harrison named him as the solicitor general of the United States. Will saw it as a stepping-stone to the Supreme Court, his ultimate professional goal. For his wife, it offered the prospect of life in Washington society as the spouse of a prominent government official. She looked "forward with interest, moreover, to a few years in Washington."[17]

In her ghostwritten memoirs published after they left the White House, Nellie Taft recalled with fondness "a life, sometimes amusing, sometimes quite exciting, but, on the whole, of quiet routine." Their daughter Helen was born in 1891. With two small children in her care at this time, she did not have the opportunity for as much entertaining as she would have liked. Nevertheless, the pace of Washington in the early 1890s suited her. "There were occasional big receptions," Nellie remembered in 1913, "but for nobody was society the mad rush that it is to-day. We ourselves lived very simply even for those simple days."[18]

Their time in Washington was short. President Harrison named her husband to a federal appeals court position in 1892. The stay at the capital did introduce Helen and her husband to other rising political stars. The most important of these was Theodore Roosevelt, a member of the Civil Service Commission. Though the Tafts became acquainted with Roosevelt and his wife, Edith, they were not yet close friends. In fact, there are strong indications that Helen Taft and Edith Roosevelt did not share the personal regard that their husbands displayed for each other. That emotional coolness between the wives would prove significant once Will and Theodore found their political fortunes interlocked after 1900.

Whatever Nellie Taft may have thought of the nomination to the federal appeals court with its base in Cincinnati, there was never any question that Will Taft would accept the coveted place. In March 1892 the Tafts returned to their hometown and settled in for eight years of living keyed to the duties of the federal bench. Will Taft took to judging at once. He enjoyed the routine of travel around the circuit that included Ohio, Kentucky, and Michigan. The couple summered in Murray Bay in Canada, which became a favored spot for relaxation before and after the presidency.

Nellie's family grew with the arrival of a second son, Charles, in 1897. Because she and her female friends did not want to emulate the large families of her parents, Nellie pretended she was not pregnant with Charles for many months until the reality could not be hidden. Among her three children, Charles would be her favorite and the one with whom she shared the closest rapport. When he went off in October 1908 to the private school that her brother-in-law Horace Taft founded, she recognized that, as she wrote, "I fear I shall never get him back."[19]

While her husband handed down rulings, Nellie Taft found herself once again involved with the music she loved. In April 1894, she was the guiding spirit behind the creation of the Cincinnati Orchestra Association Company. With other prominent women of the city, she launched a high-profile campaign to raise money to create a professional orchestra. As the money flowed in, she was named chair of the new organization and head of the board of directors of fifteen women. Soon she was elected president of the Orchestra Association. She found, she wrote later, "a practical method for expressing and making use of my love and knowledge of music."[20]

Over the next six years, Nellie Taft supervised the workings of the orchestra. She cooperated with Lucien Wulsin of the Baldwin

Piano Company in securing the services of Frank Van der Stucken as the conductor of the new symphony. A native of Texas who had studied in Europe, Van der Stucken was a brilliant young composer and conductor who had already achieved an international reputation. To meet Mrs. Taft's intention to have an orchestra that might "compete favorably with any in the country," Van der Stucken was the kind of visible hire that Cincinnati needed to be credible in the professional music world. After the acquisition of Van der Stucken's services in 1895, Nellie Taft supervised negotiations with the musicians' union, dealt with the problem of obtaining subscriptions, and helped select yearly programs. The ability to run the business side of the orchestra demonstrated Nellie's executive talent. When she left the position in 1900 to follow her husband to the Philippines, the Orchestra Association recognized her as "the creator of this organization."[21]

On the artistic side of her tenure with the orchestra, Nellie Taft supervised programs that brought distinguished musicians to perform for the citizens of Cincinnati. Among those whom she heard or invited to perform who later appeared at the White House were the virtuoso violinist Fritz Kreisler, the gifted young pianist Josef Hofmann, and the singers Johanna Gadski and Ernestine Schumann-Heink. A local magazine noted in late 1897 that the symphony had enlisted for that season "a notable array of high-grade artists."[22]

In her role as the president of the orchestra, Nellie Taft gained confidence in her ability to direct events. Like many other civic-minded women during the 1890s, she saw herself as an agent of cultural uplift. Through her association with Van der Stucken and other musicians, she developed a knowledge of classical music and the artists who performed these works that she carried forward into the White House a decade later. Few first ladies have equaled Nellie Taft in their command of music as an artistic calling.[23]

Throughout the decade of the 1890s, Theodore Roosevelt and William Howard Taft drew closer together even though their political careers diverged. In 1894 Roosevelt wrote his sister that he had seen Taft, "of whom we are really fond," at a Washington dinner. After William McKinley was elected president in 1896, Will Taft joined other Republicans in urging that Roosevelt be named assistant secretary of the navy in 1897. Senator Henry Cabot Lodge told

A card-playing first lady. Helen Taft enjoyed bridge. Here she is with her husband and two military aides on one of the trips to the Philippines. (Library of Congress)

Roosevelt that Taft, "one of the best fellows going," had been a strong supporter of the appointment. For Nellie Taft, however, competition with the Roosevelts was as important as the friendship of the two men. After Nellie's daughter, Helen, was born in 1891, the new mother noted several weeks later the birth of one of Edith Roosevelt's children. "I see that I got ahead of Mrs. Roosevelt and feel quite proud," she wrote to Will.[24]

For her husband, the 1890s brought increasing prominence as a judge involved in labor cases (where he usually ruled in favor of employers) and in antitrust law. Within the Ohio Republican Party, Will Taft's talents came to the notice of President McKinley and his political ally, Senator Marcus A. Hanna. Late in 1899, the president looked for someone to send to the Philippine Islands.

The Philippines, acquired from Spain in the Treaty of Paris of December 1898, had been in revolt against American rule since February 1899. The American army was fighting the insurrection in an ugly and difficult conflict. McKinley was eager to establish civilian government there and had already sent one commission out to appraise the situation. Now the president intended to dispatch another panel to establish civil institutions for continued rule. He looked for a respected, credible Republican to act as chair of the commission. Early in 1900, a telegram from the president summoned Will Taft to the White House. McKinley asked him to go to the Philippines to serve as head of this second commission. Taft told the president he would need a week to decide on his answer and headed back to Cincinnati.

When her husband told Nellie of the Philippine assignment, her immediate reaction was to urge him to accept. She recalled years later that "I wasn't sure what it meant, but I knew instantly that I didn't want to miss a big and novel experience." She shrewdly recognized that this was a major opportunity for her husband. If he succeeded in handling the Philippine problem, national elective office could become a real opportunity. Her dream of becoming first lady now had a chance to emerge as a reality. Will would have to leave the bench and plunge into government service. While Will worked out the details of the Philippine post, Nellie "began at once to make hasty, and I may say, happy preparations for my adventure into a new sphere."[25]

After getting his family to Japan, Will Taft went first to the islands, and Nellie, along with their three young children and her sister Maria, came in August 1900. Nellie's arrival opened four of the most rewarding and productive years of her life. Will Taft was a success as a colonial administrator. He believed that American rule was beneficial to the Filipinos, so there was no thought of granting them independence at this time. Within that imperial credo, however, he approached the task with more respect for the inhabitants of the archipelago than many of the American occupiers. Nellie Taft shared these principles and proved a strong asset to her husband in the years that followed. In many respects, her sojourn in the Philippines became a kind of ongoing rehearsal for her later role as first lady.[26]

Many of the Americans regarded the Filipinos as their racial and cultural inferiors. At home in the United States, the Tafts shared some of the prejudices of white Americans toward blacks and other minority groups. In Manila and other Philippine cities, however, the couple refused to draw "the color line," as it was known at that time. Mrs. Taft shook hands with Filipinos she met, a gesture of politeness that the United States army often disdained. Both Tafts danced with Filipinos on festive occasions and otherwise treated the members of the island aristocracy as social equals. These humane acts did much to endear the Tafts to the people during their stay in the islands. The gift for organizing and entertaining that Nellie had displayed with the Cincinnati Symphony aided her in Manila. She staged garden parties to which the local populace was invited, and she encouraged the musical events that residents of the city enjoyed so much. She took particular notice of the Luneta, a park with bandstands where residents gathered in the evenings for music, gossip, and play. It was, she recalled, an institution "whose usefulness to society in the Philippine capital is not to be overestimated." The idea of such a communal meeting spot stuck with her and reappeared when she became first lady in Washington, D.C., a decade later.[27]

By including Filipino women in the planning for these occasions, Nellie Taft further disseminated the sense of shared values that her husband's government espoused. She set up a Liga Feminina de Paz, with a board of women equally divided between Americans and Filipinas that sought to promote reconciliation among those who had fought against the United States. In addition, she toured the islands on horseback, learning to ride in the process of doing so. Treating her time in the Philippines as an adventure, she and her family provided invaluable aid to the creation of the civil government and the maintenance of the American presence in the archipelago. Many of the initiatives she developed as the spouse of the governor would reappear as part of her agenda when she became first lady in March 1909.[28]

One musical offshoot of the Taft years in the Philippines was the Philippine Constabulary Band. Authorized by Governor Taft in 1902 under the direction of Walter H. Loving, a black army lieutenant who had trained at the Boston Conservatory of Music, the eighty musicians from the islands soon gained attention for their skill and artistry. They won acclaim at the St. Louis World's Fair and would perform in March 1909 for the inauguration of President Taft.[29]

The experience of Will and Nellie Taft in the Philippines divided into two distinct segments. In the first, they implemented the policies of President McKinley, who gave his officials on the ground discretion in how they conducted their business. After 14 September

1901, when McKinley died of an assassin's bullet, their friend Theodore Roosevelt was the new chief executive. Although the two men had been roughly equal in the past in their political accomplishments, now Will and Nellie had to take into account Roosevelt's desires and decisions. At the outset of this new relationship, there were some indications that Will Taft had doubts whether Roosevelt would be as effective as McKinley had been as president. Nellie Taft seems to have shared these reservations and never really abandoned them, even when her husband and Roosevelt moved closer together in the government. In March 1903, after Roosevelt entertained her at the White House, Nellie told her husband: "I do not think his personality is agreeable and his manners are explosive and so demonstrative as to seem like an affectation."[30]

In her eyes, Will Taft and Roosevelt were implicit rivals for the presidency. During the summer of 1901, for example, there had been some passing references in the press to the possibility that Governor Taft might succeed William McKinley in 1904. Her husband did not take these trial balloons seriously. He believed that his judicial decisions against organized labor and his Unitarianism ruled him out. Once Roosevelt became president and made clear his desire for a term in his own right, Will Taft put the presidency out of his mind for the time being. He hoped that the president might find the occasion to name him chief justice of the United States, replacing the incumbent, Melville Weston Fuller.

Had such an offer come from Roosevelt, Nellie knew that her husband would jump at the vacancy. An appointment to the Supreme Court as an associate justice was another matter for both of them. Being on the Supreme Court in a subordinate position would probably rule out an elevation to chief justice. When Taft came back to the United States in early 1902 to testify before Congress about Philippine affairs, he and Roosevelt talked over the idea of a Supreme Court appointment. With no vacancy available, Taft informed the president, much to his wife's relief, that he wanted to stay in the islands until his work was completed.

Then in October 1902, Associate Justice George Shiras told Roosevelt of his desire to resign from the court. Roosevelt now made a formal offer of a place on the court to the Philippine governor. Complicated negotiations ensued by letter and cable, with Roosevelt becoming ever more insistent that Taft should take the nomination. Even Mrs. Taft, concerned about her husband's health after his work in the islands, thought that perhaps he should accept. The people of the Philippines intervened and made it clear that they wanted Governor Taft to remain at his post. A reluctant Roosevelt yielded to these considerations and made another appointment in early 1903.

Six months later, Secretary of War Elihu Root told Roosevelt of his desire to step down by early 1904. The president now asked Will Taft to be his replacement and to serve as his close adviser through the election and into the second term. Nellie Taft later wrote that "this was much more pleasing to me than the offer of the Supreme Court appointment, because it was in line with the kind of work I wanted for my husband to do, the kind of career I wanted for him and expected him to have, so I was glad there were few excuses for refusing to accept it open to him."[31] Will Taft took up his duties at the War Department early in 1904.

Helen Taft soon learned that the routine for the wife of a new cabinet secretary was one of "rather monotonous stress," without the assistance of the retinue of servants she had enjoyed in Manila.[32] The social mores of Washington demanded that she make formal calls on the spouses of members of the Supreme Court, the wives of government bureaucrats, and, for the wife of the secretary of war, the wives of the officers in the army. In addition, there were weekly meetings of Cabinet wives that Edith Roosevelt hosted as first lady. At these sessions, the women would go over pressing social issues. Mrs. Roosevelt believed in setting a tone for Washington society, and these gatherings laid down a common position for her colleagues to follow. Nellie Taft was from the outset dubious about the value of these occasions. She found extended gossipy talks with other women boring, and her negative feelings could well have gotten back to Edith Roosevelt.

It is not quite clear just what underlay the distance that existed between Edith Roosevelt and Nellie Taft, or even how well they knew each other before 1904. In 1902, Nellie asked Will about the first lady: "Is she one of the advanced women? I see she dresses on $300 a year, or did so. I wonder how she does it."[33] The two women did not interact easily. In October 1904, Will was writing his wife to ask, "Have you called on Mrs. Roosevelt? Don't you think you ought to write to her secretary and make an appointment."[34]

With alcoholism in her family, Edith Roosevelt did not approve of the hard-drinking side of Washington life. Nellie Taft, on the other hand, consumed champagne on a daily basis and enjoyed a glass of beer. Nellie Taft smoked at a time when genteel women did not. She played cards for money and was quite adept at bridge and other games. There was also some tension between a woman from New York City's upper crust, as Edith Roosevelt was, and the attitude of a leader of Cincinnati society, as Nellie Taft had been. Most important, Mrs. Roosevelt was not impressed with Will Taft's potential as a successor to her husband. Whether those negative sentiments got back to the Tafts is not known. Nellie confessed some years later that she had never liked Edith Roosevelt.[35]

Another source of difficulty between the Roosevelt and Taft families was the president's oldest daughter, Alice. She was an international celebrity, and newspaper readers all over the country followed her romances and activities with intense fascination. She and Will Taft got to know each other during a congressional trip to the Far East in 1905, a journey that Helen Taft did not make. The genial secretary of war watched Alice get more involved with Ohio representative Nicholas Longworth of Cincinnati. Out of this trip came the couple's engagement. Will Taft acted as de facto chaperone for Alice, and the Cabinet secretary and the presidential daughter had an innocent, playful relationship.[36]

Nellie was less impressed with the president's daughter. Once Alice and Nick Longworth had married in the social event of the Washington season in 1906, the couple mingled in Cincinnati society. Alice's path often crossed Helen's, and the two were civil at best. As a deft mimic, Alice enjoyed mocking the wife of the secretary of war with a nasty imitation of her speech and mannerisms. In the cloistered Washington society of that time, word of these satirical moments soon reached Helen Taft. Will Taft and Alice also indulged in good-natured teasing of each other, which Nellie did not like.

An example of how Mrs. Taft stood in relation to Alice in regard to their respective international visibility occurred when Nellie was on a trip to England in 1905. Through a mix-up, her luggage was misplaced and then located with only five minutes to go before their train departed. She hurried to the stationmaster and told him first that she was "Mrs. William Howard Taft of Washington." That statement failed to impress him. She then said, "My husband is the Secretary of War of the United States." The man remained unmoved. "You must have heard of him," she tried a third time. "He's travelling now with Miss Alice Roosevelt." The magic name worked, and "the station-master was my humble servant." Nellie bore with the gibes of her family and friends about how she was "*the* Mrs. Taft whose husband was travelling with Miss Alice Roosevelt."[37]

Throughout her years in the Philippines and in Washington, Nellie Taft kept her interest in classical music active and alert. She wrote Will from Germany in the summer of 1902, when they were both in Europe, that she found Dresden "a most delightful place where the Dresden Orchestra plays every day. The conductor is Trenkler, the same men we heard here fifteen years ago." In October 1904, she attended in Washington a concert of the Kneisel String Quartet. "It was very fine. I had forgotten how well they play." Two years later, she informed her husband about an appearance of the Philadelphia Orchestra with the opera singer Johanna Gadski. Nellie sat "in Mrs. Roosevelt's box" with friends and "enjoyed it *ever* so much."[38]

As one of the Cabinet wives and spouse of a potential presidential candidate, Nellie Taft began attracting press attention. An article in December 1905 described her as "a fragile looking woman" who had during the spring of that year "felt the insidious approach of nerves, and she took immediate steps to tone herself up." Medical considerations provided the underlying reason for the trip to England that spring. She rowed with her son, Robert, to build up her strength. She "returned to Washington looking ten years younger and with her nerves as steady as the Rock of Gibraltar." This 1905 episode may have been one of the incidents of stress and excitement that foreshadowed her stroke in May 1909.[39]

Washingtonians got to know Nellie Taft as a dedicated walker. "In all kinds of weather she may be encountered swinging at a good gait, sometimes miles from her home," reported the press. She took "a tramp just as other women take a tonic." Newspapers also recognized her avid devotion to card playing. She was, said a society item in 1907, "one of the most enthusiastic bridge players." When she took her daughter, Helen, to enroll at Bryn Mawr, she told the press that college women should not become "poor imitations of men. I am old fashioned enough to think that woman is most attractive the more feminine she is."[40]

Helen Taft's main concern in 1905 and 1906 was the impending Republican nomination for president in 1908. On election night in 1904, Theodore Roosevelt had announced that he would not be a candidate for what would have been in effect a third term in 1908. The statement cleared the way for other Republicans to launch candidacies. In addition to Will Taft, the potential field included Elihu Root, now secretary of state, the vice president, Charles W. Fairbanks, Speaker of the House Joseph G. Cannon, and after 1906 the newly elected governor of New York, Charles Evans Hughes. Roosevelt wanted someone who would carry on "my policies," and none of the hopefuls save Will Taft seemed likely to meet that requirement.

Perhaps regretting his 1904 comment and thinking of how easy a third term would be to obtain, Roosevelt did not in 1905 and 1906 make clear who his favorite potential successor was. He probably preferred Elihu Root, who was in his midsixties and a former corporation lawyer. His age and professional associations in time ruled out Root. The logical next step was Will Taft, but Roosevelt declined throughout 1906 to make his feelings known to the party and the public. As a result, Nellie Taft worried that the president might go back on his word about a third term. Ever suspicious of Roosevelt's motives, she tracked all of his statements and actions with a wary eye. She felt sure that in the end Roosevelt would serve his own interests and cast her husband aside.

The issue of Will Taft's future came up again in 1906 when another vacancy appeared on the Supreme Court with the resignation of Justice Henry Billings Brown. The secretary of war very much wanted to be chief justice, but knew that his wife opposed the acceptance of an associate justice position. Being a member of the Court, rather than chief justice, conveyed no special social status in Washington, and the actual day-to-day life of a justice was more cloistered than Nellie Taft desired. In a memorandum that he wrote for himself, Will Taft said in March 1906 that he had told Roosevelt "that Nellie is bitterly opposed to my accepting the position and that she telephoned me this morning to say that if I did, I would make the great mistake of my life." Roosevelt said that he would confer with Nellie Taft about the issue.[41]

Out of their conversation of half an hour or so came a lengthy presidential letter to Will Taft setting out the case for going on the Supreme Court. In the course of weighing Taft's options, Roosevelt emphasized that it was "a matter in which no other man can take the responsibility of deciding for you what is right and best for you to do." The implied rebuke to Nellie Taft was evident. Mrs. Taft had told the president that her husband wished to continue his work as secretary of war, with the underlying assumption that such a course might lead to the White House. Roosevelt once again did not come out and say that Taft would be his choice in 1908. Instead he called his friend "the man who is most likely to receive the Republican Presidential nomination and who is, I think, the best man to receive it; and under whom we would have most chance to succeed." Those were nice words, but they were not the same as an outright endorsement. And what did Nellie Taft make of Roosevelt's final sentence in the letter: "No one can with wisdom advise you." Leaving the decision up to Theodore Roosevelt and her husband was not at all Nellie Taft's view of the matter.[42]

Mrs. Taft's attitude toward Roosevelt and his choice for 1908 were causing some concern among the people close to Roosevelt. After visiting Nellie Taft, James R. Garfield, an Ohioan who was a close ally of the president, noted in his diary in April 1906: "am disturbed by the way she speaks of the Pres. in regard to the Sec'y's going on the Supreme Bench. I am sure she quite misunderstands the President's position."[43]

There the question of presidential succession rested through the summer of 1906. Taft campaigned for Republican congressional candidates in the autumn and bided his time before announcing his own intentions. This cautious posture suited Taft's needs, but it worried Theodore Roosevelt, who wanted to keep control of the 1908 nomination in his own hands. The president decided that his potential successor might not be moving with enough speed to solidify his position. With Taft away campaigning, a conversation with Nellie Taft seemed to Roosevelt the best move he could make.

In that context, Nellie Taft once again went to the White House in October 1906 to speak with Theodore Roosevelt at a luncheon along with several other prominent guests. The conversation, one of the very few between the president and Mrs. Taft alone, was awkward. "After lunch the President said he wanted to talk to me and drew me off to sit down in the window. As usual, it was about you, but on a new tack." In Nellie's mind, "he seems to think that I am consumed with an inordinate ambition to be President and that he must constantly warn me that you may never get there." Although Taft was his first choice, Roosevelt went on, if his friend did not appeal to Republican leaders, "it may become necessary for him to support some one else like [Charles Evans] Hughes," who was then a candidate for governor of New York. Mrs. Taft bristled inside but stayed silent: "I felt like saying 'D— you, support whom you want, for all I care,' but suffice it to say I did not."[44]

After she told her husband about this conversation, Will Taft wrote to the president to assure him that if Roosevelt had to support Hughes or someone else for the White House, "you will awaken no feeling of disappointment on my part." A miffed Roosevelt shot back that Nellie Taft had misinterpreted his comments. The president was only trying in his mind to make Will Taft more forceful in pursuing the nomination. The implication was that the two men involved could settle the problem without a woman's intrusion. The upshot of the encounter was to leave Mrs. Taft more irritated than ever with Roosevelt, and more suspicious of his motives toward her husband. At the end of 1906, the situation still seemed unsettled as far as her husband's presidential prospects were concerned.[45]

Events at the conclusion of the congressional campaign changed the situation and made Roosevelt a more open partisan for his secretary of war. In mid-August 1906, there had been a shooting episode at Brownsville, Texas. White residents blamed the detachment of African American soldiers stationed at a nearby fort for the violence. In fact, the charges were trumped up and the soldiers were not guilty. Just before the election, however, Roosevelt dismissed an entire company of black troops on the grounds that they were covering up the guilty within their ranks. A major public controversy erupted in which Senator Joseph B. Foraker of Ohio became the most celebrated defender of the accused soldiers. Foraker made the plausible case that the ousted troops were not guilty of anything and had been dismissed more because of racial prejudice than for anything they had done. It seemed likely that the white residents of Brownsville had staged the shooting in the first place.

An angry Roosevelt clashed with Foraker in public at the Gridiron Dinner of the press corps in early 1907. Now more anxious to undermine the political base of his public rival and to thwart Foraker's presidential ambitions, which grew out of his base in Ohio, Roosevelt moved toward a more formal endorsement of Will Taft. He informed Cabinet officials that they should give the secretary of war preference in making appointments. Astute Washington observers knew that Roosevelt had thrown his backing to Taft. The key point was that Roosevelt had opted for Taft for pragmatic reasons, not because of their ideological affinity. After he had made the decision, the president then convinced himself that he and the secretary of war were political soul mates. Meanwhile, Taft's wealthy half brother, Charles, had funded a campaign organization with the goal of rounding up delegates for the candidate. The Taft boom picked up momentum during 1907, and Nellie Taft's dream of seeing her husband in the White House moved closer to reality.

Nellie Taft had emerged as a de facto adviser to her husband throughout 1906 and 1907. She counseled him on such issues as the protective tariff and his relations with Theodore Roosevelt. On the contentious question of tariff revision among Republicans, she urged Will to play it down in his speeches. In other letters, she pushed him to distance himself from the president and not to identify too much with Roosevelt's policies. Although Will Taft did not follow her recommendations to give less weight to the tariff, she was part of his campaign team in a way that few prospective first ladies before her had been. As the press noticed her important role, there began to be stories about her views on such topics as divorce and the role of women in society. "If it were in my power," she told an interviewer, "divorce would be stopped entirely." As the presidency neared, Nellie Taft achieved an even higher profile within first her husband's campaign and then in his impending administration.[46]

From these events would grow the idea that William Howard Taft was a reluctant candidate for the presidency pushed toward the White House by a domineering spouse. The evidence in the Taft Papers, however, indicates that both Will and Nellie Taft shared the purpose of his becoming president. Because he could not be chief justice, achieving the presidency and implementing his ideas about foreign and domestic policy now had definite appeal to the ambitious Taft.

Yet the secretary of war believed that he could not be too assertive in seeking the Republican nomination until Roosevelt had made his preference clear. Will's letters to other politicians in 1906 and 1907 show a candidate who was involved in a substantial way in shaping the strategy for his own campaign. Nellie might prod and push him, but to some degree, that was part of his personal style as a politician. He allowed family members and friends to urge him to move in a direction that he had already chosen for himself.

With the prospect of becoming the first lady now a realistic possibility, Helen Taft began preparing her program for what she intended to do once her husband was president. She would bring better music to the nation, transform the look of Washington, D.C., and make the nation's capital the center of American social life. It was an ambitious agenda, and from mid-1907 to the spring of 1909, Nellie Taft laid her plans and prepared the ground for what she expected to be a magnificent four or eight years as the wife of the next president.

CHAPTER 2

"I LOVE PUBLIC LIFE": THE NEW FIRST LADY

As the presidential campaign for Will Taft accelerated during 1907, press attention toward his wife also increased. The sense that Helen Taft played an influential part in her husband's candidacy intensified as reporters learned more about this potential first lady. The media scrutiny of the wives of the candidates had become more sustained during the years after 1900. Yet journalists had little of substance to ponder. Ida McKinley had been a sickly recluse, while Edith Roosevelt had guarded her privacy amid the hoopla of her husband's public persona.

By 1908, however, initial signs of modern celebrity coverage had appeared. Roosevelt's emphasis on his family fed public fascination with the occupants of the White House. The sense that first ladies were relevant and important to the character of the president justified the enhanced press attention. Nellie Taft became a visible public figure between the spring of 1907 and May 1909 as well as a backstage force in her husband's presidential candidacy.

Though he did not say so in public, Will Taft treated his wife as one of his key advisers during the White House run. Like so many other candidates in that position, Taft knew that Nellie had only his interests at heart. He had consulted her on so many key decisions over the years that it was natural for him to share documents and exchange views with her, as he did throughout 1907 and 1908. He had begun doing this in a systematic way during 1906 canvassing as he traveled through the West. She remained in Washington with the two younger children, Helen and Charlie. Nellie recalled "that I was made the victim of his thinking process since he poured into them all the politics and turmoil of the hour, together with lengthy comments which kept me very much alive with interest in the campaign in which he was engaged."[1]

In their correspondence, Nellie advised him on such issues as the reduction of the tariff, which her husband emphasized in his speeches during the 1906 campaign. "I am sorry you keep bringing in the tariff as it seems to be unnecessary and not a special issue at this time, and calls down comments." To which Will Taft responded: "You say in your letter that I talk too much about the tariff, and I probably do, and you are quite right in supposing that this will be another ground for opposing me on the part of powerful interests, but it is relevant, it comes in natural." The couple continued their dialogue on such questions during their separations.[2]

Whatever personal reservations Will Taft had shown about running for the presidency had receded during 1907. "I am not quite so shy or so nervous in respect to the Presidential campaign" as he had been a year earlier, he told his friend Mabel Boardman, the leader of the American Red Cross, in September 1907. He and his wife were now committed to winning the nomination and the election. To that end, Nellie began to respond to the pleas of newspaper reporters that she sit down for extended interviews.[3]

One of these took place with Margaret B. Downing of the *Washington Post* in early May. During their conversation, Nellie spoke out for the creation of "a national musical conservatory, a national school of art, [and] higher education for women." She did not believe that the government should fund these programs. Better education in elementary and secondary schools would instill interest in the arts in younger children. Of music itself, she said, "I have studied music all my life, and I am still studying it." Her children, and presumably her husband, did not find in music "the absorbing passion which it is to me."[4]

The female reporters who interviewed Helen Taft sought to give their readers a sense of her looks and personality. These judgments tended to be contradictory in their evaluation of the prospective first lady. The *New York Times* found her "a woman of medium height" who "looks even smaller beside her portly spouse." On the other hand, in the *Washington Post,* she was described as "tall and slender with fine grey eyes and soft brown hair." That hair, concluded the *Times,* "is just showing its first touch of gray, and Mrs. Taft is doing nothing to disguise the evidence of years."[5]

When it came to her personality and intellect, however, these appraisals were equally flattering. She was "very frank, witty, and vivacious." After weighing Nellie Taft's record as a Cabinet wife, Margaret Downing concluded that "few mistresses of the White House have combined the three desirable qualities, artistic, intellectual, and domestic. Mrs. Taft shows that she has carried the trinity to the highest development." While Will Taft was a Unitarian, his wife was "an ardent Episcopalian," and she was "among the few women in high official life who have not yielded to the growing cosmopolitanism of Sunday entertainments."[6]

During the spring of 1907 Nellie followed the developing battle between her husband and Senator Joseph Foraker for control of the Ohio delegation to the Republican National Convention. In late March Foraker challenged the Taft forces to have a primary election to decide between the secretary of war and himself. Will Taft's half brother, the wealthy publisher Charles P. Taft, fired back that "we are willing to submit to the Republican voters of Ohio and the sooner the better."[7] Reading these words in Washington, Mrs. Taft was worried. "You have got yourself in an awful position" by allowing Taft's brother "to take his own way. It makes me scrunch just the way his old effusions in the Times-Star used to do, but that now it comes home more nearly. I think this all comes from being under money obligations to him. It never does, even with one's nearest relatives."[8]

Her suspicions of Roosevelt surfaced as well in this episode. She told her husband that "the [New York] Sun has one of its editorials on Roosevelt. How they hate him & they go farther than I, in insinuating that this is all part of his scheme to get himself nominated and as the only man and greets you as a 'martyr & scapegoat.'" After she spoke with the secretary of the interior, James R. Garfield, she learned that Roosevelt thought Charles Taft had gone too far. She urged Will to cable "Charlie to say nothing more till you get home."[9]

Two days later she apologized to Will for writing a "disturbed letter" and told him, "I have calmed down now." The reaction to Charles Taft's anti-Foraker action had been positive. She now recognized that her brother-in-law had been "very sure of his ground" when he issued the statement. Indeed, the Taft forces in Ohio demonstrated that spring and summer that they were in control of the situation for 1908. Foraker's candidacy faded as the extent of the Taft sentiment in the state became clear. Nonetheless, Mrs. Taft's apprehensions about the president and his long-range intentions continued.[10]

Secretary Taft had one more troubleshooting assignment to fulfill for Theodore Roosevelt. Beginning in late August and continuing for three months, the Tafts left on a round-the-world tour that took them to Japan, China, the Philippines, Russia, and then home through Europe. Nellie and their son, Charles, met her husband in Montana in mid-August and accompanied him on the remainder of his speaking tour of the West before embarking for the Orient. "Nellie has been with me since we left Yellowstone," Will told Mabel Boardman, "and has seen something of all this and has enjoyed it, although it has made her to know the strenuous character of my traveling."[11]

Nellie Taft kept a diary of her experiences on this world tour. In Seattle, she spoke to members of the newly organized Seattle Symphony Society. An orchestra had existed in the city since 1903, but these women sought a more permanent home, a better framework for conducting the business affairs, and a new conductor. Nellie Taft's expertise with the Cincinnati Symphony, and the reputation she had gained in the music world for that success, led the society members to approach her for advice: "I tried to give them my experiences in starting our orchestra."[12] Their work culminated in a new and more viable symphony for Seattle.

Throughout their visit to the Northwest, Nellie Taft indulged her love of bridge. Her commitment to the game resulted in one close brush with adverse publicity during the weeks that they moved across the West. Nellie Taft enjoyed playing cards. She was adept at bridge and played for money with friends in Washington. In April 1907 she reported proudly that she had won ten dollars while playing at a country club in Washington. Protestant churches frowned on cards, and there was little publicity about Nellie's diversion. During their extended Western swing, riding from army post to army post as Will Taft inspected installations, Nellie recalled that they "lost track of the days of the week and made what I then thought would prove to be a fatal error."[13]

After arriving at a hotel late one afternoon, she and her party played bridge to pass the time. Only later did they discover that it was Sunday. For devout churchgoers at this time, the Sabbath was a day when no such secular entertainment was allowed. Nellie and her husband fretted that the newspapers or the Democrats might learn of their cultural indiscretion. Luckily for them, the incident passed unnoticed. Once she was out of the country, Mrs. Taft played cards on their world tour. In the Philippines she was playing bridge when her hostess received word from a policeman "that the law against playing cards for prizes or money must be respected by her guests."[14]

The Tafts' three-month trip ended in December 1907. They returned to find that Will's absence had allowed his rivals for the Republican nomination to make some headway with their own campaigns. Theodore Roosevelt stepped in and reaffirmed his decision not to run in 1908. The president, Mrs. Taft wrote later, "was quite impatient at the loss of ground that Mr. Taft's candidacy had suffered and he urged him to take a more active interest in the situation." The problem soon disappeared, and the secretary of war resumed his march toward the Republican nomination. Nellie Taft was once again reminded, however, of the importance of Theodore Roosevelt's endorsement to her husband's chances for the presidency.[15]

A famous anecdote, often cited about the Tafts, dates from this period. According to the Chicago newspaper publisher, H. H. Kohlsaat, who recalled being present on the occasion, one evening when Will and Nellie were guests at the White House, Roosevelt spoke to them as follows. "I am the seventh son of a seventh daughter and I have clairvoyant powers. I see a man weighing three hundred and fifty pounds. There is something hanging over his head. I cannot make out what it is. . . . At one time it looks like the presidency, then again it looks like the chief justiceship." Mrs. Taft said: "Make it the presidency," while Will Taft responded, "Make it the chief justiceship."[16]

Because it illustrates the differences between the Tafts over the presidency, this story has become a staple of the literature on their lives. It provides evidence of how Nellie Taft pushed her husband toward the presidency. Yet it has inherent problems. Kohlsaat was not in fact at the White House in early January 1908 when the episode allegedly occurred. In any case, those who have referred to this tale usually omit a key fact. Kohlsaat first recounted the story in a magazine article in 1921. When Will Taft was nominated as chief justice of the United States in June 1921, reporters asked him about what Kohlsaat had written. "I read that story," he answered, "but the incident did not occur."[17]

Although her husband stressed his support for Roosevelt and the administration, Nellie urged him to maintain some distance from the White House and not to compare Roosevelt to Lincoln. "I do hope myself," she told him in February 1908, "that you are not going to make any more speeches on the 'Roosevelt policies' as I think they need to be let alone for the present, and you are simply aiding and abetting the President in keeping things stirred up. Let the corporations rest for a while. It is soon enough to talk about it, when something needs to be done, and whatever the West may be in the East it has an aggressive air." When Will received a letter about improving his public image, he sent it on to Nellie, adding the phrase, "Respectfully referred to my better half."[18]

By the spring of 1908, it was evident that Secretary Taft had all but wrapped up the Republican nomination. In June, the party held its convention in Chicago. Nellie Taft still worried that some last-minute event might produce calls for President Roosevelt to run again. Until her husband had received the nomination and was the official candidate of the party, her fears persisted. When the convention met, the Tafts were at the War Department, where a direct telegraph line and a telephone link connected them with events on the floor. The press reported that Mrs. Taft was "as happy and smiling as a schoolgirl on the first day of vacation. Everybody who came within her radius was infected with her enthusiasm and good cheer and she grew as excited over the fast arriving bulletins as a boy at a baseball game."[19]

The day before the nominations occurred, there had been a spontaneous demonstration for Roosevelt that went on for forty-nine minutes. The outburst did not produce a stampede for the president's renomination, but Helen Taft noted its length. She fretted that the convention delegates might break loose from their commitments and nominate the president for a third term. As the information and telegrams poured in, Nellie Taft, the press recorded, "understood every one and knew its meaning."[20]

The day that candidates were placed in nomination, the Taft demonstration began. To the group at the War Department, Mrs. Taft said, "I only want it to last more than forty-nine minutes. I want to get even for the scare that Roosevelt cheer of forty-nine minutes gave me yesterday." Her husband said, "Oh, my dear, my dear!" The cheering for Taft did not exceed the enthusiasm for Roosevelt, but the nomination of the secretary of war was not in doubt. The momentary apprehension soon passed, and Will Taft was nominated. An observer later reported: "It is needless to add that Mrs. Taft's face had more than regained its normal color. She was the personification of a proud and happy wife."[21]

A month later came the official notification to her husband that he was the nominee of the Grand Old Party. The gala event occurred outside the Taft home at Cincinnati on 28 July. In the hot sun, the presidential nominee gave a lengthy address about how he would extend the legacy of Theodore Roosevelt. Reporters found a happy Nellie Taft ready to discuss what had just occurred. "Hasn't it been glorious?" she told the press. "Everything has been perfect. I have been so interested. I love public life. To me this is better than when Mr. Taft was at the bar and on the bench, for the things before him now in which he takes part are live subjects, and the law is more abstract and harder for a woman to understand."[22]

The prospective first lady then expanded on the issue of woman suffrage. "I am not a sympathizer with the woman suffragists, for though it may be all right for women to vote, I do not believe in their holding office. We are not ready for women to vote, as not enough of them take an interest in political affairs, and until the majority of women want to vote they will scarcely be given the right. I do not question that they should have the privilege of casting a vote, but it seems to me that she should not hold office, as that forces them to neglect other duties that they cannot possibly shift to others." Just how her lack of sympathy for woman suffrage manifested itself is not clear from this statement because she had endorsed woman suffrage, if not women holding office.[23] The press duly reported what she said without exploring her apparent inconsistency on the issue.

In this interview, Mrs. Taft complained of having been mis-
quoted in previous statements she had made to reporters. She said
that her "opinions are the same as those of Mr. Taft, and I, of course,
am also an admirer of President Roosevelt." For the rest of the campaign season, she kept her own counsel. As the Republican canvass
developed, it became clear that Will Taft would have to take the
stump in his own behalf. His Democratic opponent, William Jennings Bryan, was making his usual vigorous speaking tour. Republican leaders wanted to see their party's candidate out before the voters as well. She told her son, Robert, that his father "starts on his first
tour on Wednesday also and I shall breathe much easier when I see
how he goes along. It is proving to be very hard work and I am nervous when I think of it."[24]

The 1908 campaign found Nellie Taft on the sidelines during
much of the fall. Republicans used her Episcopal faith as a counter
to the whispers that Will Taft's Unitarianism disqualified him for the
White House. Senator Foraker, who was under fire for his links to
corporations, charged in late September that the Tafts had benefited
from the generosity of a wealthy friend who made a yacht available
to the couple when they traveled on the Great Lakes. "Wasn't
Foraker's attack pointless? It seemed so to me," Nellie Taft told her
husband. She believed that they had been guests of the club where
they had stayed and the yacht loan did not matter. Throughout the
fall, Will Taft and Foraker exchanged charges about their relationship, but none of these touched again on Nellie Taft.[25]

At the end of September, Mrs. Taft conferred with President Roosevelt about the status of the race. She retained her suspicion of
Roosevelt's motives in making the request for a meeting. When the
invitation to have lunch at the White House arrived, she wondered
what lay behind the initiative. "I can't imagine what Teddy wants,
but probably only to complain of something." After asking what the
White House had in mind, she received word "that the President
only wants to see me to encourage me—that he is most optimistic."
The visit went well, and Nellie reported to her husband that there
was no cause for worry.[26]

As Will stumped through the Middle West in October, he kept his
wife informed of how the campaign was unfolding with letters dic-
tated or in some cases handwritten from his train. "I don't know

what the rest of the trip will be," he wrote her from Kansas on 3 October, "but thus far it has been a great success in the number of people who have turned out to greet me and the enthusiasm of their receptions." "It is splendid that you have had such fine success," she told him in answering another letter on 14 October, "and you must be awfully pleased with it." There was a sense as October ended that Taft and the Republicans were on their way to another presidential election victory.[27]

The long race for the presidency concluded on 3 November 1908 with a decisive success for Taft and the Republicans. In Helen Taft's estimation, the time had come to implement the changes in the operation of the White House that she had long envisioned. In so doing, however, she placed herself more and more at odds with the Roosevelts and their way of living in the mansion. Most importantly, she did not reach out to Edith Roosevelt and inform the outgoing first lady in full of her plans for the transition. Anxious to get started in her new role, Helen Taft contributed to the growing tension between the two families that marked the transition between these two Republican administrations. As she later wrote about her tenure in general, "Perhaps I did make the process of adjusting the White House routine to my own conception a shade too strenuous, but I could not feel that I was mistress of any house if I did not take an active interest in all the details of running it."[28]

There had not been anything like the shift from Roosevelt to Taft in terms of the first ladies for a decade and a half. The last such occurrence came in 1889, when Caroline Harrison succeeded Frances Cleveland. When Benjamin Harrison gave way to Grover Cleveland in 1893, the departing president's wife had just died. In 1897, Mrs. McKinley was an invalid with no disposition to impose her will on how the White House operated. Four and a half years later, after McKinley's assassination, Edith Roosevelt was in a position to do whatever suited her regarding the executive mansion and its customs. In 1909, Theodore and Edith Roosevelt believed that they had set an example of how the president and his family should live in the White House. Naturally, they felt that Helen Taft was implicitly criticizing their conduct when she pressed to make immediate changes in how the president and his spouse lived.

From Mrs. Taft's perspective, the realization of her dream to become first lady meant that she had no time to lose in getting started. Even the four-month transition from one administration to the other seemed to her hardly enough of an interval to have procedures and practices in operation in time for the inauguration on 4 March 1909. With her energies unleashed, she saw no point in hesitating about her intentions. If that rankled the Roosevelts, she gave little sign that such a result bothered her at all. In time, the family of the outgoing president would see Nellie's actions as a deliberate policy, in the words of Alice Roosevelt Longworth, "to let the setting sun know its place."[29]

The sense of urgency that Helen Taft felt about having her own way with the executive mansion soon brought her into contact with the White House military aide, Archibald Willingham "Archie" Butt. At forty-three, Butt was an impressive figure in his full-dress uniform. A native of Georgia, he knew the cream of Washington society and enjoyed hobnobbing with the cave dwellers at their round of dinners and parties. He wrote home to his mother and sister lengthy letters that conveyed the latest Capital gossip and inside information. He had been close to the Roosevelt family and worried about how he might fare with the new president and first lady.

Butt, a confirmed bachelor, shared a house with painter Francis D. Millett. He made the social rounds of the capital and was a coveted guest at Washington social occasions. He found in time that he admired Will and Nellie Taft as much as he had Theodore and Edith Roosevelt. During the months of transition, he was still learning what Helen Taft was like, but with his usual efficiency, Butt moved to help her develop a personal style for living in the White House.

The changes came rapidly during the transition. Edith Roosevelt had employed Isabella "Belle" Hagner as her social secretary to handle correspondence and to deal with the many issues that arose in hosting musicales, parties, and official receptions. As a result, the tall, statuesque Hagner became something of a Washington celebrity in her own right. Archie Butt called Hagner "the chief factor at the White House. She went there merely as the social secretary of Mrs. Roosevelt, but her sphere has broadened until it's sort of head aide, general manager, and superintendent."[30]

Nellie Taft did not see herself elevating a social secretary to the level Hagner had attained with the Roosevelts. She wanted an employee who could take dictation and act as a stenographer for her own wishes. "Mrs Taft frankly declared that she wished a clerk not a companion," wrote a newspaper at the time. Because Belle Hagner had become an extension of the Roosevelt family, however, relieving her of her duties was another instance where tensions flowed from Nellie Taft's personnel choices. Her insistence on doing everything herself added to her burdens in the White House and contributed to the health problems that marked her time as first lady.[31]

During the Roosevelt presidency, visitors to the White House had encountered men at the door of the executive mansion who had directed the arrivals to their destination. These footmen, all of them white in frock coats, did not seem to Nellie Taft to convey the proper sense of dignity and decorum befitting the residence of the president. She wanted instead to have African American men, dressed in liveried uniforms, to handle the task of meeting White House arrivals. The news distressed Edith Roosevelt, who thought first of the individuals she had known who would now be out of work. Through the efforts of Archie Butt, a compromise was arranged for several of the incumbent servants to retain their positions while supervising the new black employees. Mrs. Taft also decreed that the White House kitchens would take care of preparing meals in the future instead of the caterer that the Roosevelts had employed. Finally, she declared that automobiles would now be used to get around Washington instead of the horse-drawn carriages of the past.[32]

The shaping of the Taft Cabinet was another aspect of the transition that attracted Mrs. Taft's attention. She exercised some voice in who was selected for the official family. As Will Taft told Butt on 10 December 1908, "I was Cabinet-making early this morning, and I had thought that I had settled one place at least, and just as you were announced I had told my wife. She simply wiped him off the face of the earth, and I have got to begin all over again. The personal side of politics has always been funny to me, but nothing has been quite as funny as to have a man's career wrecked by a jealous wife."[33]

Nellie Taft responded: "Not jealous at all, but I could not believe you to be serious when you mentioned that man's name. He is perfectly awful and his family are even worse. I won't even talk about it."[34] Mrs. Taft did not have great influence on the political and regional balancing act that her husband went through in making up his Cabinet, but she did have a veto over individuals about whom she had a strong opinion on social and personal grounds.

These actions of Mrs. Taft and the determination to break with the Roosevelt legacy that they represented contributed to the strains between the two families that grew during the transition period. The Roosevelt clan learned through Washington gossip that members of the Taft family told the president-elect to be "his own king." When that happened, the amity on both sides frayed.[35]

Mrs. Taft intended to reshape first lady traditions whenever she could. To keep the focus on his successor on Inauguration Day, Roosevelt had decided not to ride back to the White House after the ceremonies but to go to the railroad station to leave for Oyster Bay. Mrs. Taft saw her chance. She decided that she would drive to the mansion with her husband. On 1 March 1909, the *New York Times* announced that "Mrs. Taft is to smash all precedents on inauguration day by accompanying her husband on the drive from the Capitol to the White House after he has taken the oath of office. This will be the first time that the wife of a President has accompanied him through the cheering thousands to take formal possession of the White House."[36] Nellie Taft disliked the practice of relegating wives of politicians to the company of other prominent ladies. When she traveled with him, "he is taken in charge by committees and escorted everywhere with honour, while I am usually sent with a lot of uninteresting women through some side street to wait for him at some tea or luncheon."[37]

Before she could make her ride, Nellie Taft experienced the ceremonies and rituals of the inauguration itself. President Roosevelt had proposed that the president-elect and his wife spend the night before the swearing-in at the White House. Neither of the wives had been consulted about this proposal before Roosevelt invited Will Taft. As Helen Taft wrote in her memoirs, "my impression is that neither Mrs. Roosevelt nor I would have suggested such an arrangement for this particular evening, but it having been made for us, we naturally acquiesced."[38] It turned out to be a very awkward event. The conversation, which Roosevelt dominated, did not ease the tension in the room.

Later, Washington gossip would say that on this or another occasion before the inauguration, Helen Taft was "reported to have re-

Helen Taft and her daughter, Helen. The first lady and her daughter strike a formal pose for a photographer during the White House years. (Library of Congress)

marked privately" to one of the other guests "that a certain piece of White House furniture would look better if put in another place." When the remark was conveyed to Edith Roosevelt, she commented that "Mrs. Taft might better have waited forty-eight hours" until she was in charge of the White House. The circulation of such stories formed part of the background in which the Taft inauguration took place.[39]

While Will Taft attended an event put on by his friends from Yale University, Helen moved to the Blue bedroom, which had once served Abraham Lincoln during the Civil War. "It seemed strange," she later wrote, "to spend my first night in the White House surrounded by ghosts."[40] The weather, which was moving toward blizzard conditions the following morning, kept Nellie Taft awake. So too did the "many petty details" of the inauguration "with which I had no reason to be concerned."[41] As the wind howled and the branches cracked outside her window, she thought of the day to come. Perhaps she also pondered how far she had traveled since the days of Rutherford B. Hayes, when she had spent time in the executive mansion as a young girl. Helen Herron Taft had come a long way from the salons of Cincinnati and the classrooms of Mrs. Nourse's school. In a few hours she would be the first lady, with a social status that would put her in the limelight ahead of Alice Roosevelt. Nellie had her plans to make her tenure as the president's wife a memorable one. Will Taft had always succeeded at everything he tried, and so the prospect was for eight years to make Washington the social capital of the United States. Nellie would bring her love of music, the lessons she had learned in the Philippines, and her intense desire to excel to the White House. Activism was part of her nature and style. In the afternoon of 4 March 1909, her quest to put her own stamp on the institution of the first lady would commence.

The day began with a blizzard that tied up Washington traffic and forced the inauguration ceremonies indoors at the Capitol. Nellie Taft recalled that riding back with her husband after the oath-taking "was the proudest and happiest event of Inauguration Day. Perhaps I had a little secret elation in thinking that I was doing something which no woman had ever done before." At that moment, she "was able to enjoy, almost to the full, the realisation that my husband was actually President of the United States and that it was this fact which the cheering crowds were acclaiming."[42]

The institution of first lady, of which Helen Herron Taft now became a member, was still evolving toward its modern form. Under Edith Roosevelt, there had been steps taken to adapt the practices and responsibilities of the president's wife to the expectations of the early twentieth century. Mrs. Roosevelt had employed a social secretary to handle the mail that the first lady received. She used the weekly meetings of the Cabinet wives to set a social tone for Washington society. During her tenure, musicales at the White House with such artists as the young cellist Pablo Casals became a custom. In many respects, Edith Roosevelt codified the rituals that would become standard for other first ladies who followed her.

At the same time, Edith Roosevelt established a zone of privacy for herself about her activities and the doings of her family. Her ebullient and charismatic husband did the publicity seeking for the couple. Nellie Taft, on the other hand, wanted attention. As her ride to the Capitol suggested, she had a sense of how to make news once she was in the White House. Edith Roosevelt had been a quiet activist. Helen Taft intended to let the world know how she planned to change the way things were done in Washington. As a newspaper story reported on 7 March 1909, she had "assumed duties without public ceremony or oath of office which, in weight of responsibility, magnitude of importance, delicacy of execution, and lack of compensation, have no comparison."[43]

Nellie Taft planned to do most of the work of the position herself, as she always had during her married life. To replace Belle Hagner in this less ambitious position of secretary to the first lady, she selected Alice Blech, who had worked at the Bureau of American Republics. Blech, the daughter of a member of the Consular Service, had been educated abroad and was "highly accomplished, speaking several languages." She was a distant relative of the family of Theodore Roosevelt's mother in Georgia. Mrs. Taft picked her over several other applicants for the place.[44]

Blech seems to have gotten along with her employer, who was a demanding boss by all accounts. She came each morning at nine and stayed through the afternoon, taking dictation from the first lady. Most of the paper trail of Alice Blech consisted of brief memoranda to Fred W. Carpenter, the president's personal secretary, over how to handle such matters as the Taft family's bookplate or the demands from temperance groups that Nellie Taft not serve liquor to her White House guests. At one point, the first lady noted that "Miss Blech takes so much time about" preparing lists of people to be invited to a dance for Helen and Robert Taft. In November, Blech became engaged to Lieutenant Richard Wainwright Jr., the son of a naval officer. Their wedding was scheduled for the spring of 1910, at which time Mrs. Taft would have to find a replacement. Blech remained anonymous and in the background.[45]

Mrs. Taft's reluctance to have more than one clerk/secretary was odd in view of the ambitious goals she had for what the first lady could do in American society. Though she made no official statement of her intentions, there were a number of newspaper articles even before the inauguration that conveyed her intentions to enhance the status of Washington, D.C. In an interview with Viola Rodgers of the *New York American* in November 1908, the future first lady outlined her sweeping aspirations. She did not go on the record herself, but allowed her husband to speak for her at this juncture: "Without bold, aggressive, or radical changes, but with tact and dignity, which she possesses to an unusual degree, Mrs. Taft is destined to go down in the history of White House mistresses as one that has counted in the making and molding of a real American society built upon intellectual and thoroughly democratic lines."[46]

By the time Will Taft took office, the forecast was "that the Taft administration will be brilliant beyond any similar period in America's social history" in "the opinion of the Washingtonians who have observed Administrations come and go." The *New York Times* noted that the morning meetings of the Cabinet women under Edith Roosevelt would not be continued because they had "proved far from successful in the past Administration." The press spoke of her intention to make the White House more accessible than it had been under the Roosevelts. "Keep the White House open. Let them come in. This is their White House, and I want them here," she reportedly told the White House staff.[47]

The breadth of what Mrs. Taft wanted to do became clear in the days after the inauguration ceremonies. The *New York American* reprinted that part of her November 1908 interview in which she asserted that "geographically and logically, Washington should be the representative social city of the land" and hoped "one day to see it the recognized social center of the land." Predictably, New York women were skeptical. Mrs. Rhinelander Waldo, a New York City matron, said that "Mrs. Taft's idea of making Washington the social center of America is as absurd as it is impracticable." The president of the Daughters of the American Revolution, also a New Yorker, observed that "the best society to be found in the country is to be found in New York." Mrs. Fenton B. Turck, "a social leader of Chicago," defended the first lady. "The country is fortunate in having Mrs. Taft as mistress of the White House, because she is of the higher intellectual type."[48]

Though Theodore and Edith Roosevelt have a well-deserved reputation for making the White House an American version of a European salon, the presidential couple was not much committed to the formal side of White House entertaining. President Roosevelt observed in January 1908 that "formal social entertainments are rather a nightmare to me." Will and Nellie Taft, on the other hand, enjoyed giving parties and receptions as much as they enjoyed attending such events. In her memoirs, Mrs. Taft spoke of informal dinners "nearly every night as a matter of fact" while only "once in a while we dined alone." If the Tafts did not qualify as the Progressive Era equivalent of "party animals," the pace of their entertaining and cultural activities made them the most intense social couple in the White House of the four administrations between 1897 and 1921.[49]

The new first lady adopted a hectic schedule of activities to show what she had in mind for the national capital. She took her twelve-year-old son, Charlie, and his school friends to an "illustrated lecture" on Russia at the Columbia theater. Although she wanted a conventional gasoline-powered automobile of her own, the president said no to that. She did obtain "an electric machine" in late April and "took her first spin in it, handling the levers and the steering bar herself." The vehicle would have "a horn of a peculiar sound" in order to achieve a distinctive "honk-honk" that would tell other cars that Mrs. Taft was driving. The *Washington Post* said in an editorial that "no greater contrast can be found between the pomp and state of a European court and the democracy of America than to see the wife of the President driving her own automobile in the streets of Washington."[50]

During the early weeks of the new administration, Nellie Taft also showed that she intended to have a voice in the patronage policies of her husband. When she mentioned finding an appointment for a personal friend in the Justice Department, Gist Blair, a member of the prominent Blair family from Maryland, the president sent her a jocular memorandum: "If you are going to give Gist Blair a place in this Administration you had better talk with the Attorney General about him. He has the power of appointment over his Department. Don't come to me, who have very little influence in this Administration."[51] Blair did not obtain the post he was seeking.

Nellie Taft's reputed involvement in a high-profile diplomatic appointment proved to be another step in the fraying relationship of the Tafts with Theodore Roosevelt. Since the time when Henry White had sent Will and Nellie Taft on the second-choice visit to the Royal Stables in 1886 on their honeymoon, the diplomat had become one of the major players in American foreign relations. Theodore Roosevelt esteemed White's abilities and used him on numerous foreign assignments. White had been named the American ambassador to France in the spring of 1907, where he gained even more respect from President Roosevelt. In the mind of the retiring president, few members of the diplomatic corps equaled White in skill or knowledge. Roosevelt expected that his friend would be retained when the new administration took office.[52] For the Tafts, on the other hand, White had remained an irritant when they encountered him during their travels in Europe in the Roosevelt presidency. Will Taft had called him "such an infernal snob and toady," while Charles P. Taft had avoided any contact with White during a visit to London.[53]

White was something of a snob who cultivated those who could help him and looked down on those who could not do so. Soon after the election, there was talk in Washington that he was "to be removed owing to private adverse influences." A worried White wrote the president-elect about his situation. Will Taft replied that he would not turn to "foreign appointments" until after the Cabinet had been confirmed. He assured White "that the fullest consideration will be given to your desire to continue in the diplomatic service and no change will be made without due notice and opportunity for discussion." Henry Cabot Lodge told his friend that Taft planned to retain him. "So that anxiety, if it is one, you may dismiss from your mind."[54]

In fact, the president had already decided to replace White. He planned to name another close Roosevelt ally, Robert Bacon, a J. P. Morgan partner and former State Department official, in White's place. That gesture would, in Will Taft's mind, compensate for the ouster of White. If that was what the president and his wife decided to do, the ploy did not work as they had hoped. White was indeed told that he would not be retained. "I am at a loss," wrote White to Lodge, "to imagine what can be the cause of the President's change of mind in regard to myself but suppose someone has got at Mrs. Taft and said something untrue about Daisy [Mrs. White] or me or both of us on some point respecting which she is sensitive." A British diplomat wrote of White: "One is sorry for him, though one cannot help smiling at the thought of how he has been paid out for what was a snobbish sentiment."[55]

Nellie Taft had her revenge, but it came at a substantial political cost. The episode rattled Senator Henry Cabot Lodge, a friend of both White and Theodore Roosevelt. Secretary of the Navy George von Lengerke Meyer noted in his diary on 11 March 1909: "Cabot seems disturbed over the influence that Mrs. Taft is going to have in this administration. She has fixed ideas & intends to assert herself. The Taft family are he believes trying to prejudice him against every thing Roosevelt even against many of the former president's friends."[56]

Roosevelt was then on safari in Africa when he heard about White's removal. He wrote his friend that he could not criticize Taft over the situation, but he made it clear that he thought White's case had been badly handled. The episode contributed to the sense of alienation from Taft that Roosevelt developed while he was in Africa. By the time it occurred, Nellie Taft had become ill and she never commented on what happened to Henry White. Meanwhile, White was writing influential friends within the Republican establishment that the episode "shakes my faith in the strength of character of the President whom I have always thought a strong man as if he can be influenced by his wife's personal feelings in my case he can also be in others & still more serious ones."[57]

During the busy first two months of her husband's presidency, Nellie Taft made frequent appearances in the newspapers as she started her various charitable and cultural commitments. She had been named the honorary chair of the woman's department of the National Civic Federation in December 1908. That organization, looking to promote better relations between capital and labor, had received a petition about the status of female employees in govern-

Helen Taft and feathered hat. The first lady favored the fashionable feathered hats of the early twentieth century for her garden parties and out-of-doors events.
(Library of Congress)

ment agencies such as the bureau of printing and engraving. The document was sent on to Nellie Taft, and her letter reached the *Washington Post.* Although she could no longer be the formal chair of the committee on "welfare work for government employees," she was "just as much interested in the progress of the work" and was "glad to have you send me anything relating to your work." The first lady agreed to appear when the federation met in Washington at the end of April 1909.[58]

On the cultural side, Mrs. Taft demonstrated her commitment to the musical community in Washington. On 16 March she "occupied a box at the National Theater" when the Boston Symphony Orchestra performed. A month later, a singer named Leila Livingston Morse gave a song recital at the White House that featured works by Schumann and Strauss as part of the program. A dance for Robert and Helen Taft also occurred on 13 April. This was part of a process that in time made the musicale "one of the favorite vehicles of formal entertainment at the Executive Mansion. Indeed, it has had preference over all other forms of entertaining."[59]

To facilitate her musical ambitions, Nellie Taft took advantage of an offer she had received from her old friend, Lucien Wulsin of the Baldwin Piano Company in Cincinnati. For years, Steinway & Sons had furnished their instruments to the White House and managed the appearances of musical artists at the mansion for cultural events. On 2 February 1909, Wulsin asked Helen Taft to "buy from us, for one dollar, love and affection, two pianos or whatever you may need for the White House." Noting that Steinway had provided pianos for the Roosevelts, Wulsin was "vain enough to believe that we would offer for your acceptance, instruments that you need not be ashamed of having in the Presidential Mansion."[60]

Nellie Taft waited until she was in the White House to inform Wulsin that "there is still room for another" piano in the mansion. She wrote him "with many thanks and great pleasure" that she would place his piano in the Blue Room. The piano was made during the summer of 1909 and arrived at the White House during the fall. The first lady told Wulsin that she would use the Blue Room for the smaller musicales that she intended to give during the spring of 1910. She was grateful "for this splendid gift which has given me so very much pleasure."[61]

The press soon noted Helen Taft's musical emphasis. In April, there was talk about how "Mrs. Taft sets fashions in Washington." One example of the change from Edith Roosevelt was the placement of "a magnificent grand piano" in the Blue Room of the mansion. "Mrs. Taft, as everybody knows, is an artist of no mean worth and a patron of music, so nobody wondered much at the 'glorification of the piano.' "[62]

The round of White House receptions and dinners was on in the spring of 1909. The new president invited members of Congress without regard to whether they had supported or criticized him, a departure from the practice under Roosevelt. Ellen Maury Slayden, the wife of a Texas representative, came on 1 May 1909 and recorded her impression of the new first lady. "She was direct and sincere as I have always found her, but she looked dreadful and spoke of not being well. I thought the inauguration had tired her, but she said she had suffered of nerves all through the campaign while Mr. Taft was so constantly traveling in crowds where there was danger of accidents and bombs."[63]

The appearance of Washington itself was another priority for Nellie Taft in this early phase of her time as first lady. From a Washingtonian named Eliza Scidmore, she received the suggestion that the planting of Japanese cherry trees would beautify some of the roadways of the city. She responded on 7 April 1909 that "I have taken the matter up and am promised the trees" from Japanese diplomats, who had offered her two thousand trees. David G. Fairchild, who conducted research on plants for the Department of Agriculture, knew the first lady and echoed Scidmore's suggestion about cherry trees. Mrs. Taft informed the government's landscape gardener at the time that she wanted cherry trees planted "so as to form masses, or continuous lines of bright color in the spring and early summer months when these trees bloom." By August the Japanese government had pledged five thousand trees. The *Washington Post* said that it would "delight the kindly soul of Mrs. Taft" to have Potomac Drive "glorified by the umbrageous beauty of the cherry trees." The trees were scheduled to arrive in the United States early in 1910.[64]

On 4 April 1909, Nellie Taft spoke with Archie Butt of her intention "to try to make the speedway in the Potomac Park what the Luneta was to Manila, the Malecon to Havana, and Hyde Park to London." She had already mentioned her idea to the press, and articles appeared the same day about how "the erstwhile repellant and fever-breeding 'flats' are to be transformed into a sort of fairyland of music, gayety, and athletics."[65]

The first semiweekly band concert occurred on 17 April with an attendance that Archie Butt described as a "crush." The first lady, he added, had "really provided a long-felt need here in the Capitol City." She attended the second concert on 28 April, "when any question as to the permanent success of this innovation was answered affirmatively." A longtime Washington resident recalled of these events that "delightful afternoons in May and June saw all Washington turn out in gala array to enjoy the sky and the river."[66]

In May *Harper's Bazaar* looked at "Interesting Women of the Capital." Nellie Taft led the list. "It is too early to appreciate Mrs. Taft in the White House, but not too soon to prophesy an exceptional social administration." The new first lady was "phenomenally executive. She forms her own plans, establishes her own methods, and in delightful self-reliance personally supervises everything till she is satisfied that those upon whom she wishes to depend are fully capable of executing her wishes according to the system she inaugurates. Whatever the White House is, it will be Mrs. Taft."[67]

The potential problem with this highly personalized approach, of course, was that it depended on the energy, strength, and good health of Nellie Taft herself. Should she falter, there was no way for her ideas for the institution of the first lady and the national capital to be implemented through the work of others. The president said on 12 May that "I am very proud of the way Nellie has taken hold of things at the White House." It was not easy to follow the Roosevelt administration, Will Taft continued, "but I really feel she has impressed her individuality on the few entertainments she has given so far."[68]

The only small worry was the health of their son, Charles. In mid-May he needed an operation on his tonsils, and surgery was scheduled for the 17th. Mrs. Taft was concerned about what her favorite child had to undergo, but she assured Captain Butt that everything was all right. That afternoon, however, Nellie Taft's tenure in the White House took a dramatic turn that brought an end to the bright hopes she had brought to the position of first lady since the inauguration.

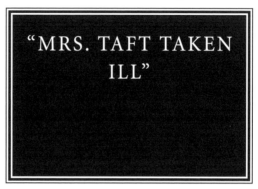

CHAPTER 3

"MRS. TAFT TAKEN ILL"

After two and a half months in the White House, Nellie Taft had good reason to be satisfied with her performance as first lady. On 16 May, the *Kansas City Star* and other newspapers told readers "that the complete social success of the Taft administration has been fully established within three months of its inauguration." The reporter praised the Friday afternoon receptions for eight or nine hundred guests and singled out the band concerts on the Esplanade as "already assuming a place in Washington life similar to that played by Hyde Park in London or the Bois de Bologne in Paris."[1]

Mrs. Taft was also often seen in the Senate gallery, where she went, according to another account, "three or four times a week, whenever any important speech is about to be made." Her aim, said the writer, "is trying to get on to the political situation so that she can advise the President. She is going to be one of the strongest women who have ever presided over the White House. She is changing the whole aspect of things in Washington." On 26 April, for example, she was in the gallery when flamboyant Democratic senator Joseph Weldon Bailey of Texas spoke on the protective tariff during the debate on what would become the Payne-Aldrich Tariff of 1909.[2]

In the White House itself, Nellie Taft had taken over with a firm hand. Long concerned about the family's finances, she now had the security of her husband's $75,000-a-year salary. She and Will Taft hoped to save several thousand dollars a month while in the presidency. At the same time, they would be personally responsible for many of the expenses of the presidential mansion. Accordingly, Nellie Taft decided to move away from the previous arrangement where the White House steward ran the building and private caterers handled the ceremonial dinners and other events. The goal of the new president and first lady was to "have it managed just as any other big home where considerable entertainment was necessary would be managed."[3]

To accomplish all that she had done and to plan even more elaborate programs for the future, the first lady had been driving herself with mounting intensity since the end of the presidential campaign. The self-imposed pressure should have been a warning to her and to the president. In the past when she had overextended herself, Will Taft wrote later, she had experienced "attacks which seem to proceed from nervous exhaustion, and in which her heart functions very feebly." Her husband believed that "it is not an organic trouble of the heart, but it seems to be some nervous affection." Henry Adams learned from the widow of John Hay that Mrs. Taft's attack in May 1909 was "the third time she has had something of the kind."[4]

It is not clear when such episodes occurred or how frequent they might have been in the past. In February 1902, she wrote her husband that her doctor had "given me something today for my rapid pulse which seems to be the cause of my discomfort and I hope to feel more comfortable after this."[5] Traveling in Europe in 1902, she had complained of various ailments. Her recuperative trip to England with her son, Charles, in 1905 may have grown out of similar conditions. By mid-May 1909 her hectic schedule had caught up with her. The insistence on making all the decisions about the living arrangements in the White House heightened the tension for her. Imperious and abrupt, she expected the White House staff to fulfill all her wishes with unquestioning efficiency. Relaxation was not part of her daily routine.

On Monday, 17 May 1909, personal worries added to her burdens. Charles Taft was scheduled for a hospital visit to have his adenoids removed. In the era before antibiotics, such an operation posed evident risks to all patients. She wished to be present when her favorite child went through the procedure. Although she did not see him being operated on, she felt the apprehension in the air throughout the facility. She was relieved but somewhat shaken when the operation was over. As Archie Butt reported, "there was a good deal of blood, and the poor boy was hysterical when he came from under the ether."[6]

The president came to the hospital with Attorney General George Wickersham, Butt, and others, and they went on to the Navy Yard to board the yacht for the scheduled trip to Mount Vernon. As they got under way, the attorney general "said something" to the first lady, "which she did not answer." Wickersham became concerned and told Archie Butt: "Mrs. Taft has fainted. See if there is any brandy aboard." The vessel turned around and headed back toward Washington and the White House. The president reported to his son, Robert, that "she did not lose consciousness, but she did have a very severe nervous attack, in which for the time being she lost the muscular control of her right arm and her right leg, and of her vocal chords, and the muscle governing her speech." Butt recalled that "the President looked like a great stricken animal. I have never seen greater suffering or pain shown on a man's face."[7]

Once back at the White House, the decision was made to treat the first lady there. The daily diary that recorded her activities for 17 May read: "Mrs. Taft Taken Ill." At no time was any thought given to a hospital stay for her continuing convalescence. The president turned instead to the White House doctor, Major Matthew A. Delaney of the army's medical corps, for Mrs. Taft's therapy and recuperation. A graduate of the University of Pennsylvania medical school in 1898, the thirty-five-year-old Delaney had joined the army's medical corps in 1901. He was a surgeon and does not seem to have had particular expertise in the area of strokes and their treatment, even by the standards of 1909.[8] As time passed, however, the president brought in specialists to handle his wife's continuing recovery.

While Mrs. Taft rested upon returning to the White House, her husband carried through with a formal dinner that evening. The press received a formal statement from the president himself. "Mrs. Taft is suffering from a slight nervous attack. She was attended by specialists this morning, where Charles Taft underwent a slight operation for the throat. She was with him for several hours. She then started with the President and a party of friends on the Sylph for Mt. Vernon. The excitement, heat and exertion were too much for Mrs. Taft's nerves and the party was obliged to turn back before reaching Alexandria." Only to close friends did Taft mention the severity of his wife's condition.[9]

Many years later, Helen Taft's daughter shed further light on what had taken place with her mother. In 1964, *Time* magazine did a story about Lady Bird Johnson and the Democratic National Convention of that year. As a sidebar to the main narrative, a photograph of Helen Taft was included along with the statement that as first lady, she had attended Cabinet meetings. Helen Taft Manning wrote to correct the record on that point. In the process, she made the most extensive public statement of what had happened to her mother. "Within two months of my father's inauguration, my mother suffered a brain hemorrhage which rendered her unconscious for four or five days and from the effects of which she never fully recovered. For the next two years she had, most unwillingly, to accept the role of invalid. During the whole period of my father's presidency I doubt whether she visited the executive offices half a dozen times."[10]

Yet it was not long before word of what had happened leaked out to the gossipy Washington community. Edith Roosevelt knew some of the details of her successor's illness within two days and was writing her son Kermit, who was with his father on safari in Africa, about the background of Mrs. Taft's "nervous collapse."[11]

Will Taft's public announcement of his wife's illness represented a small step forward in presidential candor. During the McKinley presidency, the epilepsy of Ida McKinley was well known in official Washington but never alluded to in the press beyond the most vague generalities. Edith Roosevelt guarded her privacy, and there was no knowledge of her two miscarriages while her husband was in office. The medical bulletins about the first lady, such as they were, did not mention a stroke and left the impression that the first lady was exhausted or had experienced a nervous breakdown.

Helen Taft had suffered a stroke that left her unable to speak. The paralysis in her right arm and leg eased within an hour, but her vocal cords and throat did not function. She seems to have experienced a form of verbal apraxia that entailed "the inability to perform complex or skilled speech acts."[12] A more precise definition of apraxia says that the "patient has trouble speaking because of a cerebral lesion that prevents his executing voluntarily and on command the complex motor activities involved in speaking, despite the fact that muscle strength is undiminished."[13]

The lingering effects of the stroke on her speech persisted for the remainder of her life. After the presidency, she was able to speak with more fluency. In 1909, however, an articulate and bright woman found herself unable to use her voice to make her feelings and needs known to family and friends. In essence, Nellie Taft had to learn with painful slowness to speak all over again. Her husband wrote that "after two or three days she began to talk, but this was slowly and with difficulty." A month after the stroke, Washington insiders commented that "she is improving, and is now able to talk a little, but has to be taught like a child." Archie Butt told Edith Roosevelt on 16 June 1909 that "Mrs. Taft is still too wretchedly ill to see anyone."[14]

Modern treatment for strokes emphasizes having the patient become as active as possible as soon as feasible. During the Taft presidency, the consensus of doctors was that patients needed rest and quiet to overcome what had happened to them. Given Nellie Taft's inability to speak with any degree of clarity, public appearances were out of the question for the immediate future. Guarded medical comments came from the White House about her condition. "Mrs. Taft's Health Better" was one typical headline that newspapers carried during July and August 1909.[15]

Behind the scenes, the president and his family evolved a regimen for caring for his now-invalid spouse. Mrs. Taft's sister, Eleanor More, came to help her with the daily routine. Her daughter, Helen Taft, took leave from her studies at Bryn Mawr College to assist her mother. They began a process of teaching her how to speak again. As the president reported to his sister on 25 June 1909, "she reads aloud and Eleanor and Helen read aloud to her and each week we can see a decided improvement in her fluency of speech." One sentence which she learned to repeat to her doctor was, "I am as obstinate as a mule."[16]

Two days later, on 27 June 1909, the president was positive about his wife's situation with their close friend, Mabel Boardman. "Am glad to say," he told her, "that Nellie is getting stronger and better. She has been out riding two or three times, and expects to go again this afternoon. We can see from week to week that her speech is becoming more fluent, although it will take quite a time for her to entirely recover it."[17]

President Taft himself participated in the therapy process for his wife as she relearned "the whole art of speech." Elizabeth Jaffray, the housekeeper at the mansion, recalled "the scores of times that I saw him sitting by her side on a sofa, with his hands over hers, saying over and over again: 'Now please, darling, try and say "the" —that's it, "the." That's pretty good, but now try it again.'"[18]

The whole process was a very slow one for an active woman such as Nellie Taft. She had kidney stones and anemia in the month after her attack. Some aspects of the treatment must have been difficult for the first lady. Two weeks after the stroke, "the Doctor gave her a machine for applying electricity to her throat in order to facilitate the return of the control of the muscles and nerves governing vocal expression."[19] Helen Taft was candid in evaluating their mother's situation when she wrote her brother: "She talks a little better each day but she can say very little unless she repeats after you. She can repeat almost anything and can read out quite fluently though not very distinctly." The president looked on the positive side of these developments and remained optimistic that some rest and recuperation at their summer residence in Beverly, Massachusetts, "will bring about a complete restoration of her strength and health and power of speech." Will Taft then added, "I am not working too hard, and but for Nellie's illness I should be enjoying much my experience."[20]

For the first two months after her stroke, Nellie Taft becomes visible only through the comments of her husband and family about her condition. What the experience of living upstairs in the White House as an invalid was for her is not recorded. Archie Butt noted on 1 June that "she only comes into the corridor of the White House when she can do so without running any danger of seeing anyone." The president had been planning to include a visit to Washington State and Alaska for his transcontinental trip during the autumn of 1909. Out of deference to his wife, he decided to abandon that portion of the journey. When he told her of the decision, he reported that "it has had a very beneficial effect upon her, and I think she worried over my leaving her more than any of us suspected, for she realized that she could not go with me."[21]

As the first lady recuperated, one of her social initiatives for Washington faltered. With the onset of the heat of the summer in the city, attendance at the band concerts on Potomac Drive receded. By late June 1909, Colonel Spencer Cosby, the officer in charge of the buildings and grounds at the White House, told the president's secretary that there had been "insignificant attendance at the last two band concerts on Potomac Drive." He recommended that the events be suspended through the summer and they were.[22]

In an era predating air-conditioning, affluent residents of Washington and most senior government officials left the city during the summer to escape the swamplike heat and humidity of the capital. Even before Mrs. Taft became ill, she and the president had identified Beverly, Massachusetts, as the place for them to spend the summers. For years the Tafts had summered in Murray Bay in Canada. Continuation of that practice had to end while Will Taft was president. Chief executives by tradition did not leave the continental United States during their term of office. As one family member quipped, "if we could annex Murray Bay, the summer plans of the President would be easily settled."[23]

The announcement that the Tafts were seeking a summer home set off a wave of applications from various communities for the honor of hosting the president and his family. Beverly, Massachusetts, was on the coast, and it had ready access to the railroads that served Boston. There were in addition several nearby golf courses where the president could indulge his passion for the game. Helen Taft took the lead in making the selection of a house where her family could live during the summer. She worked with their wealthy friend, John Hays Hammond, to identify a large structure that provided a seaside dock where the presidential yacht *Sylph* could be anchored. With golf courses at hand and roads on which the traveling Taft could ride, Beverly seemed an ideal refuge after the cares of Washington.[24]

In 1909, however, the president could not take care of his wife during her convalescence at their summer residence until mid-August. Taft had called Congress into special session in April to revise the tariff laws. By early July, the Senate was still in the midst of its deliberations. It was clear that the completion of the tariff measure would consume the rest of the month and stretch into August. Mrs. Taft could not remain in Washington with any degree of comfort during that time. She and the rest of the family went to Beverly while the president made some ceremonial trips and then settled down in the White House to oversee the tariff struggle. The political future of the administration hinged on the outcome of the legislation.

As he had done during his travels as secretary of war and presidential candidate in 1908, William Taft wrote his wife daily with a review of what had happened about the tariff and Washington affairs in general. In a series of letters, the president described how each day developed, the people he met, and the decisions he reached. At the same time, from a distance, he encouraged her recovery. When their children, along with his half brother, Charles, arrived at Beverly, Will Taft hoped that "you will feel more like making the effort to talk with them than you have heretofore, because it is practice that brings about the changes you seek." He craved news of her improvement. "I hope that you are getting the good effects of the sea air," he told her on 14 July. "You do not write me anything about yourself. I wish you would."[25]

The handwritten letters that he received from his convalescing spouse gave news of the activities of their children on vacation. She commented occasionally about his lengthy reports on the tariff negotiations. "How interesting all your talks about the tariff are," she told him on 17 July. "I see today you made a statement as to what you were going to stand for. I hope you won't have to come down much on it, dear." Her letters provided a few indications of the continuing effects of her stroke, with words and letters crossed out here and there, but her overall meaning was always clear.[26]

Will Taft used his authority as president to be sure that his wife's recovery was as smooth as possible. The newspapers announced that "Mrs. Taft will not entertain or be entertained by the Summer colony on the North Shore." The Secret Service men guarding the president and his family were instructed "that under no circumstances was Mrs. Taft to be disturbed."[27] Bulletins came from "the summer White House," and Dr. Delaney noted that the first lady "has showed a marked improvement in health." Nonetheless, strict limits on her strength remained in place. "She is not receiving friends at present, and though she is getting very much stronger, it is necessary for her to remain very quiet," Will Taft instructed one potential visitor.[28]

In early August, the president signed the Payne-Aldrich Tariff, and Congress adjourned the special session after months of wrangling over customs duties. Will Taft hurried to his wife's side in Massachusetts. When the president left the train and climbed into the waiting car where his wife and her sister waited, "he presented both his wife and Mrs. More with a resounding Taft smack, squarely on the lips and affectionately impressed. This, the belle dames of Beverly say, was awkward to say the least. Mr. Taft, however, as well as his wife and Mrs. More, did not appear to consider the incident at all unusual."[29]

During the following month, the president and his family took what vacation time they could amid the duties of the presidency. Will Taft and Nellie went on daily motor trips, with the driver instructed to keep the speed down to twenty miles an hour. The president played golf with his customary intensity and mediocre scores. On the business side, he dealt with the emerging controversy in the Interior Department about the record of its secretary, Richard A. Ballinger, and the criticism of the chief forester, Gifford Pinchot. Most of all, Will Taft looked ahead to a two-month tour of the continental United States that would begin in mid-September and end in November. The president had decided to make a stop in Washington and Oregon, but had remained true to his pledge not to travel to Alaska. Nonetheless, the excursion would be a strain on his wife first in Beverly and then after mid-October in the White House.

With the president now on the scene, the condition of the first lady seemed to be getting better. Archie Butt confided that she was "improving very rapidly now, and the President is very optimistic that she will be able to resume her duties in the winter, but I fear she will not be able to do so." Will Taft was encouraged that his wife seemed to be returning to her old ways. He wrote to his brother, Horace, that "she is quite disposed to sit as a Pope and direct me as of yore, which is an indication of the restoration of normal conditions, which you will fully realize."[30]

By the middle of September, it was time for the presidential party to leave for the West. For the next two months, Will Taft poured out his comments on the people he saw, the political situation, and his concern for his wife's well-being. Throughout his trip, he kept up the flow of encouragement and praise for her efforts to regain her ability to speak with fluency. "I am glad to hear from you and from Carpenter, of your going to the theatre and of your taking an interest in so many things, and I hope that gradually—not too rapidly, but gradually—you will continue to see your old friends, and that the embarrassment will wear off and the confidence in yourself return."[31]

Her letters talked of her daily routine, some bridge playing, and the shopping trips she made in Washington and New York. In mid-November, the president's half brother reported that "We saw Nellie for two or three days in New York and were delighted to see what progress she made since last summer. I am sure you must feel especially grateful."[32] By the time the president returned from his cross-country trip, only a month remained before Congress convened for its regular session and the social season at the capital got under way.

While the president was on the road, Mrs. Taft returned to Washington in October to prepare for her first full social season. During that period, the White House physician, Dr. Matthew A. Delaney, consulted with Dr. Lewellys F. Barker of the Johns Hopkins University medical school. A specialist in circulatory problems and the nervous system, Barker visited the White House and examined the first lady. "I am sure Mrs. Taft is very much encouraged at what he told her," Delaney reported to her husband. Barker "found her practically normal except for the one trouble—articulation—and told her that that only required rest time and the same treatment she has been receiving to restore her to health." Unhappily, Barker "could not say just how [long] it would take but judging from the rapid progress she has made since you saw her it will not be too long."[33]

The two physicians agreed that it would be good to engage "someone to re-educate the speech muscles, and Dr. Barker thinks this is a very good plan, and we are going to start this just as soon as we can get a proper teacher." Delaney concluded on an upbeat note. "Mrs. Taft is very much better, is constantly improving, and is now very optimistic about herself." Despite these encouraging signs, the first lady's progress would be slower than Delaney's forecast.[34]

At the end of November, Mrs. Taft's secretary, Alice Blech, announced her engagement to Richard Wainright Jr., a naval officer. The newspaper stories on her impending marriage said that Blech was "averse to the notice of the public." Blech had withstood Nellie Taft's insistence on being her own social secretary. The first lady had signed every piece of her outgoing mail that left from the White House. Blech worked long hours in what was the job of a clerk without much influence on her boss. The example of Belle Hagner and her role with Edith Roosevelt was one that Helen Taft was still determined should not occur during her tenure. Blech's departure meant that a new secretary would have to be found before her wedding occurred during the early spring of 1910.[35]

The first lady experienced a significant disappointment for one of her projects to beautify Washington, D.C., in late 1909 and early 1910. The cherry trees that were sent from Japan arrived in the United States during December. When the Department of Agriculture inspected them, however, they were found to contain "root gall works, certain fungus diseases, and insects pests, some of the latter hitherto unknown in this country." In addition, the trees were "entirely too large for replanting" and would not have survived in any case. The infected trees were destroyed, and regrets were expressed to the Japanese government and the mayor of Tokyo. In Japan, preparations for sending other trees began, but it would be more than a year and a half before the second shipment of cherry trees arrived to be planted.[36]

The return of Congress in December 1909 came at a time when President Taft's political fortunes had declined from the optimism of the postinauguration period. The enactment of the Payne-Aldrich Tariff had been a difficult process that left the Republican Party split between conservatives and progressives. There were also signs of tension within the administration because of the emerging feud between Secretary of the Interior Richard A. Ballinger and the chief forester, Gifford Pinchot, over conservation policy. Because Pinchot was a close friend of Theodore Roosevelt, any controversy over his role threatened to expose reservations that Will Taft now had about his predecessor and his policies. Resurgent Democrats looked to make gains in the 1910 congressional elections. The Taft administration faced a difficult winter and spring during the long session of Congress.

Theodore Roosevelt planned to return to the United States from his African safari in the spring of 1910 as well. By then, the strains in the friendship of Taft and Roosevelt were the stuff of Washington gossip. The Roosevelt camp was convinced that Mrs. Taft in particular had been determined to overshadow the former administration in every way that she could. Her disdain for Alice Roosevelt Longworth impelled her to take steps to frustrate her more prominent social rival in matters large and small. The first lady boasted to Archie Butt that she had been the deciding element in blocking an attempt by Nicholas Longworth to obtain an appointment as minister to China. As she told Butt, "she simply would not have it, as she thought neither Nick nor Alice fitted for this post under present conditions."[37]

Nellie Taft's action has been seen as one of the steps in the deterioration of relations between the Roosevelt and Taft camps. It is not clear, however, just when Mrs. Taft exercised her negative influence. The post of minister to China came open when President Taft decided to move W. W. Rockhill, the incumbent holdover from the Roosevelt administration, to St. Petersburg. Will Taft then offered the post to a former senator, who declined. The president turned to his personal friend, John Hays Hammond, who also said no. Finally, at the urging of the Chicago business community, Charles R. Crane of that city got the nod. Taft informed Nellie on 14 July 1909 of Crane's willingness to serve, and the White House announced his selection two days later.[38]

The question of Nicholas Longworth arose in a conversation that President Taft had with Archie Butt on 18 July. Should Longworth be defeated in the 1910 election, Taft said, he hoped to find a congenial patronage position such as governor of Puerto Rico, to console the defeated candidate. China was not mentioned because Crane was already the designated choice for the post.[39]

In mid-October, however, Crane's selection ran into trouble. He leaked documents to the press and took positions against what the White House wanted. Secretary of State Philander Knox recalled Crane, who was on his way to Beijing, and dismissed him. The administration now had an opening. At this point, Nick Longworth could well have asked, as Archie Butt paraphrased Mrs. Taft's report, "to be sent to China and was willing to resign his seat to accept the mission." According to Mrs. Taft, while Longworth's candidacy was being considered, she stepped in and vetoed the appointment. Her decision seems odd on the merits. Sending the Longworths to China would have placed her bitter social rival thousands of miles away and rendered Alice's malice irrelevant. Once she spoke about her decision to Archie Butt, she probably mentioned her maneuver to others. In the hothouse of Washington gossip, her words likely reached the former president's daughter. The first lady had added her contribution to the growing tension between the Taft and Roosevelt camps without really helping her husband in any meaningful way.[40]

In any event, Nick Longworth's name did not come up in the deliberations that Secretary Knox and the president had about the China mission. After some searching, they settled on William James Calhoun, a supporter of William McKinley in the 1890s and a special envoy under Theodore Roosevelt as well.[41] The extent to which Mrs. Taft's influence operated in the China mission for any candidate is still unclear.

The onset of the official social season in December revived rumors about the fragile state of Mrs. Taft's health. She intended to play as large a part as possible within the limits of her physical condition. At the same time, her sisters would provide valuable assistance in dealing with the demands of the large receptions and official dinners that made up the Washington season. As these arrangements became public, the White House battled rumors that the first lady was going to defer to her sisters or even Mabel Boardman. Alice Blech spoke to the press and told them that "Mrs. Taft will be the White House hostess during the coming season, contrary rumors notwithstanding."[42] At the annual presidential reception for the people on New Year's Day, Mrs. Taft "seemed rather pale" but stayed in the receiving line through the Cabinet, the diplomatic corps, and the Supreme Court justices.[43] Despite these successful appearances, newspaper columnists noted that "it is commonly known that the president is alarmed over the state of her health."[44]

Mrs. Taft launched several innovations at the initial state reception of her tenure as first lady on 3 January 1910. The White House provided refreshments for the throng "for the first time in many administrations," and the guests enjoyed "oysters, salads, ices, and champagne punch." Mrs. Taft cut back on the number of invitations in an effort to have "every guest present" feel that they were "the personal guest of the President and his wife." To that end, this reception made no distinction between those who were invited into "the Blue Room circle," as had been done under the Roosevelts, and those who were not. The previous practice of "separating the sheep from the goats" disappeared.[45]

Throughout the winter and spring of 1910, Nellie Taft appeared in public with her husband to convey a sense of recovery and a return to normal. She was at the ballpark of the Washington Nationals on opening day, 14 April 1910, when the president threw out the first ball for the season in what would become an annual spring rite for subsequent presidents. That same month, she was listed as one of the sponsors of the Sister Marie Louise Guild to help the work of orphan asylums in Japan that the guild operated. The Brightwood Park Citizens' Association praised the president and the first lady for their efforts to beautify Washington in general.[46]

The spring of 1910 brought the resumption of a practice that Mrs. Taft had initiated before her stroke. The *Washington Post* called the garden parties that she hosted "a series of al fresco entertainments in the picturesque grounds around the White House." These events were not open to the public. As the president's secretary explained to a citizen seeking an invitation, "the Garden Parties at the White House are distinctively Mrs. Taft's affairs. They are entirely different from the regular public receptions of the winter."[47]

The parties began on 6 May 1910 with the president and Mrs. Taft receiving the guests. The president had been traveling in the Middle West but he hurried back to be there on that date because "Mrs. Taft has a garden party . . . which she is very anxious to have me attend." As the guests mingled on the grounds, "the Marine Band played throughout the afternoon, their scarlet uniforms lending a picturesque touch of color to the scene." The second party on May 13 fell victim to cold weather and was moved inside. Two more parties followed during the rest of May 1910. The first lady had even more ambitious plans for the White House grounds.[48]

In mid-June, an afternoon performance of *Twelfth Night* took place at the White House. The young actor Charles Coburn and his wife, Ivah Wills Coburn, with their Coburn Players, staged the play. Although he would become famous for his movie roles as an older

Charles Coburn on the White House grounds. A young Charles Coburn paused at the White House for a photographer as he prepared to stage Shakespeare for Mrs. Taft and the president in June 1910. (Coburn Papers, Hargrett Library, University of Georgia, Athens)

man in the 1940s and 1950s, the thirty-three-year-old Coburn in his early career was devoted to spreading theater to the masses. The Coburn troupe had been in existence since 1906, giving out-of-doors productions of "all Shakespearean plays that were written for such a setting" around the country. In this instance, the actors came to the mansion at the invitation of the first lady. The *Washington Times* told its readers that "for the first time in the history of the White House a theatrical performance will be given on the lawn at night." The event would occur, said the advertising, "through the courtesy of Mrs. Taft."[49] The program was scheduled for 16 June 1910, but rain caused a twenty-four-hour postponement. Despite clouds and a threat of more rain, the Coburns went ahead as planned on the afternoon and evening of 17 June with both of their productions. President Taft was there for the afternoon performance, sitting in the back with his program like any other guest.

When the Coburns presented *As You Like It* that night, President and Mrs. Taft remained in their seats "even though a few gentle drops of rain stampeded some of the listeners." The two plays benefited the Playground Association of Washington, and the persistence of the Tafts, despite the weather, made the occasion a success. A happy Charles Coburn wrote to a friend two days later: "We are still palpitating with the excitement of our delightful experience at the White House. It is a memory the Coburn players will long keep. President and Mrs. Taft used such discretion through the trying weather conditions and helped to make our appearance there most happy."[50]

As for Nellie Taft herself during the winter and spring of 1910, the president remained hopeful that his wife would make a full recovery from her stroke. "Nellie is getting along well," he informed his brother Horace in March. "At times when she is nervously tired her speaking is with less facility than at other times, but I think she is steadily improving." Doctor Barker had come to the White House again from Baltimore to see his patient. He assured Will Taft "that she made remarkable progress in the preceding two months." It would be the end of the year "before she will feel herself again; but meantime I think she is enjoying life more than she has in the past."[51]

This bright picture of his wife's condition was at odds with other elements of life in the White House. In March 1910, the first lady's

Shakespeare at the White House. In mid-June 1910, Charles Coburn and the Coburn Players staged a production of Twelfth Night *outdoors on the White House grounds. (Charles Coburn Papers, Hargrett Library, University of Georgia, Athens)*

brother-in-law, Thomas M. Laughlin, committed suicide because of business failures and the imminent exposure of his embezzlement. The family attempted to keep the cause of death a secret, but word leaked out that he had shot himself. Mrs. Taft was not strong enough to accompany the president to the funeral. In late May, Mrs. Taft's father, John W. Herron, was reported gravely ill and likely to die soon. That judgment proved premature, but family worries shaped the first lady's existence during these months.[52]

To replace Alice Blech as her secretary, Mrs. Taft recruited a young woman, Mary Dandridge Spiers, from the Department of the Navy to fill the post. When her appointment was announced, the newspapers emphasized the crucial nature of her role in assisting the first lady. Mrs. Taft expected her secretary to serve a clerical function while the first lady herself "personally selects the guests she wishes at each tea, musicale, or small dinner party, her secretary merely writing the note of invitation."[53]

Spiers began work on 2 April 1910, and within two weeks, she was out. News of her resignation appeared in the newspapers on 15 April 1910. In a letter to President Taft asking to be restored to her previous position or located elsewhere in the government, Spiers noted only that Mrs. Taft wished to make a change. The first lady had already acquired a reputation as a difficult taskmaster. Her granddaughter would later note a propensity on Mrs. Taft's part to discipline employees in front of friends and family. It is likely that some such incidents or episodes along those lines convinced Nellie Taft that Mary Spiers would not be satisfactory.

After Spiers departed, a woman named Katherine Letterman who worked at the Department of State succeeded her and stayed on for the next three years. Born in Philadelphia in 1875, Letterman proved to be the capable and efficient assistant that the first lady had been seeking.[54]

Nellie Taft's inability to delegate her responsibilities to her aides contributed to her ongoing problems as first lady. She wished to expand the commitments of her position in cultural and social affairs while also taking on roles in various charitable organizations. The demands on her time were intense, especially for a person with continuing physical issues arising from her stroke. Her insistence on doing everything for herself taxed her limited energies and impaired her effectiveness in the White House.

By the spring of 1910, the return home of Theodore Roosevelt from his African hunting expedition was only weeks away. During the year when he was out of the country, relations between the president and his predecessor had deteriorated. Substantive policy differences over conservation, for example, had resulted in the firing of Gifford Pinchot, the chief forester, early in January 1910 in a blow to Roosevelt. At the same time, Nellie Taft's actions had exacerbated tensions. The transition from Edith Roosevelt to Nellie's regime had been difficult. The dismissal of Henry White from the embassy in Paris had been another move that the Roosevelt camp placed on Mrs. Taft's head.

Nicholas Longworth, writing to his father-in-law in late April 1910 to bring Roosevelt up to date on political developments, put most of the responsibility for the change in relations on Nellie Taft. The president, Longworth said, "has not changed a bit in his personal feelings either to yourself or to the things you stand for." This was true despite the differences in methods between the two presidents. The problem, Longworth believed, lay elsewhere. "He is surrounded by influences which are opposed to you, and I doubt very much if he knows it; and those influences, I believe, are largely in his own family." The approach of the White House to members of the Roosevelt family, Longworth concluded, "was, to say the least, extraordinary."[55]

Nick Longworth laid the blame for the unhappy situation at the door of Helen Taft. "The colored gentleman in the wood-pile was not a gentleman at all, but was Mrs. T. As you know, I have known her all my life and her family intimately. I know how the minds of the Herron family work, and I am just as sure that I sit here that from election day on she planned in every way to make the new Administration as different as possible from the last." But whatever Mrs. Taft's culpability in producing this state of affairs, "I don't believe anybody could have any other feelings but one of sympathy now, because today the person most responsible is one of the most pathetic figures in the country."[56] Roosevelt's reply to this letter, if one was sent, has not survived.

In Nellie Taft's defense, the Roosevelts, particularly Longworth's wife, acted in 1908–1909 as though the presidency was on loan to Will Taft and his wife. The family of the outgoing chief executive interpreted many things that Nellie Taft did as negative reflections on Theodore and Edith's tenure in the White House. They did not recognize the likelihood that changes would occur, given the different tastes and ideas of the couple that succeeded Roosevelt in office. Alice in particular conducted herself as if she should still be treated as a resident of the mansion and a famed presidential daughter.

With that said, Nellie Taft herself behaved as though her husband did not need the political support of Theodore Roosevelt in his projected reelection in 1912. Some solicitude for the feelings of the Roosevelts would have been appropriate and wise. The president had to urge his wife to write a bread-and-butter letter to Edith Roosevelt at one point. Had Nellie Taft been more politically astute, she could have found simple ways to behave in a polite and thoughtful manner to the Roosevelt family. Instead, as in the case of Henry White, she took actions that left few doubts about what she sought to do in asserting her own sense of social superiority.

By the spring of 1910, the Taft administration had rebounded from the problems of the first year and had achieved some success in the long session of Congress. The Republicans confronted rocky prospects for the congressional elections in the fall. The achievements of the White House, however, gave Taft and his aides some confidence that they might overcome division in their own party and hold down Democratic gains. The great unknown was what Theodore Roosevelt would do upon his return to the United States. Taft bought some much-needed time by naming his predecessor to serve as the representative of the United States to the funeral of King Edward VII in London in late May. The president endeavored to fill Roosevelt in on the political situation in a lengthy handwritten letter of 26 May 1910. Although the bulk of the document dealt with the accomplishments and problems of the administration, Will Taft also summed up Nellie's health situation.

"My year and two months have been heavier for me to bear because of Mrs. Taft's condition," he wrote. "A nervous collapse, with apparent symptoms of paralysis that soon disappeared, but with an aphasia that for a long time was nearly complete, made it necessary for me to be as careful as possible to prevent another attack. Mrs. Taft is not an easy patient and any attempt to control only increased the nervous strain. Gradually she has gained in strength and has taken part in receptions where she could speak a formula of greeting, but dinners and social reunions where she has had to talk she has avoided."[57]

In a subsequent letter of 14 June 1910, carried by Archie Butt to Roosevelt when he arrived home in New York, the president asked his predecessor to come to visit him in the White House. The request was noteworthy for what it implied about Nellie Taft. "Mrs. Taft is leaving for Beverly via New Haven, in a few days, but I shall be here until Congress adjourns, and it would be a great joy to me to see you both here before I go to Beverly." If that invitation did not work, the Tafts could see the Roosevelts at their Beverly residence during the summer. The thrust of the message was that getting Edith and Theodore Roosevelt together in the same room with Will and Nellie Taft would not be the wisest course to follow.[58]

Along with his own letter to Roosevelt, Will Taft insisted that Nellie write a similar note to Edith Roosevelt asking her to come to the

White House. As Archie Butt put it, if the note were sent, "it can never be charged in the future that there was the slightest discourtesy toward Mr. or Mrs. Roosevelt from the White House. If either now feels aggrieved that more attention had not been shown to the children, not understanding Mrs. Taft's condition of health, I think a note of invitation from Mrs. Taft will set this right." The president had to push his wife to discharge this social obligation, but she did so. Archie Butt was not sure "that it will be altogether welcomed, for when women get at cross purposes it is hard to get them straightened out again."[59]

The letter from Nellie Taft did not achieve the warmth of what her husband had written to Theodore Roosevelt. Addressed to "My dear Mrs. Roosevelt," it extended "to you and President Roosevelt and your family a hearty welcome. I congratulate you that your husband and Kermit have returned to you safe and sound. Mr. Taft has invited you and President Roosevelt to visit us at the White House soon after your return. I earnestly second that invitation. I am sorry that I shall be at Beverly after June 22nd where I go to recuperate after the season. If you find it impossible to come to Washington now, Mr. Taft and I would be delighted to have you and Mr. Roosevelt visit us in the White House next December after Congress meets."[60]

For two women whose husbands had been friends for two decades and who had met weekly during the Roosevelt years, this document had a bloodless and detached quality. It conveyed no sense of an eagerness to meet with Theodore and Edith Roosevelt. No doubt those sentiments reflected Nellie Taft's genuine feelings. Although her continuing problems with her voice probably shaped the first lady's attitude regarding a visit from the former president and his wife, she was not willing to go further to conciliate Roosevelt than this empty gesture. Of course, neither did Edith Roosevelt encourage her husband to meet Taft halfway. The stored-up grievances that had been submerged during the 1908 campaign were now becoming evident.

Roosevelt and his wife declined the invitation on the lame grounds that former presidents should not come to Washington or visit the White House. Because previous former presidents had done these things, Will Taft concluded that Roosevelt for some reason did not wish to see him. However, the two men did get together in Beverly on 30 June in an awkward meeting that Helen Taft and her daughter attended, along with Henry Cabot Lodge and Archie Butt. Nellie Taft spoke up only once, according to Archie Butt. When the men discussed the possibility of having the retired industrialist, Andrew Carnegie, head a commission to pursue peace in Europe, she said, "I don't think Mr. Carnegie would do at all"—a judgment with which the men present concurred.

In her memoirs, the first lady observed that she "was glad on this occasion to find the old spirit of sympathetic comradeship still paramount and myself evidently proved to be unwarrantably suspicious." As the meeting passed off in a pleasant way, Roosevelt succeeded for the moment in "convincing me that he still held my husband in highest esteem and reposed in him the utmost confidence, and the rumors of his antagonism were wholly unfounded."[61]

If Nellie Taft had enjoyed any confidence in Roosevelt's intentions toward her husband's administration, she had kept them well hidden during the first year of the presidency. Her actions toward Henry White and Nick Longworth indicated a desire to remind the Roosevelt family of who was now president and first lady. The treatment of White had been especially galling to Roosevelt. As White himself told his wife, "T. has particularly resented the Presidential action regarding me after his promises before assuming office and seems quite unable to get over it."[62] A greater generosity of spirit about White's actions many years before would have served Nellie Taft well in 1909.

Theodore Roosevelt's support could not assure the success of the Taft administration, but his open enmity could guarantee that the president would not gain a second term in 1912. Nellie and Will Taft did not have to treat Roosevelt as a kind of copresident, but neither did they have to follow policies that seemed designed to emphasize the failings of his own administration. Nellie Taft obtained her revenge for the perceived slights she had experienced at the hands of Edith and Theodore Roosevelt. Her insistence on these actions, however, contributed to the events that led to the split between Taft and Roosevelt in 1912. In so doing, she ensured that her tenure as first lady would fall short of the ambitious agenda she brought to the White House.

In one area, however, Nellie Taft achieved some of the purposes that had animated her desire to be the first lady. The musical events that she staged in the White House brought to the mansion a variety of classical artists of the first rank. Even more than Edith Roosevelt, Mrs. Taft sought to use the White House as a cultural center to bring to the public the best in the music that she had enjoyed since her youth. The Tafts did not receive much credit for this phase of their four years in Washington. The political failure of the administration meant that their accomplishments in the social and cultural realm have largely been forgotten and neglected. Yet in the years before the outbreak of World War I, Nellie Taft set a high standard of artistic achievement for the first ladies who would follow her.

CHAPTER 4

MUSIC FOR NELLIE
TAFT, 1909–1910

When the subject of music in the White House arises, Helen Taft is not the first name that comes to mind. Edith Roosevelt and Jacqueline Kennedy hosted cellist Pablo Casals six decades apart. Florence Harding studied piano and had musicales, and Grace Coolidge invited Sergei Rachmaninoff and many other artists to perform during the 1920s, as did her successor, Lou Henry Hoover. Eleanor Roosevelt protested the banning of the African American singer Marian Anderson by the Daughters of the American Revolution in 1939. Even Richard Nixon, who thought Guy Lombardo played jazz, had Duke Ellington appear for a celebrated tribute in 1969. Jimmy Carter sang "Salt Peanuts" with Dizzy Gillespie, and Bill and Hillary Clinton invited a diverse array of popular and classical artists to perform at the executive mansion.

Mrs. Taft's extensive role as a patron of music, however, has receded from memory. The standard work on music at the White House by Elise Kirk has four informed pages on the gifted musicians who appeared during Nellie's tenure, but the narrative does not do justice to the breadth of talent that the first lady recruited. The first lady's biographer devoted only two pages to this phase of Nellie Taft's career in the presidency. Otherwise, what Mrs. Taft did to bring the best classical music and its performers to the White House has now been forgotten.[1]

Yet over the long history of American first ladies, few occupants of that position did more to promote an understanding of classical music among her fellow citizens than did Nellie Taft. Despite the persisting effects of her stroke and the limitations that her physical condition imposed on her, she conducted a sustained campaign to bring distinguished artists to the White House to perform the works of both recognized and rising young composers. She made a special effort to feature women musicians, particularly pianists, and she fostered the music she loved at every opportunity.

Because of the sad fate of her husband's presidency and the fragmentary records of what she did, Nellie Taft had not received much recognition in this area. The William Howard Taft Papers contain the programs and some press accounts of the first lady's musicales. For one artist, the singer Beatrice Bowman, there is a file about how her appearance was arranged. No such material exists for the other prominent musicians who came to the White House to perform for Mrs. Taft. Even more disappointing is the absence of information about the working relationship between the first lady and Joseph Burr Tiffany of the Steinway & Sons who booked the artists. Only two brief telegrams from Mrs. Taft to Tiffany have survived. Yet notwithstanding these source problems, a careful review of the musicales she sponsored and the artists she invited indicates just how wide-ranging and innovative her musical taste was.

Music and theater had been integral parts of the cultural interests of Will and Nellie Taft since the days of their courtship during the 1880s. In the White House, they continued to be frequent attendees at operas, musicals, and drama in Washington and New York. Their letters recount the many plays they saw and the operas where they were in the audience. Newspapers in Washington noted how much the presidential couple did to patronize the arts in the capital.

Within the White House, President Taft enjoyed playing records on the primitive phonographs of that day. He had, his wife recalled, "a Victrola in the Blue Room and he never failed, when opportunity offered, to lay out a few favourite records for his evening's entertainment." The president's tastes ran to "Melba and Caruso, the Lucia Sextette, some old English melodies, a few lively ragtime tunes." It was for the Tafts "as pleasant a diversion as one could desire." Archie Butt obtained the latest popular songs for his boss, and they enjoyed hearing the disks in the evenings after a hard day of political work. The president's musical tastes were not on the sophisticated level of his wife, but he enjoyed the operas they attended as a couple. He had a penchant for the showy and dramatic, while Mrs. Taft had deeper knowledge and more tolerance for artistic innovation.[2]

Both the president and the first lady enjoyed theatrical productions and took in the shows and plays that came to Washington during their time in the White House. There was a presidential box at the local theaters that Mrs. Taft often occupied for such artists as Lillian Russell and the popular Irish actor-singer, Chauncey Olcott. In 1912, she saw Olcott perform in *Macushla,* "a romantic comedy about an Irish landowner and his race horse," and called it "a good play and he sang well seeing that he is sixty years old." Olcott was fifty-four when the first lady viewed that production.[3]

During the Christmas holidays of 1910, the president and his wife went to a production of a musical comedy, *Marriage a la Carte,* at the Belasco Theater. Their visit was not announced until just before the performance began. The play's company scrambled to arrange a suitable tribute to the presence of the first couple. When the Tafts and their party arrived, "the 25 men dressed in the brilliant uniform of English Hussar officers, stepped to the front of the stage, facing the President and drawing swords saluted, while the principals and chorus, standing in a semi-circle behind them, sang 'The Star-Spangled Banner' accompanied by the augmented orchestra of 40."[4]

Although he did not have his wife's expertise about serious music, the president enjoyed the musical interludes in his hectic schedule. In January 1910, the flamboyant New York impresario, Oscar Hammerstein I, sent his Manhattan Opera Company to Washington "for the most magnificent season of grand opera in the history of the Capitol." The charismatic Hammerstein brought his big-name stars, Mary Garden, Luisa Tetrazzini, and Lina Cavalieri, and a company to perform seven operas, including *Lucia di Lammermoor* and *The Daughter of the Regiment.* "I intend to give Washington a brief season of grand opera," Hammerstein told the press, "such as it has never had before—real grand opera." He also wired Will Taft, offering the first couple a box for the week's performances. "The President replied yesterday that he would accept the box with pleasure and that he would attend personally four of the six performances."[5]

Luisa Tetrazzini, 1909. The flamboyant Italian diva, Luisa Tetrazzini, as she looked at the time she sang for President and Mrs. Taft in Washington. (Library of Congress)

The president and the first lady were present for "the most brilliant first night of grand opera that the Capital of the nation has ever witnessed."[6] In his diaries, Archie Butt noted that the opera was *Lucia di Lammermoor*. Tetrazzini, in her account, stated that it was *The Daughter of the Regiment*. Recognizing that the president had come to the performance, she noted that "his magnificent, kindly face was beaming a welcome, and so I responded by marching right across the stage until I could almost step into his box. Then I gave 'him my cheeky little salute. The President broke into a roar of infectious laughter, and all the crowded house joined with him."[7]

The clever Hammerstein pulled off a second public relations coup when his performers visited the White House the next day to talk with the president and Archie Butt. Mary Garden, a soprano who also headlined the Hammerstein operas, joined Tetrazzini and the popular young tenor, John McCormack, for a conversation with the president. The nervous McCormack and his wife "walked twice" around the mansion before he went in. Inside, the president and Mary Garden chatted about promoting opera in Washington.[8]

During his conversation with Tetrazzini, Will Taft told her that one of his favorite tunes was the "Polonaise" from *Mignon*. She asked him in her less than perfect English if "you come tonight?" To which Taft replied, "Madame, not all the Cabinet dinners in the world could keep me away."[9] Aides for the Oscar Hammerstein I organization that was putting on the opera rushed to get the musical scores from Philadelphia for the president's request. At the evening's performance, "the President and Mrs. Taft were plainly pleased when the orchestra played the opening strains, and the audience, which had not been let into the secret, enthusiastically applauded." When her stay in Washington was over, Tetrazzini "called at the White House to say good-bye to Mr. and Mrs. Taft. To please the wife of the President, I sang a few songs." Will Taft gave her an autographed photograph with the inscription "in remembrance of 'Polonaise.'"[10]

The encounter of the diva with the president garnered extensive press coverage. "It is pleasant to note," wrote the *Kansas City Times,* "that President Taft heard Tetrazzini in 'Lucia di Lammermoor' last night. Every President ought to study the methods of those who have learned how to take a high note in a mad scene." "Mr. Taft is a grande papa," Tetrazzini told reporters. "I am glad he is fat. It is a pleasure to sing to him." The San Jose *Mercury News* quipped that "Mme. Tetrazzini recently sang for President Taft and showed him how to be entrancing though stout." A year later, when she was singing on the West Coast for charitable causes, the president sent a telegram thanking her "for what she has done for the Red Cross" and "the great pleasure she has given to the people of the United States and particularly the people of San Francisco." In return, the diva sent Taft "the little silver seal of the City of San Francisco" as a token of their friendship.[11]

Will Taft's enthusiasm for the music his wife admired helped the first lady plan an extensive program of concerts and recitals from the outset of her time in the White House. Her musicales built on the precedent that Edith Roosevelt had set between 1901 and 1909. Mrs. Roosevelt invited numerous prominent musicians to perform at the mansion. The young cellist, Pablo Casals, was one such notable guest. Later the Polish pianist and champion of his country's nationalism, Ignacy Jan Paderewski, was a featured artist. Edith Roosevelt's efforts went on despite the difficulty with her frenetic husband. He enjoyed ragtime but tended to become distracted and tense when required to listen to longer classical pieces.

In the case of the young pianist, Fannie Bloomfield-Zeisler (1863–1927), the performer turned down an invitation in December 1903 to perform for Mrs. Roosevelt when she learned that she would not be the only artist at the event. Joseph Burr Tiffany, who handled the booking of White House musicians for Steinway & Sons, told Bloomfield-Zeisler "that these musicales are purely social affairs and rigid adherence to the musical part is not necessarily observed." The first lady intended to "have a vocalist also for that evening, probably someone in the social circle to sing one or two selections." Bloomfield-Zeisler declined the request that she appear when an amateur musician was also on the evening's program.[12]

Edith Roosevelt's musicales were linked to the formal Washington social schedule that began when Congress reconvened each year and then extended on until Easter. In the summers, official Washington fled the swamplike atmosphere of the capital city in an era before air-conditioning. During the late autumn and through the winter, elaborate rituals of White House dinners and receptions for the diplomatic corps, Congress, the judiciary, and the military kept the political elite of the city busy. The president and first lady were the focus of these occasions. Edith Roosevelt used them to impart the cultural tone to the capital that she desired, and did so with a high degree of success.

When Will and Nellie Taft came to the White House, Washington was a city of more than three hundred thousand residents, two thirds of them white and the remainder African American. Within the structure of racial separation that made the capital a very Southern city, Washington responded to the chronological rhythms of the political year in its musical events and performances. As far as music was concerned, Washington did not have a symphony orchestra. An effort to establish one had faltered during the early years of the new century. Efforts to revive the symphony idea came to little during the Taft and Roosevelt presidencies.[13]

Yet this bleak picture did not do full justice to Washington's bustling musical scene. The capital was one of the many venues that prominent orchestras and renowned concert artists visited on their frequent tours of cities in the Northeast and mid-Atlantic states during this period. In the winter months, opera companies came to Washington for a week or two to present their current attractions. Although Washington lacked the large number of practicing professional musicians that existed in Boston, New York, or Chicago, polite society was exposed to the extensive variety of serious music that characterized the United States when Nellie Taft was the first lady.

In fact, the Tafts brought their musical interests to the national capital at a moment when American music itself was undergoing important changes. At the outset of the twentieth century, no clear line of demarcation separated serious music and what would later become popular music. Opera attracted large audiences, and the famous singers were treated in the manner of modern rock stars. Newspapers followed the tours of such artists as Tetrazzini and Enrico Caruso with rapt attention. For their appearances, the most famous of these singers received annual salaries that, in the case of Caruso, were more than double the $75,000 that President Taft earned. Other performers with a strong fan base garnered in excess of $100,000 per year. The Manhattan Opera House of Oscar Hammerstein I challenged the longtime supremacy of the Metropolitan Opera in New York City. In the world of the musical theater, it was the era of Franz Lehar and *The Merry Widow*, of Victor Herbert and *Naughty Marietta*, and of George M. Cohan and *Forty-Five Minutes from Broadway*.[14] The pulsing rhythms of Irvin Berlin and "Alexander's Ragtime Band" in 1911 would signal the emergence of new composers of popular songs that eventually supplanted serious music as a democratic art.[15] The onset of World War I and the temporary suppression of German artists and music would further end the milieu in which Nellie Taft functioned as first lady. In those brief prewar years, however, Mrs. Taft brought first-rate musicians to Washington for her guests to hear. She deserves to rank among the presidential wives who did the most to elevate the taste of the American people from her privileged setting.

Nellie Taft was not just someone who listened to and enjoyed music as a recreational activity. She followed developments in the classical music world with close attention and attended concerts and recitals in New York and Washington several times a week. In November 1910, for example, she went to see the production of *The Mikado* with the Austrian singer, Fritzi Scheff, and the veteran comic actor Digby Bell. She reported to her son Robert that "Fritzi Scheff did it very well and Digby Bell made a wonderful 'Lord High Executioner.'"[16]

When Oscar Hammerstein I produced Richard Strauss's controversial opera *Elektra* early in 1910, the first lady wired the empresario for tickets so that she could see the production.[17] Newspapers reported on other events where she spoke with musicians and soon thereafter invited them to perform at the White House. Aware that a request to play for the president and the first lady could not be declined, Nellie Taft capitalized on her chance to have the very best of American and foreign touring musicians play for her on a regular basis.

The first lady also saw to it that her husband took her to the opera productions she wished to see. During the spring of 1911, she wanted to attend a production of Jules Massenet's 1881 opera *Herodiade* about John the Baptist and Salome. Nellie Taft induced Archie Butt to ask the president whether he wished to go to the opera that evening. "Don't tell him what opera it is," she warned, "for he has never heard of it and will be sure to think it poor and not go." After Butt broached the idea, the president said: "Well, if you think I will enjoy it and Mrs. Taft has nothing else to do, see if you can get a box." Told of her husband's response, the first lady laughed: "Well, I don't think he will enjoy it, but we will." Will Taft dozed through the performance, but his wife achieved her goal of seeing the opera. Archie Butt found the work "a most delightful surprise."[18]

In her own ambitious vision to make Washington the center of the nation's cultural life, Nellie Taft went beyond what Mrs. Roosevelt had done and sought to locate her musical interests at the focus of Washington's social season. Because her husband's presidency began in March 1909, it was not possible to have a full schedule during her first spring in the White House. By the time she and the president settled in, there was only the opportunity for three musicales before her stroke took her out of the public eye.

In the first concert on 6 April 1909, the Philippine Constabulary Band, which had come to Washington for the presidential inauguration, performed twelve selections including a medley of "Filipino Airs," "Minuet No. 1" by Paderewski, and Beethoven's "Moonlight Sonata."[19] Since its establishment in 1902, the band had scored a triumph at the St. Louis World's Fair and become a recognized attraction under its director, Walter Loving. Taft had made a point of inviting the ensemble to be part of the inaugural festivities, and the eighty-six men had come to Washington to play for "the big Governor." The wind and snow at the inauguration had not deterred the musicians from performing. "The President," said one of the officers with the group, "is the only man on earth these little fellows would have tramped through that blizzard for." After a triumphant tour of New York and New England, the band was heading homeward, but not before it played for the president and Mrs. Taft at the White House.[20]

A week later, on 12 April 1909, Mrs. Taft hosted her first late-afternoon "song recital." Soprano Leila Livingston Morse (1878–1977), granddaughter of the inventor of the telegraph, Samuel F. B. Morse, appeared. This event signaled that Mrs. Taft intended to provide women artists with a prominent venue in the capital. Leila Morse had sung for Edith Roosevelt in 1902 and appeared with some frequency in New York and other cities. She sang a dozen songs by composers such as Schumann and Strauss. The Washington newspapers called it an "informal musical tea" and "a song recital" for "a few friends at the White House." The society reporter for the *Washington Herald* said that the occasion was one where "formality was skillfully mixed with informality" and was "one of the most charming affairs possible."[21]

A second recital on 22 April 1909 brought the pianist Estella Neuhaus to the White House along with "a number of specially invited guests" for a program that included works by Robert Schumann and Claude Debussy. Neuhaus gave "a number of excellent piano selections."[22] Although creditable professional artists, neither Morse nor Neuhaus stood among the most distinguished of American musicians, and Mrs. Taft would elevate the level of performances during the next year.

Mrs. Taft's stroke put an end to her musical activities until the return from Beverly, Massachusetts, to Washington for the 1909–1910 social season. These three initial concerts/recitals indicated her intention to present her guests with music that she considered worthy of their attention. The booking of two female artists also reflected the first lady's intention to give women musicians greater recognition at a time when they received fewer offers and smaller honoraria than their male counterparts. Women pianists, even those as prominent as Olga Samaroff, routinely received about half of what a male artist might get for a performance. Over the course of her musicale productions, Mrs. Taft succeeded in giving a number of women artists the boost that a presidential appearance could provide in terms of better bookings and greater financial returns.[23]

Despite her stroke, Mrs. Taft had ambitious plans for the year to come. No record remains of the process by which the first lady arranged her musical schedule for the first half of 1910. She had decided to use the Lenten season to hold four musicales at the White House with performances by distinguished concert artists of the day. During Lent in the Taft years, society gave up dancing for the season of abstinence. Churches added an extensive program of services and sermons that kept parishioners active in their devotions. Fasting was the norm during this "season of self-denial." The first lady and her daughter, Helen Taft, "set an example in the matter of Lenten church going. Every afternoon found the President's wife and daughter listening to the evensong at Saint John's, the little church across Lafayette Park, visible from the windows of the White House." Listening to serious music at the White House, therefore, conformed to the sobriety and restraint of Lent.[24]

The first lady used the services of Steinway & Sons and their representative, Joseph Burr Tiffany, to line up the musicians she wished to have. At fifty-three, the Cornell-educated Tiffany was the founder of what was called the art department at Steinway in 1897. He had worked first with Ida McKinley and then with Edith Roosevelt since 1902 on her musicales. By 1911, he was "in almost absolute control of the arrangements of these affairs" and was known as the chargé d'affaires for White House music. In the case of Nellie Taft, he submitted the names of the potential performers to the first lady, and she made it clear which ones she preferred to use.[25] Mrs. Taft also reviewed the program and approved individual selections for each of the musicales. However, on some occasions, friends of the president and first lady would suggest names of performers. In other cases, there would be a personal or political link that would determine whether or not an artist would be invited to perform.

Tiffany and the first lady took advantage of a larger than usual array of musical artists and performers who had signed contracts to perform in Washington during the winter of 1909–1910. From Fritz Kreisler to Isadora Duncan, from the Boston Symphony Orchestra to the Manhattan Opera Company, the coming attractions aroused great anticipation among music devotees in the capital. Looking at the lineup in September 1909, the *Washington Times* observed that "local music lovers are certain that the coming season is to be the richest in the history of the city."[26]

The four musicales of 1910 presented an impressive roster of talented artists. On 11 February, the American-born pianist Olga Samaroff (Lucy Hickenlooper) played and accompanied F. Ver Treese Pollack, tenor. Ten days later, the Hess-Schroeder Quartet of the Boston Symphony Orchestra, with Ernest Hutcheson as pianist for one selection, were the featured artists. On 11 March, Karl Jorn, tenor, sang and Yolando Mero, pianist, played. Finally on 15 April, the violinist Fritz Kreisler played on the same program with the distinguished pianist Fannie Bloomfield-Zeisler.

From the outset, the Taft musicales took a standard form. Before the four or five hundred guests arrived, the president and the first lady hosted a small dinner. Occasionally, the musicians were invited to the dinner. Otherwise they waited in the Red Room of the White House for the event to begin. The Tafts greeted the artists at around 9:30 P.M. Meanwhile, the invited audience lined up in the East Wing halls and reception rooms until twelve uniformed ushers guided them to their seats. "Mrs. Taft is generally seated part way back, so that if she is overtired by the crowds or the lights, she can slip out." The musical selections then followed, in most cases without encores, and refreshments were provided after the music finished around midnight. The gold Steinway piano, given to the White House in November 1903, stood at the north end of the East Room surrounded by palms and flowers. The spectacle of uniforms, gowns, flowers, and jewelry made some of these evenings dazzling events for the attendees.[27]

In her first 1910 musicale, Nellie Taft featured one artist who is now little remembered. Frank Ver Treese Pollock sang under the names of Frank Pollock with the opera company of Oscar Hammerstein. Born in 1878 in Abingdon, Illinois, he was educated at Knox College before starting his professional career. He was also featured in productions by John Phillip Sousa and Victor Herbert. In 1912, the *New York Times* commented that in England, where he was then performing, Pollock was "another instance of the extraordinary success gained by an American born and bred among the operatic artists of Europe."[28] For his evening with the Tafts, Pollock rendered such melodies as Frederick Clay's "I'll Sing Thee Songs of Araby" and "The Year's at the Spring," the best-known song by the American composer, Mrs. H. H. A. Beach. After his White House appearance, Pollock returned to the musical comedy and operatic stage before his career ebbed during the 1920s.[29]

Olga Samaroff (1880–1948) was a young American pianist who had adopted her professional name because "Lucy Hickenlooper" was not a name that looked good on a program or marquee. Born in Texas in 1880, she had shown great promise as a young performer. She studied piano in Europe with teachers in France and Germany. An unfortunate marriage interrupted her career, but by 1905, she was divorced and back in the United States. She made her American

Olga Samaroff in a formal pose. Her performance for Mrs. Taft and the president in 1910 confirmed her reputation as one of the best American pianists of that day. (Library of Congress)

debut with an orchestra led by Walter Damrosch. A tour of Europe followed in 1909, and her White House appearance was part of a series of concerts she gave during 1910. In 1911, she married Leopold Stokowski, who would become a legendary conductor.[30] They divorced during the 1920s, and she became a revered and renowned piano teacher until her death in 1948. Her reputation as a teacher has endured to the present day.

For her concert at the White House, Samaroff "wore a ruby colored velvet gown, which helped to create a really stunning picture which the exquisitely painted and gilded piano and the flowers and palms completed." It was Samaroff herself, however, who made the lasting impression. After playing the "Prelude in G Minor" by Sergei Rachmaninoff and the "Nocturne for the Left Hand Only" by Aleksandr Scriabin, she pleased her appreciative audience by ending her performance with a virtuoso solo piano arrangement of Wagner's "Ride of the Valkyrie" prepared by Ernest Hutcheson, one of her teachers. In response to her dazzling rendition, President Taft gave her an autographed photograph of himself with scribbled compliments about her artistry. A year or so later, while being interviewed, Samaroff mentioned the picture to a reporter, who wrote a story with the headline "President Taft Takes Wild Ride through Clouds with Young Pianist."[31] The pianist hastened to inform the president that she meant nothing disrespectful in her comments. Taft assured her that he had taken no offense.

The appearance of the Hess-Schroeder Quartet at the second musicale in mid-February indicated that the first lady and the Steinway company booker were well aware of recent developments in the concert and chamber music world. Willy Hess, a violinist and concertmaster of the Boston Symphony Orchestra, teamed with cellist Alvin Schroeder to create the quartet in 1908. Emil Ferir, a violist with the symphony, and Julius von Theodorowicz as second violin, rounded out the group. Their goal was to program new compositions as well as the customary works for a string quartet. The *New York Times* said in January 1909 that "the new organization starts out with the potentiality of making a high place for itself."[32] The Boston Symphony Orchestra was in Washington during February 1910 for a concert. It was thus natural for the first lady to invite the quartet to perform for her guests.[33]

Three or four hundred prominent Washingtonians gathered at the White House at 10 o'clock on 21 February 1910 for a diverse program that included two movements from a string quartet by Edvard Grieg, "Tema and Variazini" by the American composer Arthur Foote, two movements from a string quartet by Claude Debussy, and finally a quintet by Robert Schumann, with Ernest Hutcheson serving as the pianist. Within a few years, the Hess Schroeder Quartet had disbanded as some of its members returned to Germany. Mrs. Taft and those in attendance thus had a rare opportunity to hear these talented musicians, who displayed, according to one critic, "the quality of excellent musicianship, a sound and sane artistic sense and unselfish devotion to the music."[34]

In March, Mrs. Taft's third musicale of the season brought two artists new to the United States to the White House audience. Karl Jorn (1873–1947) was a handsome German tenor who joined the Metropolitan Opera in late 1909. His performances attracted enough attention that by Christmas Eve 1909 he had received an invitation to sing at the White House the following spring. Either Steinway's manager pitched his name to the first lady or, in a more likely scenario, Mrs. Taft read the favorable review of his appearance in *Lohengrin* in the *New York Tribune.* Early in 1910, he became a naturalized citizen of the United States. Before he left Germany, he participated in an early recording session with excerpts from *Carmen, Faust,* and the second act of *Tannhauser.* The first lady's guests were thus being treated to an opera singer much in the news at the time of his performance.[35]

At the musicale itself, Jorn sang the "Prize Song" from *Die Meistersinger,* a selection that President Taft enjoyed and soon wished to hear again. The tenor also performed selections from *Pagliacci* by Leoncavallo, *Faust* by Gounod, and works by Max Liebling and Meyerbeer.[36] Jorn continued his operatic work into the 1920s before he retired to live on his investments in Colorado. When he lost money in the stock market, he returned to teaching until his death in 1947.

The other artist at this musicale was Yolanda Mero (1887–1963), a young Hungarian pianist who had made her American debut in New York in 1909. She had started her professional career in 1902 with the Dresden Philharmonic. Over the next five years, she toured

Karl Jorn. The German tenor in formal dress for an evening on the town or a musicale at the Taft White House in early 1910. (Library of Congress)

Europe, where she won "golden opinions in London and on the Continent." Charles Steinway listened to her in London and signed her to play in the United States. She was the last European musician that Steinway brought across the Atlantic. "After me," she later recalled, "he was through."[37]

Mero's playing at her second appearance in New York during November 1909 proved her musical talent. She "has technique, fire, passion, and a pair of iron wrists." To have such a talented young woman pianist entertain at the White House suited Mrs. Taft's agenda. Mero played works by Chopin, Liszt, and Rachmaninoff. Later in life, Mero left the concert stage to work with organizations devoted to providing assistance to indigent professional musicians. The third musicale of 1910 occurred under something of a cloud. Mrs. Taft's brother-in-law, Thomas Laughlin, had died early that day from a self-inflicted gunshot wound, but the news came too late "to recall the invitations."[38]

The final musicale of the 1910 Lenten season, held on 15 April 1910, capped off Mrs. Taft's first series with two of the most famous solo artists of the period. Her invitations, written by her secretary and signed by the first lady, went out to special friends inviting them "to take tea at five o'clock Friday afternoon to meet Fritz Kreisler and Mme Bloomfield-Zeisler, who will be present." Then came the musicale in the evening.[39]

Fritz Kreisler (1873–1962) had been a virtuoso violinist, "to many minds the greatest of modern violinists," since his childhood in Austria. Tours of Europe had confirmed the brilliance of his playing, and he visited the United States in 1888 on the first of what evolved into an annual tour of the country. By the time he appeared for Mrs. Taft in 1910, Kreisler was an international musical superstar. "Kreisler has returned," said the editors of *The Etude* in December 1909, "and convinced New York he is unapproachable as a violinist." For the Tafts, he played one of his own compositions "Caprice Viennois," and selections by Cecile Chaminade and Antonin Dvorak.[40]

Fannie Bloomfield-Zeisler was regarded as the preeminent female pianist in the nation in 1910. Known as "the [Sarah] Bernhardt of the piano," she, like Kreisler, was born in Austria. Her family moved to the United States when she was two years old. By the early 1880s she was embarked on a solo career that continued for the next three decades. Ten days before she played at the White House, she gave a recital in New York where the critic for the *New-York Tribune* praised the "generosity of her offering and its excellence." At the White House, she performed three works by Chopin, one of Mendelssohn's "Songs without Words," and works by Franz Liszt and Robert Schumann.[41]

The president and first lady had invited the Congressional Club, made up of the wives of lawmakers, along with their husbands as the guests for the evening. While the formal concert was being played, President Taft interrupted the program to ask Fritz Kreisler to perform the "Prize Song." The violinist knew the piece, but his accompanist did not have the necessary music. The president's aides rushed out of the White House, hailed the first car that came by, and hurried over to the nearby home of Representative Nicholas Longworth, who was in attendance with his wife, Alice Roosevelt Longworth. An accomplished amateur violinist himself, Longworth had a copy of the score among his music. "Inside of eight minutes from the time the President had expressed his wish the 'Prize Song' was being played for him."[42]

Kreisler and Bloomfield-Zeisler continued their prominence as concert artists for years after their White House performances. The violinist survived the persecutions of World War I when his Germanic background drove him from the concert stage for several years. He regained his fame during the 1920s and continued his round of recitals, recordings, and radio programs until the 1950s. Fannie Bloomfield-Zeisler also performed across the country into the early 1920s to great acclaim. She died of a heart attack in 1927.

The Bloomfield-Zeisler program ended the first season of the Lenten musicales. With the adjournment of Congress in June and the onset of the Washington summer heat, the president and first lady were away from the White House until the lawmakers returned for the session of Congress that opened in early December 1910. During that month, the White House hosted two concerts that further disclosed the diverse nature of Nellie Taft's musical tastes. As she told her oldest son, "we heard the Liederkranz sing" and "Scharwenka played."[43]

On 7 December 1910, the Liederkranz Society of New York gave an afternoon concert for the president and first lady. There were at the White House eighty-five members of the German American male chorus that had been performing in New York City and on tour since 1847. Directed by Arthur Claasen, the society's members had made two previous White House appearances, including a concert for President and Mrs. Roosevelt. The Liederkranz had close ties with the Steinway Piano Company as well. Their program in-

Fritz Kreisler in 1913. The virtuoso violinist Fritz Kreisler in a photograph taken three years after his appearance at the White House. (Library of Congress)

cluded works by Schubert, Haydn, Schumann, and other German composers. They ended their contribution to the afternoon with "My Old Kentucky Home."[44]

By chance, the famous Polish composer Xaver Scharwenka (1850–1924) was in the United States on a brief tour to play with the New York Philharmonic. Born in 1850 in what is now Poland, the pianist gained fame as a performer and teacher in Europe for his interpretations of Fredric Chopin. Gustav Mahler, who was conducting for the Philharmonic during these years, arranged for Scharwenka to appear during the fall of 1910. In mid-December, he received warm approval from the New York audience for his playing of Beethoven's "Concerto in E Flat Major" (Piano Concerto No. 5, "Emperor," Op. 73). In his White House program, Scharwenka played the Chopin "Fantasie-Impromptu," the selection for which he was best known. He also performed "a number of his own Polish dances, known to most of the piano players and students in this country. Mr. Scharwenka made a great triumph before a distinguished group of music lovers."[45] The pianist returned to Europe and performed there until his death in 1924.

A week later, the Tafts hosted their final recital of 1910 in a program with a distinct Ohio tone to the affair. The occasion was a dinner honoring the members of the Cabinet and their spouses, with governors of five states and other guests rounding out those in attendance. The two artists who sang were H. Evan Williams (1867–1918), a tenor, and Gertrude Ferguson Penfield Seiberling, a contralto, of Akron, Ohio. The two singers had been suggested to the president and first lady by Senator Charles W. F. Dick of Ohio. He believed that Williams and Seiberling "might provide a musical evening of considerable pleasure" to the Tafts and their guests.[46]

Born in Mineral Ridge, Ohio, in 1867, of Welsh parents, Williams worked in coal mines as a boy and gained fame as a tenor singing with a Welsh choir in his native state. By the mid-1890s, he was a soloist in Europe. After returning to the United States, he taught and sang "with leading choral societies both in England and the United States."[47] At the White House, he performed selections from Handel and Haydn. He also sang the "Prize Song" for the president and provided the larger share of the evening's entertainment. Williams remained a popular singing attraction through the beginning of World War I before his death.

The other performer, Gertrude Seiberling, was the wife of the president of the Goodyear Tire and Rubber Company in Akron. She sang with the Tuesday Musical Club in her hometown and in opera productions at the Academy of Music, a local opera house run by her father-in-law. She performed three selections at the White

House, the "Hindoo Song" by Herman Bemberg, "Po' L'il Lamb" by Carrie Jacobs Bond, and "Charity" by James G. McDermid. The two performers closed out the program with a duet, "Passage Bird's Farewell" by Eugen Hildach. Archie Butt pronounced the singing for the evening as "not bad, although there was too much of it."[48]

The *Washington Herald* called the musicale at the first state dinner of the 1910–1911 social season "a delightful innovation." The fifty-two invited guests gathered in the East Room amid a bevy of flowers including "tall bunches of flesh-tinted carnations," creating "a beautiful effect with the rich gold hangings." The event brought the musical programs of the first lady for 1910 to a successful close.[49]

At the end of her first full year of musical entertainment as first lady, Nellie Taft had reason to be proud of what she had accomplished. The Lenten musicales were an immediate success with Washington audiences. Mrs. Taft made sure that her guest list was as prestigious for the third and fourth musicales as for the opening performances. In the past, "invitations to all functions were so obviously graded to the supposed importance of their recipients, that the third or fourth company—reception, dance, or musicale—became by comparison so ordinary that the invitation to it lost all value as well as all compliment." With such a social strategy, the first lady had gone a long way toward assuring that the audience for her musicales remained worthy of the artists that she and Joseph Burr Tiffany had enlisted to play for her.[50]

For the year ahead, Mrs. Taft had already begun lining up the musicians for the Lenten musicales of 1911. To give the artists a sense of the appreciation that she and her husband felt for their unpaid appearances, she was thinking about devising some tangible way of conveying their gratitude for the evening's entertainment. During the last three social seasons of her husband's presidency, Nellie Taft would broaden the focus of the musicales and continue her impressive campaign to provide the best in serious music to official Washington and the society of the Capital.

CHAPTER 5

MUSICALES AND
MEDALS, 1911–1913

Having managed the first group of successful musicales during the winter and spring of 1910, Nellie Taft looked forward with enthusiasm to 1911 and the roster of famous artists whose talents she could secure. For the 1911 series of Lenten musicales, Nellie Taft and Joseph Burr Tiffany arranged for another lineup of distinguished classical performers. They opened with the Kneisel Quartet, the most famous American chamber music ensemble of the day, and pianist Arthur Friedheim on 10 March. Two weeks later, the first lady featured two singers, Alexander Heinemann and Lilla Ormond, and a pianist, Alma Stenzel. On 7 April Josef Hofmann, the renowned pianist, was the sole performer. The season closed out on 21 April with Frances Alda, a prominent soprano from the Metropolitan Opera, and Alice Sovereign, a contralto.

With a year's experience in handling musicians and staging these events, Nellie Taft wanted to provide the visiting artists with a more tangible token of the occasion than the autographed photographs President Taft had given to previous performers. She collaborated with Tiffany and Company in New York City to create gold medals that could be presented to the musicians on behalf of her and the president. The medals carried the presidential seal and were inscribed on the back. There was some disagreement on how the decoration looked. "They were pinned, like an Order, on the chest of the performer" in what one person who attended a musicale called "a very graceful recognition, and one which gave enormous pleasure to those so honored."[1]

Ernest Schelling, an American pianist who performed for Mrs. Taft in 1913, recalled for the press his different experience when he received the medal. He noted that when appearing in Europe he had been able to avoid getting paid in medals. "I have always preferred the other alternative—cash. All the same, I have got a medal. I was at the White House when Mrs. Taft hung a large gold one about my neck with a silk ribbon. Several diplomats inquired afterward what order it was."[2] Other musicians spoke with pride of the receipt of the medals and mentioned the award in their publicity releases and their memoirs.

The first ensemble for Mrs. Taft's Lenten musicale guests in March 1911 was the most famous and influential string quartet in the United States. The Kneisel Quartet had been active for more than two decades since its founding in 1885. Bankrolled by the Boston philanthropist Henry Lee Higginson, the quartet, organized by the young Franz Kneisel (1865–1926), functioned first as an offshoot of the Boston Symphony and then, after 1903, as an independent unit. Tours of Europe added to its sterling reputation as a premiere attraction for American music lovers. In January 1907 the quartet played for President Theodore Roosevelt and his wife at the White House.[3]

The first lady was well acquainted with the artistry of this ensemble. Since hearing them in October 1904, she had been present for one of their recent performances. The quartet had been in Washington in April 1909 to entertain Mrs. Jonkheer Loudon, wife of the Dutch minister to the United States, and they performed for Mrs. Loudon's guests again in late November 1910. On the second occasion, Mrs. Taft was in the audience. Whether she then decided to engage the quartet for her musicale series is not known for certain. In any event, she was already well acquainted with their international reputation as an ensemble.[4] The Kneisel Quartet performed for another six years before it disbanded during 1917.

The second artist on the program, Arthur Friedheim (1859–1932), was renowned for being the last student of the legendary pianist Franz Liszt. Born in 1859 in Russia, Friedheim began his studies with

Liszt in 1880 and in time became his secretary. During his career, Friedheim was "acclaimed by critics as one of the foremost pianists of the world." He performed in the United States and Europe between 1891 and 1911. In late 1910, he gave a recital in New York, where he had not played in almost twenty years, which involved "very little preliminary announcement" of his intention to perform. The critic for the *New York Times*, while complaining that his tone sometimes had a "hard quality," concluded that "his technique was wholly master of the difficulties of the music and there was at times a splendid sweep in his performance." Once again, the first lady took the opportunity to add a musician who was in the news to her repertoire of musicale artists. Friedheim settled in the United States in 1915 and six years later accepted a professorship at the Canadian Academy of Music. He died in New York City in 1932.[5]

At the White House on 10 March 1911, for an audience of four hundred, including Cabinet members and the elite of the diplomatic corps, Friedheim performed six selections from Liszt, Beethoven, and Chopin. In his memoirs, Friedheim said nothing about the Kneisel Quartet's presence on the program. "Outside of Russia," he recalled, "I had never seen a gathering as stately, rich and brilliant as that before which I played that evening." Along with the quartet, he received the first of the gold medals that the Tafts gave to artists. Friedheim noted that when he wore the decoration at a concert during World War I, he was hissed "by overzealous wartime 'patriots' who mistook the American red, white and blue for the colors of Germany."[6]

For their contribution to the evening, the Kneisel Quartet played Edvard Grieg's "Quartet in G Minor," a Bach sonata in D major for violoncello alone, and portions of a quartet by Serge Taneiew. The program, said the *Washington Post* the next day, was "delightful," and the *New York Herald* said that the assembled dignitaries made up "a brilliant and appreciative company."[7]

Two weeks later, on 24 March 1911, five hundred guests gathered to hear Alexander Heinemann (1873–1919), a singer of German lieder, Lilla Ormond, a popular mezzo-soprano, and Alma Stenzel, a young pianist who had been born in Washington, D.C. Heinemann had "attained high repute in Germany" for his art before coming to the United States late in 1910. His recitals in New York were well received. The critic for the *New York Times* had some reservations about Heinemann for "his excessive use of vocal power, when the beauty of the voice is affected, and at times even its intonation suffers," but concluded that overall "he is heard with great pleasure." Once again, Tiffany and Mrs. Taft presented their audience with an artist who was much in the minds of classical music devotees during the spring of 1911.[8]

Lilla Ormond (1883–1976), a native of Massachusetts, had a concert career in Europe and the United States before retiring from the stage after her marriage to Harold Ray Dennis in 1912. She toured extensively in 1910 and 1911, giving some ninety-four concerts in all. In 1910, the music critic for the *New York Times* said that she performed "with splendid vocal power and rich melody."[9]

Alma Stenzel displayed talents on the piano that led her parents to send her to Europe to study at the age of twelve. She remained in Europe for a decade. One of her teachers was the great Russian/Polish pianist Leopold Godowsky. According to the *New York Times*, "she has played with many of the leading orchestras of Europe."[10]

At the musicale itself, Heinemann performed songs by Anton Rubinstein and Ruggero Leoncavallo. He closed the program with works by Schubert and Schumann. Alma Stenzel played selections by Chopin, Mendelssohn, and Strauss-Tausig. Lilla Ormond sang "From the Land of Sky Blue Water" and other numbers. According to the first lady, "she made a great hit."[11]

The third musicale on 7 April 1911 featured just one artist, the renowned pianist Josef Hofmann (1876–1957). Hofmann had been an international sensation since he emerged as a piano virtuoso during the late 1880s. The prodigy from Poland had, according to press reports, appeared for Frances Cleveland at the White House in the 1880s, "when he was in his knickerbockers." As one critic put it, he played "not only like an artist, but like a master." For the Tafts, Hofmann "gave a programme to a delighted audience of the country's most distinguished diplomats and officials."[12] The works that he played included four selections by Chopin, as well as compositions by Scriabin, Rachmaninoff, Anatol Liadow, and Liszt.

A week later, on 15 April, President Taft and the first lady held a dinner for the new senators elected in 1910, including several Democrats and Republicans identified as "insurgents" against the administration. A young Welsh violinist named Haydn Gunter "gave several selections." In his account of the dinner, Archie Butt called Gunter "an inferior violinist" and identified him as a constituent of Senator Robert L. Owen, an Oklahoma Democrat. In fact, Gunter was from Muncie, Indiana. So tepid was the response to Gunter's playing that Butt recorded the first lady as observing "that she will do a good deal to propitiate the insurgents, but in the future she will draw the line on admitting their musical friends to the White House."[13]

Mrs. Taft's second full season of musicales came to an end on 21 April with the appearance of two female singers. Alice Sovereign was a contralto who sang as a solo performer during the two decades after 1900. She also made a few records around the time she appeared at the White House. In 1917, reviewing a concert she gave at Aeolian Hall in New York, the critic for the *New York Times* observed that "Mrs. Sovereign unfortunately sang flat a good deal."[14]

Frances Alda (1879–1952), unlike Sovereign, was an opera singer whose reputation has continued down to the present time. Born in New Zealand in 1879 as Fannie Jane Davis, she grew up in Australia and went to Europe around 1901 to study. After making her debut in 1904, she sang at such opera houses as the Royal Opera House Covent Garden and in Italy at La Scala in Milan. In 1908 she broke her European contract and came to the United States to sing with the Metropolitan Opera. She arrived amid allegations of a campaign to discredit her with the critics. In an interview with the *New York Times*, she said, "I broke a three years' contract to come here, and here I intend to remain until my contract expires. If they think they can get rid of me, frighten me off, they are mistaken. They have got to hear me for three years."[15]

In 1910, the feisty and opinionated Alda married the director of the Metropolitan Opera, Giulio Gatti-Casazza. To avoid suggestions of favoritism, she did not sing at the Met during the 1910–1911 season, but rather embarked on national tours that brought her in April 1911 to Washington and Helen Taft. On that evening, Alice Sovereign sang six works by Brahms and Rachmaninoff, among others. Frances Alda for her part performed nine selections by Debussy, Massenet, and Moussorgsky. The several hundred listeners present once again heard "From the Land of Sky Blue Water" that Lilla Ormond had sung a month earlier.[16]

Although the Lenten series was over, the first lady hosted other artists during the early summer of 1911. Congress was still in session, and audiences remained to be invited to the mansion. Mrs. Taft brought a Russian cellist named George Rogovoy, "one of the favorite artists of the czar," to give a private concert in late April. Two weeks later, for her second garden party of the outdoor season, she and her four hundred guests heard the Marine Band and the Mozart Society of New York in an outdoor concert. The first lady had learned of the existence of the Mozart Society from Arthur Claasen when the Liederkranz Society appeared at the White House in December 1910. At that time, he asked the first lady whether she would like to hear this women's chorus. "Mrs. Taft expressed a desire to do so, and invited the society to come to Washington this spring." The 132 female singers sang three selections: a lullaby by Mozart, "The Rosary," and "By the Beautiful Blue Danube."[17]

The musical activity at the White House abated during the summer and fall of 1911 with the president in Washington during June and July and the first lady resting at Beverly, Massachusetts. Then President Taft embarked on a nationwide tour in the autumn that took him away until mid-November. Soon after he had returned, the White House hosted the Salt Lake Tabernacle Choir, a forerunner of the Mormon Tabernacle Choir, for a concert on 15 November 1911. The touring chorus sang selections from Gounod, Puccini, and Victor Herbert. They also rendered a work about Utah itself, "The Irrigated Region." The *Washington Post* reported that "spurred on by the applause of the President, Mrs. Taft, and a number of army and navy officials, the singers gave a great exhibition."[18]

The event with the Salt Lake Choir brought to the White House another prominent touring artist, this time from the world of the theater. Lady Isabella Gregory and the Irish Players of the Abbey Theater of Dublin were on an extended visit to the United States. Mrs. Taft and Archie Butt went to see the Irish Players and invited Lady Gregory to the White House to hear the choir sing. In her memoirs, Gregory reported that "I arrived there late but the music was going on. It was a very pretty sight, the long white room with fine old glass chandeliers, and two hundred Mormons—the men in black, the women in white and about fifty guests." She heard one other selection and the "Star-Spangled Banner." "Then we moved about and chatted, and was presented to the President, pleasant enough, but one doesn't feel him on the stage like Roosevelt."[19] The impromptu invitation to Lady Gregory reflected the willingness of Helen Taft to have a diverse audience for the musicales she staged at the White House. Lady Gregory and the Irish Players went on to New York, where the plays they presented had already aroused opposition among Roman Catholics in the United States because of their vivid and often critical portrayals of Irish life. As a result their productions sparked protests in the theater when they played in New York City.

The first lady and Tiffany were already laying plans for the Lenten season of 1912 with another roster of young women musicians and singers in mind. *Town and Country* reported that "the formal evening musicales, which have become the smartest entertainment of this very hospitable administration," would commence in February.[20] Sensing that this series might be her last full opportunity to present the music she loved, given the political troubles of her husband's presidency, Nellie Taft followed some of her own personal inclinations in deciding whom she wanted to hear in the East Room.

In January and February two popular female opera singers launched Mrs. Taft's musical year with musicales during the Washington social season. Elise Baylor was a soprano from Chattanooga, Tennessee, who had studied in Germany with Franz Proschowsky. She was a cousin of the writer-politician, Thomas Nelson Page, and the daughter of the founder of the Baylor School in Chattanooga, Tennessee. With her accompanist, Alice Burbage, Baylor gave a program after the diplomatic dinner that featured works by Debussy, Johann Strauss, and Carey Roy Smith's "My Wee Birdie." The *New York Times*, which did not usually report much about the musicales, said that she received "enthusiastic approval of her excellent rendering" of her program. In the years that followed, Baylor sang in German opera companies before the outbreak of World War I.[21]

The musicale on 17 February 1912 brought to the mansion one of the biggest singing stars of that era. Alice Nielsen (1872–1943) was forty in 1912 and had been a major performer in opera and operettas for more than a decade. Born in Indiana, she grew up in Kansas City and was singing professionally by the mid-1880s. Within ten years she was a popular attraction in the United States and Europe. She

Frances Alda: the diva as driver. The soprano Florence Alda made two singing
appearances at the Taft White House. (Library of Congress)

toured with John McCormack and had a number of successful
records for songs such as "Home, Sweet Home" and "The Last Rose
of Summer."

Years later, Nielsen remembered her White House recital. "I was
taken to an official reception given by Mrs. Taft. An imposing gold-
laced officer led me to the small platform to sing." The president was
not there for the start of the singing "but presently one of the doors
opened and it was the unmistakable expansiveness of the chief executive. He sat down on one of those ridiculously small gilt chairs,
completely hiding it. My sense of humor imagined him suspended
in mid-air. Suddenly there came to me while I sang the sounds of
snoring. There could be no mistake—they beat above the piano
notes. The President had fallen asleep. The kid glove applause awak-
ened him and he clapped vociferously."[22]

The Lenten musicale season got under way on 1 March 1912 with
the return of Frances Alda and her opera colleague, a Spanish baritone named Andres de Segurola (1873–1953). Alda called him "someone with a grand sense of humor" who added "zest to the party."[23]
She invited her colleague to meet Joseph Burr Tiffany at her New
York apartment, where a formal invitation was made to sing at the

White House for an evening reception in honor of the governor of Maryland and other dignitaries. Segurola considered the occasion "one of the most memorable of my artistic life and friend Alda felt equally gratified."[24]

When the singers came to the White House, they found "a crowd as brilliant and picturesque as any I had seen in other principal capitals." Segurola sang works by Mozart and Grieg while Frances Alda performed songs by Cecile Chaminade and others. The two singers finished the program with a duet on "Plasir d'Amour" by Jean Paul Martini. When the program was finished, President Taft presented the artists with the new gold medals. "Why don't you put it around your neck?" asked the chief executive. "It will be a privilege for me, Mr. President," responded the singer. As Segurola recalled in his memoirs, the postmaster general, Frank H. Hitchcock, asked the singer to render a popular song for Taft. Taking the then popular favorite, "Has Anybody Here Seen Kelly?," Segurola changed the words to

> Has anybody here seen—Teddy?
> Spell it!
> T-E-double D-Y

Coming in the midst of the bitter battle between Will Taft and Roosevelt for the Republican presidential nomination at a time when the president's fortunes were in the ascendant, the improvisation from the basso drew approving laughter from the president and the other guests.[25]

Two weeks later, the first lady's second musicale featured another famous opera singer, Johanna Gadski, and a rising young American pianist, Arthur Shattuck. The Prussian-born Gadski (1872–1932) had sung with the Philadelphia Orchestra in Washington in October 1906, and Mrs. Taft had "enjoyed it *ever* so much." The singer had then joined the Metropolitan Opera in 1907 and shone in Wagnerian roles. Mrs. Taft had heard her sing again in January 1911 when she performed with Gustav Mahler and the New York Philharmonic Society in its first Washington concert. Gadski's pro-German sympathies during World War I would cause her to be deported as an enemy alien, but during the Taft years, she was a sought-after attraction. Her performance on 16 March included songs by Schumann, Edward McDowell, and Richard Strauss.[26]

Arthur Shattuck (1881–1951), a Wisconsin native and heir to the Kimberly-Clark tissue fortune, studied for seven years in Vienna with the famous piano teacher, Theodor Leschetizky. Shattuck started performing with European orchestras at the age of twenty and had returned to the United States for a concert tour in 1911. One critic called him "a rich amateur" during this phase of his life, but others believed he was a genuine talent. During World War I, his relief efforts for musicians enhanced his reputation, and his playing improved as well. In his appearance at the White House, he played selections by Brahms, Wagner, and Liszt.[27]

The third musicale that followed on 12 April 1912 assembled three promising artists who reflected the ability of Tiffany and Helen Taft to locate new talents. Prominent members of the diplomatic corps and four hundred other guests gathered to hear the young Canadian piano prodigy, Ellen Ballon (1898–1969), the Russian-born twenty-two-year-old violinist, Efrem Zimbalist (1890–1984), and the soprano, Anna Case (1888–1984). Born in Montreal in 1898, Ellen Ballon had already achieved renown for her precocious pianistic abilities. The public hailed her debut concert in New York City in March 1910 when she played with the New York Symphony with Walter Damrosch conducting. She gave recitals in New York City in February 1912 that were well received. When the news was announced that Ballon would appear at the White House, the former prime minister of Canada, Wilfred Laurier, wrote her to say, "I am happy to hear that you are to play at the White House. You can certainly tell President Taft that I claim you as a friend & that I take a very deep interest in your success."[28]

For the first lady and her guests, the Canadian prodigy played works by Chopin, Liszt, and Schubert. Later in life, Ballon would return to the White House to play for Franklin D. Roosevelt in 1934 and Dwight D. Eisenhower twenty years later. She kept the gold medal the Tafts gave her, and it remains with her papers at Dalhousie University in Nova Scotia.[29]

Anna Case was another young singer with the Metropolitan Opera during this period. Four years after her White House appearance, she entertained at a private party for millionaire Clarence H. Mackay. Case became his mistress and some years later married him. Her marriage made her the stepmother of Mackay's daughter, and thus she also became the step-mother-in-law of composer Irving Berlin. Anna Case later appeared in movies, one of which featured the eight-year-old girl who would become better known as Rita Hayworth. At the White House, among her eight selections, she sang two songs by Cecile Chaminade and a composition by Amy Beach.[30] When she died in 1984 at the age of ninety-five, Anna Case Mackay left the value of her furs and clothing to the American Theater Wing.[31]

The third performer for this musicale was the twenty-two-year-old Russian violinist Efrem Zimbalist. In inviting him, Taft and Tiffany once again reached out to a rising musician who had just arrived on the American musical scene. After making his debut in Germany and playing in England, Zimbalist came to the United States in 1911 for a national tour. The critic of the *New York Times* labeled him "an artist of truly remarkable powers." He would emerge as one of the leading violinists of the twentieth century. At this time the Russian musician was also smitten with the singer Alma Gluck, whom he would marry later in 1912. Mrs. Taft heard Gluck perform in Washington in March 1912 and reported that she liked her singing "very much." Zimbalist had begun to make records for RCA Victor during April 1912, and he shared with the White House guests some of the works that he played in what were then primitive recording facilities. These included Dvorak's "Humoresque" and "Oriental" by Cesar Cui.[32]

The sinking of the *Titanic* and the loss of hundreds of lives cast a pall over Washington society during that spring. Despite the tragedy, Mrs. Taft held her fourth musicale on 20 April 1912 as scheduled. The audience comprised "young girl students of the seminaries in and near Washington," several hundred of whom were invited to the White House. This program had a distinct Southern flavor. The pianist was Anne Atkinson Burmeister, who grew up in Columbia, South Carolina, where her father was president of the women's college there. Identified as a prodigy on the piano at an early age, she went to Europe to study at the Dresden Institute, whose director was a gifted pianist himself, Richard Burmeister. She prospered as a pupil, and the couple were married in 1899. "Frau Burmeister," as her local paper referred to her, continued her playing career with performances in Europe for various orchestras. By 1912, she had established a studio in New York City where she taught piano. It was while she was there that Mrs. Taft invited her to appear at the White House. At the musicale, Mrs. Burmeister played a Liszt sonata, another composition by Debussy, and "Spring Song," written by her husband and Frank Van der Stucken. Her marriage to Burmeister ended about this time and she remarried in 1915.[33]

The other featured artist was a Georgia woman named Louise Alice Williams, whose specialty was "Negro Folk Songs and Stories." A resident of Atlanta and the daughter of a Confederate veteran, Williams made a long career out of singing and recounting "plantation stories" to the American upper class at Newport, Rhode Island, Harvard University, and other venues well into the 1930s. She delivered these presentations in "a gown belonging to a famous belle of old Virginia, Cordelia Randolph, granddaughter of Thomas Jefferson, and worn by her at a White House ball." According to the *New York Times*, which faithfully recorded her various professional engagements over the years, she had gained "considerable distinction as a Southern raconteur." For the guests of the first lady in 1912, she offered "A Darkey Ghost Story" and other "Log Cabin Anecdotes of Old Negro Humor." Williams seems to have been an important if now neglected figure in sustaining the mythology of the Old South among the American aristocracy during the first third of the twentieth century.[34]

One young artist who was not part of the musicale program as such came to the White House in late April. Donna Easley, a native of Kansas, was an aspiring singer, but she was also the daughter of Ralph M. Easley, the head of the National Civic Federation that lobbied for improved business–labor relations from the perspective of corporations. Given Mrs. Taft's close ties with that organization, it was natural for her to want to encourage the ambitions of Easley's daughter. Donna Easley hoped to have a professional singing career under the sponsorship of another close friend of the president and first lady, Mrs. John Hays Hammond. After some initial misunderstanding within the White House about whether Donna Easley would appear at all, Mrs. Taft gave a small tea on 28 April at which Easley sang and "charmed the friends of Mrs. Taft." Later that year Easley made a successful professional debut in New York City, where she "made a good impression on those who heard her."[35] In the years that followed, Easley entertained American troops during World War I.

During the summer and fall of 1912, Mrs. Taft was away from Washington. She spent the summer in Beverly, Massachusetts, while Will Taft struggled with the Democratic Congress as the election of 1912 neared. The fall months saw the Tafts still in Massachusetts. The president, following the custom of the day, did not campaign for re-election through speaking tours. He and Mrs. Taft made a number of quasi-political appearances around New England.

By the time they returned to the Capital for the opening of Congress in December, she knew that her husband had lost his reelection bid. Woodrow Wilson had won the White House, while Theodore Roosevelt and the Progressive Party had run second. Will Taft was a badly beaten third-place finisher. Now only a few months remained of Nellie Taft's time as a promoter of music and the arts in the White House. She decided to make the first two months of 1913 a sustained period of musicales and other entertainment. Mrs. Taft proved successful in cramming as much music into that brief period as she possibly could. Six musical events took place in as many weeks.

The first lady began on 11 January with an artist from the Netherlands, Julia Culp (1880–1970), who was in the United States on a concert tour as a singer of lieder. The thirty-two-year-old Culp, who became known as "the Dutch Nightingale" in the United States, had performed for Queen Wilhelmina of the Netherlands and at the court of the German Kaiser. In the United States, she was, said the *Washington Post*, "known only to those who follow the continental triumphs of musical artists," but Helen Taft knew of her and invited her to the White House. On 10 January she gave her initial concert at Carnegie Hall before an admiring audience. The next day, she repeated the program of works by Schumann, Schubert, and Brahms for Mrs. Taft and her guests.[36] Culp returned to Europe after her American tour.

Ten days later, Mrs. Taft experienced a striking change of pace when the American folk singer Loraine Wyman (1885–1938) headlined the next musicale. The invited guests included members of the Supreme Court and a number of male friends of President Taft. At twenty-seven, Wyman had been presenting her program of English ballads and songs in Old French for only about three years. Born in 1885, she studied with the French singer Yvette Guilbert in Paris be-

Julia Culp, the Dutch Nightingale. During a visit to the United States in early 1913, the renowned lieder singer entertained Mrs. Taft and her guests. (Library of Congress)

fore returning to the United States to pursue a career as a diseuse. She was the mistress of a New York doctor, Henry McMahon Painter. Moreover, as a young woman, she was strikingly attractive when she appeared in costume to sing for audiences in public and private. This personal background may explain Mrs. Taft's cryptic remark in a letter to her son Robert after Wyman appeared: "She has a great vogue with old men."[37]

At the White House, Wyman rendered a series of English ballads and French folk songs including "The Outlandish Knight," "Petit Tambour," and "I Know Where I'm Goin'." During the next several years, Wyman would shift the focus of her art and emerge as a song catcher who transcribed melodies in the mountains of Kentucky and other states to preserve original American folk songs. Helen Taft presented her in Washington just as her fame was about to expand with her new interest in native folk tunes.[38]

The hectic pace of musicales continued on 25 January 1913 with a recital by Ludovic Breitner (1855–?), a famous French piano teacher then on the faculty at the Peabody Conservatory in Baltimore, and songs by a popular German tenor, Paul Reimers (1877–1942). Breit-

ner had made his reputation in France and Germany as a teacher for
Olga Samaroff, among others, and came to the United States in 1912.
Before an audience of fifty guests, he played selections by Mendels-
sohn, Chopin, and Beethoven. One of his students, Asdrik Kavo-
okdji, joined him for four-hand performances of works by Saint-
Saens and Strauss-Tausig.[39]

Paul Reimers was a lyric tenor from Germany who came to the
United States in 1910. His first concert in New York caused a critic to
assert that "there is something to admire in the excellence of Mr.
Reimers' diction, sometime of his phrasing." He sang three songs, by
Faure, Debussy, and Dvorak at the White House. He later sang for
President Woodrow Wilson and taught at the Julliard School of
Music in New York City from 1924 until his death in 1942.[40] The first
lady had heard Reimers sing at the home of the secretary of the
navy, George von Lengerke Meyer, on Thursday, 23 January 1913. She
invited him to join the musicale with Ludovic Breitner and his student the following Saturday.[41]

Beatrice Bowman, a singer with the Montreal Opera, followed on
31 January 1913. More than for any other singer that Mrs. Taft had at
the White House during her tenure as first lady, Bowman's recruitment for the engagement is well documented. The president's secretary, Charles D. Hilles, acting on Mrs. Taft's request, approached a
friend of the singer, Edmund Dwight of New York City, to convey
the invitation to perform. Dwight reported back that "she will be
delighted to accept an invitation" and "is greatly pleased by the
knowledge that she may appear on this occasion and regards it as in
the nature of a command."[42]

With this commitment in hand, Hilles informed the first lady
that "Miss Bowman has been the Prima Donna of the Montreal
Opera Company and has a very remarkable soprano voice. She ren-
ders Spross' 'Will-o-the Wisp' brilliantly." The performers understood "that neither Miss Bowman" nor her pianist "will receive a fee
for the entertainment. The program will be limited to one hour and
she will submit her list of vocal and instrumental numbers for your
criticism and approval."[43]

A problem soon developed. Bowman wanted to bring the composer and accompanist Charles Gilbert Spross with her and asked
Dwight "if Spross might have two numbers for the piano only."

Dwight responded that "there would be no objection to it." Best known as an accompanist of such performers as Mary Garden and Enrico Caruso, Spross also wrote art songs and was the organist for a church in Poughkeepsie, New York. However, Hilles replied, "it was not Mrs. Taft's intention to have Mr. Spross play anything but Miss Bowman's accompaniments." Because Dwight had made a commitment for Spross to play, "Mrs. Taft feels that it will be necessary to have him play but wishes it be limited to *one number only.*" Happily for the White House, Spross dropped out the day before the musicale, and Bowman went forward with another prominent accompanist of that period, Mark Andrews. Bowman performed works by Debussy, Verdi, and Gounod, along with "Will o' the Wisp" by Spross and "When Roses Blow" by Mark Andrews.[44]

The final two musicales of Helen Taft's tenure as first lady finished off her activity as a patroness of serious music in high style. On 6 February, the pianist Ernest Schelling and the tenor Leo Slezak were the stars of the evening. The thirty-six-year-old Schelling (1876–1939), a native of New Jersey and a pupil of Leopold Godowsky and Ignace Paderewski, came to Washington for a week's stay that included his White House appearance and an afternoon recital at the Columbia Theater a week later. The critic for the *Washington Post* called him "a scholarly interpreter, with a technical facility little short of marvelous."[45] Before an audience that included Joseph Burr Tiffany and Alice Roosevelt Longworth, Schelling played two of Mendelssohn's "Songs without Words" and five pieces by Chopin.

The invitation to Leo Slezak (1873–1946) reflected Mrs. Taft's close knowledge of the American opera scene. Long famous in Europe as an excellent interpreter of both Wagner and Mozart, Slezak, at six feet, seven inches "an amiable giant of a tenor," had come to the United States in 1909 with a three-year contract to sing at the Metropolitan Opera. Anecdotes surrounded the charismatic Slezak. The most famous occurred when he was performing in Wagner's *Lohengrin.* At the end of the opera, he was to stand in a boat, pulled by a swan, and exit for his Wagnerian destiny. A stagehand missed a cue and the swan went off alone, leaving Slezak standing by himself on stage. He turned to the audience and said in German: "What time's the next swan?"[46]

By early 1913, Slezak's contractual obligation to the Met was end-

Leo Slezak, the German tenor and star of Wagnerian productions. Slezak had captivated audiences in the United States for three years. His White House performance was one of his last in the United States before returning to Germany.
(Library of Congress)

ing and he would soon be returning to Germany. He made his last appearance in New York to enthusiastic applause and repeated curtain calls three days before he sang at the White House. His program at the White House included songs by Liszt, Richard Strauss, and Englebert Humperdink. After hearing him sing for her, Nellie Taft told her son that he was "the equal of Caruso. I think he is anyway."[47]

The concluding musicale for Nellie Taft came on 21 February with Otto Goritz (1873–1929), a German baritone, Paul Kefer (1875–1941), a cellist, and Ernestine Schumann-Heink (1861–1936), a contralto. The event was, said the *Washington Post*, "one of the largest the President and Mrs. Taft have given." The artists dined with the Tafts, the president's military aides, and fifty invited guests. Six hundred visitors then heard the musical presentations. The two male artists were well known to followers of serious music before World War I. Goritz was a frequent cast member in Wagnerian productions at the Met. His pro-Germany sympathies after 1914 cast a shadow over his American career. The gold medal he received from President and Mrs. Taft was stolen in a burglary in 1919.[48]

A native of France, Paul Kefer had been the principal cellist for the New York Symphony Orchestra but was now commencing a career as a freelance solo artist. A year later, he formed the Trio de Lutece with the outstanding flutist Georges Barrere and harpist Carlos Salzedo. His marriage ended in divorce, and his daughter, Rose Hobart, became a movie star in the 1930s and 1940s before being blacklisted for alleged communist ties.[49]

On that evening in February 1913, with time running out on the Taft administration, the two male musicians entertained the audience, including Robert A. Taft, with selections that captured their impressive talents. Goritz performed an aria from Wagner's *The Flying Dutchman* and works by Schumann, Schubert, and Hoffmann. Kefer played "Chants Russes" by Edouard Lalo and "Hungarian Rhapsody" by David Popper.

The star attraction that night was Schumann-Heink. "Deep voiced" and "brilliantly musical," she had joined the Metropolitan Opera in 1898. By the early years of the twentieth century, she was one of the most popular and well-paid opera singers in the country. Estimates of her income went as high as $130,000 annually. Her ability to sing in English added to her appeal to audiences nationwide. In her as-told-to memoirs, Schumann-Heink recalled that President Taft urged her to eat before her performance, which she declined to do. After she had sung her songs, he gave her a tray heaping with food and an autographed picture of himself.[50] In her portion of the program, the contralto performed two songs by Schubert, one other song by Reimann in German, and then closed out the singing with

Ernestine Schumann-Heink. By 1913, Ernestine Schumann-Heink
was one of the highest-paid and most famous operatic voices in
the world. (Library of Congress)

four English tunes, including the "Cry of Rachel" and the "Kerry Dance."

One of those in attendance at Schumann-Heink's performance was Mary Randolph, later the social secretary for Grace Coolidge and Lou Henry Hoover. In her memoirs published many years later, she remembered "the gorgeous golden voice in a great flood of melody. One beautiful song after another delights our ears; every one is entranced—thrilled—carried away; and when at the end of the program she sings the lament of 'Rachel weeping for her Children,' there isn't a dry eye in the room."[51]

The Lenten musicale tradition that Nellie Taft launched continued for several administrations until it ended after the presidency of Franklin D. Roosevelt. Under Woodrow Wilson, the emphasis shifted back to the mixture of amateur and professional performers that Edith Roosevelt had instituted. Florence Harding and Grace Coolidge hosted musicales during the 1920s. The custom of classical music continued through the Hoover administration, and the artists and offerings became more eclectic and diverse during the administration of Franklin Roosevelt.

Nellie Taft enjoyed two more musical moments before the Taft presidency ended on 4 March 1913. The president and first lady dined at the palatial home of a wealthy friend, Mrs. Richard Townsend, and her thirty-four guests. There was, Nellie Taft wrote her son, "a musicale afterwards in which were three Metropolitan singers, and they dressed in Spanish costumes and sang Spanish songs." On 3 March, they went to the home of their friend Mabel Boardman and "the Misses Hoyt sang Indian and Romanian songs to us." It was fitting that the last social event of Nellie Taft's tenure in Washington involved music.[52]

Comparisons among first ladies concerning their cultural activities is always difficult because of varying tastes in art and music, the differences in the historical context of the terms of their husbands, and the changing ways in which the public learns about what presidential wives have done. Nellie Taft conducted her campaign for music at a time when there was no radio or television. Phonograph records were in their infancy. There is no way to tell what the quality of the performances was at her musicales. All that can be said with certainty is that she recruited some of the finest American and foreign musicians of the early twentieth century to appear. In the case of women musicians, she provided for them a showcase that other venues of the artistic world did not match.

The musical pursuits of Helen Taft became a tuneful backdrop for the unfolding of her husband's presidency from 1910 to 1913. The large number of musical performances that she presented and the relaxed atmosphere that surrounded these occasions contributed to the reputation that she and Will Taft gained as presidential hosts. Yet for all her cultural accomplishments, Helen Taft could not fully enjoy her social triumphs. As she recuperated from her May 1909 stroke, she watched as the Taft administration encountered more and more political trouble. In the process, her intense suspicion of Theodore Roosevelt intensified, and she became more and more convinced of his intention to oppose her husband in 1912. The ensuing tension between the two onetime friends meant that Helen Taft's chances of another four years of musicales disappeared during 1910 and 1911.

CHAPTER 6

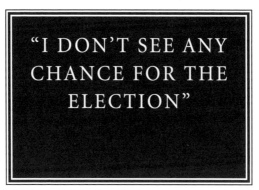

**"I DON'T SEE ANY
CHANCE FOR THE
ELECTION"**

The musicales and the performing artists that she brought to the
White House provided pleasant interludes for Nellie Taft in what
was proving to be a very difficult presidency for her husband. By
mid-1910, the bright hopes that surrounded the inauguration in
March 1909 had given way to a sense of an administration under
siege. Will Taft had not proved the heir to Theodore Roosevelt that
many progressive Republicans had wanted. The tensions with the
former president further eroded Taft's standing with the American
people. With the congressional elections facing them in the fall of
1910, the president and first lady prepared for a second summer at
Beverly, Massachusetts.

The first couple never established a comfortable yearly routine
during their four years in the White House. After their uneasy meeting with Theodore Roosevelt at the end of June 1910, Nellie and Will
Taft settled into their vacation activities at the Massachusetts shore.
These three months would be the only time during their four years
in the White House when they vacationed together as they planned.
Their son, Robert, was with them from Yale, Helen had finished her
first year at Bryn Mawr, and Charles Taft was home from the Taft
School. Newspapers reported that the younger Helen Taft "will act
as her mother's social aide at the summer capital at Beverly." By the
end of the summer Nellie's daughter had decided not to return to

Helen Taft in the public eye. Mrs. Taft joined her husband in an appearance at the Washington Senators baseball game on 9 June 1910. (Library of Congress)

college and "will act at such times as Mrs. Taft may wish to delegate the duties of her position to assistants."[1] The first lady's unwillingness to use her social secretary as a surrogate meant she had to carry much of the responsibility for White House affairs despite her uncertain health.

Throughout the summer, Nellie Taft's recovery from the effects of her stroke seemed to be progressing well. Unhappily for her husband, the intensifying tension over Roosevelt's political plans and the future of the administration made the stay in the cooler clime far from a pleasant one. On two occasions, her worried reaction attracted Archie Butt's notice.

Will Taft's first personal secretary, Fred W. Carpenter, had not performed well in the White House. Although he had been with the president through the years in the War Department, he had failed to effectively manage the president's press relations. Reporters complained about their lack of access to the president and Carpenter's inefficient response to their needs. Accordingly, he was eased out during the spring of 1910 and became the minister to Morocco. His successor, Charles Dyer Norton, had a penchant for intrigue and a desire to prove himself as Will Taft's presidential alter ego. Unfortunately, the former Chicago insurance executive lacked both astuteness and a sure sense of public relations. As Nellie Taft watched with trepidation and dismay, Norton's elaborate schemes to bolster the president had exactly the opposite of their intended effect. By the end of the summer, Norton's machinations had further strained the Tafts' relations with Theodore Roosevelt and widened the rift among the Republicans.

A major liability for Will Taft at this time was his secretary of the interior, Richard A. Ballinger. The bitter controversy over conservation policy with Roosevelt's close friend, Gifford Pinchot, during 1909–1910 had resulted in Pinchot's ouster as chief forester early in January 1910. A congressional probe of Pinchot's differences with Ballinger followed. The inquiry did not find serious guilt on Ballinger's part, but revelations regarding the White House handling of the episode had weakened Will Taft in the public mind. By the spring of 1910, Ballinger was a drag on what were already gloomy Republican prospects in the impending congressional elections: On his own, Norton decided that the White House should pressure the secretary to resign. He persuaded the president to go along with this initiative. Working with a leading conservative, Senator Winthrop Murray Crane of Massachusetts, Norton spun his plots and issued leaks to the newspapers about Ballinger's impending departure.[2]

As these political gambits unfolded, Nellie Taft grew uneasy about their potential negative impact on her husband's administration and reelection chances in 1912. One morning in early August 1910, when Archie Butt took up several matters with the president and gained his approval for each of them, the first lady erupted: "Will, you approve everything—everything Mr. Norton brings you, everything Captain Butt brings to you, and every thing everybody brings to you." Taft laughed and said: "Well, my dear, if I approve everything, you disapprove everything, so we even up on the world at any rate."[3]

Nellie responded that it was "no laughing matter. You don't want to fire Ballinger, and yet you approve of Senator Crane and Mr. Norton trying to get him out. I don't approve of letting people run your business for you." Taft countered, "I don't either, my dear, but if you will notice, I usually have my way in the long run." To which his wife responded, "No you don't. You think you do, but you don't."[4]

A president and first lady postcard. Increasing popular interest in the first family led to postcards that depicted the presidential couple with the White House. (Author's collection)

Three weeks later, Nellie Taft again raised her fears with Butt. By this time, the complex scheme to oust Ballinger had collapsed in public, much to the embarrassment of the White House and Norton. The secretary of the interior remained in office and the president had to assure Republicans that he had no intention of removing Ballinger. In addition, Taft and Roosevelt were at cross purposes over New York politics. They had mishandled the impending Republican state convention in that state, which would select candidates for the congressional and gubernatorial election in November. A Norton scheme to humiliate Roosevelt had collapsed with much recrimination in the press about what had taken place. Newspapers speculated whether Roosevelt would challenge Taft for the GOP nomination in 1912. The summer was turning into a political disaster for the Taft administration.

Nellie asked Archie Butt if he had talked to the president about these developments. The aide said he had not, to which Nellie Taft added: "I have not asked him anything and he has not talked to me. But this Roosevelt business is perfectly dreadful. I lay awake all last night thinking about it, and I don't see what is going to be the outcome." Butt urged the first lady to warn the president that he should stop listening to Norton and depend on his own judgment. "I think so, too, and I think Will sees it also," Nellie Taft said. She worried, however, that it might be too late to mend the damage that Norton had done to the president. If she did consult with her husband, she did not succeed in diverting him from his approach to national politics as the summer of 1910 wound down.[5]

The subsequent events of the autumn of 1910 bore out her worst fears. Will Taft and Roosevelt did manage a face-to-face meeting in New Haven, Connecticut, in mid-September that did nothing to clear the air between the two men. If anything, their open dispute in the press over who had sought the encounter made the political atmosphere more toxic for these onetime friends. The president, who had gone on a political trip to Ohio after seeing Roosevelt, wrote Nellie that Roosevelt had been "playing for position" and was involved in "small politics." These developments, Will assured her, "only furnish me amusement in revealing his present character, which is a development of that which I knew, but a development in a direction that I did not expect." Despite this optimistic interpretation of these events, Will Taft got the worst of the publicity out of the episode. The event marked the onset of a difficult election season for the president and the Republicans.[6]

For Nellie, the months of her vacation in Beverly brought one other unpleasant incident. While driving through Salem, Massachusetts, on 10 October, the car with Mrs. Taft and two of her sisters as passengers "struck a little 6-year-old boy and slightly injured him." The child ran out into the street without warning. Mrs. Taft and her chauffeur took little Wilfred E. Crowell to the hospital, where he was released the next day. He had suffered only some contusions in the accident.[7]

The Republican Party was not so fortunate in the 1910 balloting. As the president told a friend three days before the voters went to the polls, "Everything is chaotic politically. I shall not be surprised at our general defeat."[8] The rising cost of living gave the advantage to the Democrats. Republican factionalism between Roosevelt progressives and Taft-leaning conservatives further weakened the prospects for the Grand Old Party.

On election night 8 November 1910, the first lady invited Mabel Boardman, several members of the Cabinet, and other friends to learn about the decision of the voters when the results came in over the wires at the White House. As the press account noted, "few were encouraging, but the party received the returns with good nature."[9] The Democrats made impressive gains in the Senate and recaptured the House of Representatives for the first time since 1894. When the lower house of Congress convened in 1911, the president would face a Democratic majority. The outcome of the elections, which included a victory for Woodrow Wilson as governor of New Jersey, seemed to foreshadow difficult reelection prospects for Will Taft in 1912. There was only some consolation in the reverses that Theodore Roosevelt suffered as the candidate he had endorsed for governor of New York, Henry L. Stimson, was beaten in the Democratic tide.

Their mutual political setbacks led to the revival of a fragile rapprochement between Will Taft and Theodore Roosevelt at the conclusion of 1910 and during the early months of 1911. The two men resumed their long-interrupted correspondence, and the press spoke of how they had regained some of their previous harmony. At year's end, President and Mrs. Taft made a small positive gesture in that direction toward Edith Roosevelt. As Roosevelt's presidency wound down, his wife had expressed a wish to take with her to private life a sofa that she had purchased in 1901 to decorate the executive mansion. President Roosevelt wrote Speaker of the House Joseph G. Cannon to obtain legislative permission for her request. The Speaker, who by this time was deeply at odds with Roosevelt, leaked the news to the press, much to the embarrassment of the outgoing first lady. She departed without the piece of furniture, and the absence of the cherished sofa remained a source of emotional pain to the Roosevelts.[10]

Thanks to a timely reminder about the situation from Archie Butt, President Taft and his wife arranged to have another sofa acquired and then sent the original piece of furniture in question to Edith Roosevelt at Oyster Bay. With it came a warm letter from Will Taft to Mrs. Roosevelt explaining the circumstances of the gift and hoping "you will accept it as New Year's token of my earnest wish that the coming year may be full of happiness for you and yours. I hope the settee will bring back to you the pleasantest hours at the White House."[11]

At the same time, the first lady decided to use the china that Mrs. Roosevelt had purchased for the White House as her own. She spent her own funds to fill out the set that Mrs. Roosevelt had acquired. This public bow in the direction of first lady continuity pleased the Roosevelts as well. Archie Butt believed that these two gestures "will do much to establish the *entente cordiale* between the two families, for the Roosevelts are more susceptible to personal kindness than any I have ever known. Anything like this goes straight to the heart." Roosevelt himself told the president "how very nice it was of you to send that sofa to Mrs. Roosevelt."[12]

For Will Taft, an upward turn in his wife's health also compensated for the election setbacks. "I am glad to say," he wrote a friend, "that Nellie continues to improve. Helen's coming out this winter is giving her something to think about and to make plans for." The president had planned an inspection tour of the Panama Canal at the end of 1910, and Mrs. Taft very much wanted to go with him. Indeed, she expected to accompany him. The president decided otherwise. "I do not expect to go to Panama now because your Father thinks it would be too much of a junket," wrote the first lady to her son Robert.[13]

After the exertions of the election year and the planning for her daughter's debut in polite society, Nellie Taft was very tired by the time 1911 began. In late January 1911, for example, she attended a luncheon that Mrs. John Hay, widow of the former secretary of state, gave for her. Henry Adams reported that the first lady "had a faint turn and had to lie down, but got up and came back, green but plucky."[14]

The coming out of presidential daughter Helen Taft attracted extensive newspaper attention during the fall of 1910. Of course, nothing equaled the furor that the presentation of Alice Roosevelt to society sparked in the press in 1902. The Taft's only daughter did not have the magnetism of her Roosevelt counterpart. More reserved and quiet than the mercurial Alice, Helen had early demonstrated the academic bent that would lead her to a doctorate in history and a long productive tenure as a dean at Bryn Mawr.[15]

The younger Helen Taft had begun her undergraduate work at the woman's college outside Philadelphia in the fall of 1909. After completing her first year, it became clear to both her and her father that her mother's recovery from the stroke would be slower than anticipated. The manifold duties of the first lady were more than what Nellie Taft could manage on her own. Even with Nellie's sisters to help out during the social season, the first lady needed the support and emotional assistance that only her daughter could provide.[16]

Helen Taft was nineteen during the autumn of 1910. Attractive and self-possessed, she had an independent streak in her thinking about public issues. Her mother was suspicious of woman suffrage and dubious about how much women, other than herself, should be involved in politics. The younger Helen spoke out about the working conditions of the poor and evidenced a democratic bent that pleased the press. She also favored woman suffrage but remained quiet on the subject while her father was in office.

The daughter of the first lady did not have the innate charisma of Alice Roosevelt, though newspapers tried to identify her with "Helen pink" along the lines of "Alice blue." One thing she did share with Alice Roosevelt was a love of books. "Miss Taft has always been an inveterate reader," but she was more systematic and focused in her interests than her predecessor. Helen was "a wholesome attractive girl, with never a trace of pose or affectation in manner or conversation. She possesses a sufficient sense of humor, inherited from her father, to prevent her head being turned by the attentions she has received."[17]

The round of parties and dances associated with her coming out began during late 1910 and continued into the winter of 1911 for Helen Taft. Her father came to several of the more visible events and in the words of the reporters covering these occasions "tripped the light fantastic" with his daughter and other ladies in attendance. "Mrs. Taft was not well enough to go," reported Archie Butt, "in fact, the President discourages her from going to these entertainments with him." Although Helen Taft's debut did not match the glitter of Alice Roosevelt's, it did represent a nice triumph for the first lady in showing off her talented daughter to Washington society.[18]

In her own quiet way, Nellie Taft continued breaking precedents during the winter of 1911. On 19 January, she and a group of friends went to the Supreme Court to listen to arguments in the antitrust case that the administration had filed against the Standard Oil Company of New Jersey. Newspapers noted that this was the first time a wife of the president had visited the third branch of government.[19] During the winter of 1911, Will Taft was engaged in pushing a trade agreement with Canada to lower tariff rates between the two countries. The ensuing controversy gained the title Canadian reciprocity. The president hoped that this initiative might revive his lagging political standing as 1912 approached. There was, however, a good deal of resistance among Republicans in both the House and the Senate to this significant departure from the protectionist policy of the Grand Old Party. To woo GOP lawmakers to support the agreement, the president capitalized on the formal events during the social season.

One of these moments was the annual dinner for the outgoing Speaker of the House, Joseph G. Cannon. Will and Nellie Taft had added this occasion to other events of the formal winter social season. Cannon and Taft did not like each other, and the crusty lame-duck Republican Speaker was a leader in the forces opposing the president on Canadian reciprocity. Will Taft, who needed every vote from House Republicans for reciprocity to succeed, sent out numerous invitations to members of Congress, eighty-five in all, for the dinner in honor of the Speaker and his daughter on 14 February 1911. Almost seventy lawmakers were present, and the president told his wife "that he hoped great things from this dinner, and that she would find everyone at it whom he hoped to cajole into voting for reciprocity."[20]

Despite this social initiative and the gracious hospitality of the first couple, Cannon remained adamant against the legislation, a point that the first lady stressed to her husband. "So you see this entire dinner is wasted. Twenty-five would have done just as much good as seventy-two. Now I do wish you would consult me before you do these things. I could have told you that nothing will move that old Cannon when he gets his head set, and it is a waste of good material to lay a dinner before him."[21]

The Speaker and other Republican opponents of the reciprocity legislation prevailed in the short session of Congress that ended on 4 March 1911. The enabling legislation for the trade agreement was not approved. The beleaguered president had to summon a special session in April to have the lawmakers continue work on his trade initiative. As the legislative proceedings got under way, it became clear that Congress might be in the special session throughout the summer. If so, once again the president and the first lady would be separated.

Helen Taft's active schedule during the late winter and spring of 1911 reflected her improving health and her awareness that the celebration of the couple's twenty-fifth wedding anniversary in June was approaching. In fact, the tempo of her White House routine accelerated as her innate activism expressed itself. She held her four Lenten musicales, sponsored dances for her daughter and friends, attended the opera and other musical events, and welcomed large groups such as the Daughters of the American Revolution to the White House. Archie Butt noted this intense energy on the part of the president and the first lady: "How Mrs. Taft stands the strain is more than I can see."[22]

With her returning vigor, Mrs. Taft also received press plaudits about what journalists called her "delicate wit." One story told of a dinner for diplomats where "a distinguished French traveler . . . boasted a little unduly of his nation's politeness." The Gallic gentleman said, "We French are the politest people in the world. Everybody acknowledges it. You Americans are a remarkable nation, but the French excel you in politeness. You admit it yourselves, don't you." To which the first lady responded: "That is our politeness."[23]

On another occasion, the first lady heard a fellow guest say about a woman from the West: "She is beautiful but not at all accomplished." To which Nellie Taft reportedly commented: "My dear there is no accomplishment more difficult than to be beautiful."[24] How these supposed quips accorded with her continuing speaking difficulties arising from her stroke was not discussed. Although the first lady had a quick mind and a fast response before her illness, some of these press tales sounded more like the creations of White House publicity than accounts of actual conversations.

The first lady's effort to introduce cherry trees into the Washington landscape had stalled when the Japanese gift had proved to contain diseased plants. While she waited for another healthy shipment to be prepared, Mrs. Taft arranged for the planting of some Japanese cherry trees of her own. On 30 April 1911, the presidential couple, along with Archie Butt, drove to the location of the trees near the

Mall. "Mrs. Taft actually clapped her hands in delight when she saw the cherry blossoms."[25]

During the first week of May, delegates arrived for the meeting of the "women's welfare" department of the National Civic Federation, which took place in Washington. The women gathered at the home of Mrs. John Hays Hammond, a close friend of Nellie Taft and the president. Newspaper accounts observed that "Mrs. Taft took an active part in the meeting" as those present discussed how to bring capital and labor closer together. After their session, the delegates went to a garden party at the White House with the Marine Band. When her husband asked what the Civic Federation did, the first lady told him that it stood "somewhere between the suffragettes and the women who don't believe in doing anything."[26]

In mid-May the first lady accompanied the president on a brief speaking tour in New York City. Will Taft addressed a group of lawyers in New York on the evening of 13 May. As the president spoke, Archie Butt watched Mrs. Taft and observed "how truly pretty she was and how well she was looking." That evening, at the home of the president's brother, Henry W. Taft, the talk turned to the interview an unnamed senator had given to the press attacking the president. Mrs. Taft told the group that if she knew the name of the culprit, "she would never again invite him to the White House or have anything to do with him." Agitated and tired, the first lady went to bed soon thereafter.[27]

A few hours later, Butt heard the president "come into the hall and call loudly for his brother Harry." Mrs. Taft had suffered another stroke. She experienced what the White House termed for the public a "nervous attack" during the banquet for the president. The press was told that "the attack was not at all alarming." Nonetheless, it was decided that she should not accompany Will Taft for the remainder of his speaking engagements in Pennsylvania and then his scheduled return to Washington. Instead, she would remain in New York. Their daughter left Bryn Mawr to be with her mother. "I am glad to think that the attack from which Mrs. Taft has suffered will not be as severe as the one she had two years ago," the president wrote to a political ally, "and the Doctor gives me hope that in the course of a month she will be restored to what she was before the attack came on. I sincerely hope this may be true."[28] The first lady did bounce back from this episode with more resilience than she had evidenced in the spring of 1909. Nonetheless, the episode emphasized Mrs. Taft's need to conserve her strength.

At this time, the president was making changes in his Cabinet, one of which included naming Henry L. Stimson as secretary of war. A New Yorker, Stimson stopped in at Henry Taft's residence to ask about Mrs. Taft's condition. "The President saw me and gave me a long and personal description of Mrs. Taft's illness. This was, as I afterward learned, characteristic of him. He was absolutely devoted to her and was tremendously appreciative of any interest shown in her. With all this feeling, he could discuss phases of her illness which would have been quite impossible to some men of different temperaments, feeling as strong as he unquestionably did."[29]

As he traveled and when back in the White House, the president wrote his convalescing wife his customary long letters about the reaction to his speeches and changes in her condition. "I am longing to have Thursday come, my darling," he told her, "so that you may be safely housed in the White House and begin directing matters again and so that I can see you grow better & stronger under my eye." Six days later he was again "longing to see you. The White House is not the same without you. Flowers are wanting and that essence or atmosphere that you alone can supply. I hope you will look out from your window on the Garden party."[30]

Once she returned to the mansion, her condition improved. The White House informed the public "that it was unnecessary for her to go to Hot Springs, Va., or to Beverly to recuperate." The president was relieved at this change in his wife's situation. "I am glad to say," Will Taft wrote Mabel Boardman, "that Nellie is getting on as well as we could hope. She has nothing but an obstruction of her speech, through the drawn condition of her tongue which is improving from week to week." The president was more expansive in a letter to his brother, Horace. "There is nothing except the tongue which interferes with distinct enunciation, but which is improving with use from week to week. The Doctor gives us every hope that this obstruction to clear speech will disappear within a month, so that I am still counting on having a silver wedding. We have induced Nellie to stay in bed, so that she does not come down stairs at all, and while she resents this treatment, I think she realizes the necessity for care."

The first lady remained unwilling "to see people because of the defect in her speech."[31]

The strains between the president and the Roosevelt family persisted even during this second illness of his wife. The third garden party of the spring went on as scheduled even though the first lady could not attend. Mabel Boardman's sister came with Alice Roosevelt Longworth. As the two women were leaving, Longworth chanted, "Ya! Ya! Ya! Mrs. Taft you won't be here much longer." Boardman attributed this behavior from "the immediate Roosevelt family" to "a great jealousy at having the President in the White House though he had been so consistently a good and loyal friend to them."[32]

By early June, the political fortunes of President Taft were dependent on the outcome of the special session of Congress that he had summoned to address the issue of trade reciprocity with Canada. He was pushing the Democratic House to approve the agreement and dealing with potential Republican opposition in the Senate. At the same time, the delicate improvement in Taft's relationship with Theodore Roosevelt had stalled. The two men met in Baltimore during the first week of June to mark the jubilee of Cardinal James Gibbons of Baltimore. The onetime friends had a friendly encounter. As they sat together chatting, the audience broke into spontaneous applause. Press accounts argued that the episode meant that Roosevelt would endorse Taft for another term in 1912. An irritated Roosevelt bridled at this suggestion and there were no further letters sent from the former president to the incumbent of the White House during the remainder of the presidency. Relations between the two men cooled throughout the remainder of 1911.

Amid these political troubles, the imminence of the anniversary provided a bright spot for the first couple. The preparations for the observance of the twenty-fifth anniversary for the Tafts had been in the works for some months. The only previous occasions when a presidential couple had marked twenty-five years of their marriage had come during the Grant era and then during the administration of Rutherford B. Hayes, an event that Nellie Taft remembered.

Helen Taft later recalled that "it did not seem unfitting to me that this anniversary should be spent in the White House or that we should seek to make it an event not to be forgotten by anybody who happened to witness." She devoted elaborate attention to the preparations for the gala festivities. "I thanked the happy fate that had given me a summer wedding-day because I needed all outdoors for the kind of party that I wanted to give."[33]

The White House sent out invitations to members of previous presidential families to be present. More than four thousand guests were expected to appear when the festivities started. "At the silver wedding celebration refreshments will be served, there will be dancing in the East Room, and an 'overflow' garden party in the White House grounds." The president wrote his son, Robert, at the Harvard Law School that "your mother would very much like to have you at the silver wedding, if it is possible, on the 19th of June." Will Taft recognized that there might be "some examination that you had, but "it would gratify your mother very much if you could be with us. We don't like to have a wedding without the presence of our three children. Let me hear definitely from you about this."[34] The whole family was together for the occasion.

Newspapers informed their readers of the circumstances of the courtship of Nellie and Will Taft during the mid-1880s. There were also discussions of Nellie Taft's role in her husband's political rise. A "friend" of the president conveyed to the press Will Taft's own appraisal of his wife's influence on his career: "Mrs. Taft always had ambitions for me. She has aided me tremendously since our marriage and has supplemented my work in an effective way. My own inclination and desire was to go on the Supreme bench. She felt I was presidential timber, and vetoed my wish."[35] In taking this deferential tack on his own ambitions, the president contributed to the notion that he was less desirous of the nation's highest office than in fact he was.

The news of the silver wedding festival produced an outpouring of presents from across the country and around the world. In this period, there were no obstacles in law or custom to the presidential couple accepting gifts from private citizens for a personal occasion such as a wedding anniversary. Legal restraints of that kind and questions about conflict of interest were still many years in the future. "That silver was showered upon us until we were almost buried in silver was incidental," wrote Nellie Taft. "We couldn't help it; it was our twenty-fifth anniversary and we had to celebrate it." The president and the first lady urged friends not to send expensive gifts, but there was no stopping some individuals who wanted to make an impression on the White House.[36]

As Archie Butt wrote, "I never knew there was as much silver in the world. It is hideous to see such profligacy. It begins to look as if this feature might be the occasion of considerable embarrassment." Gifts from the head of United States Steel and the Rockefeller family were so expensive that the White House kept the amount of these presents quiet. A present from brewer Augustus Busch irritated the proponents of temperance. Nonetheless, there were grumblings in private about the dimensions of the gift giving that the Tafts had produced. The wife of a Democratic House member said, "It isn't exactly politics and is still less a social gathering of friends. It looks to me as if the idea had 'jes growed' instead of being wisely thought out, and is now beyond control."[37]

Although there were forecasts of rain in the Washington area, the weather cooperated with the Tafts and the event went off as scheduled. At 9 o'clock on 19 June, the president and Mrs. Taft descended the main staircase of the mansion to the sound of the wedding march. They moved out onto the lawn until the couple reached a place where an electric sign had been erected. Throughout the proceedings, the sign flashed "1886–1911." President Taft told the crowd, "Mrs. Taft and I are deeply touched and grateful for all the many expressions of good will that have come to us."[38]

Newspapers praised the event as one that "will go down in the history of the White House as the most beautiful function ever given there." The first lady's stamina in greeting all the invited guests also drew press approval. "That Mrs. Taft, ill as she was, had the immense pluck and ambition to engineer such a large function and to remain at her post and to greet each and every guest of the five thousand or more, none can gainsay, and it is a matter of great satisfaction to all to know she stood the ordeal so well and had no second setback in consequence."[39] President Taft agreed. He told his half brother, Charles, that "we had a great silver wedding last night. It did not rain and the White House grounds were beautiful with lights and decorations. Nellie, I am glad to say, stood the strain well, and is up this morning and happy from the successful outcome."[40] In her memoir, the first lady informed her daughter and her readers that she had "a right to be enthusiastic in my memory of that party be-

The Taft family during the presidency. The president and Mrs. Taft with their
three children, Robert, at left, Charles Phelps, and Helen Taft. (Library of
Congress)

cause without enthusiasm it could not have been given at all. And
why should not one be frankly grateful for success?"[41]

The anniversary celebration fulfilled one of Nellie Taft's girlhood
dreams. Once it was over, however, she returned to Beverly, Massachusetts, for the summer while the president stayed in Washington
to deal with the special session and the looming challenge from
Theodore Roosevelt. The president once again began his daily letters
to her about the events of his trips and the progress of administration legislation in Congress.

By now, Taft had replaced the unreliable Charles D. Norton with
a new secretary, Charles D. Hilles, a New York Republican. Hilles
brought efficiency and order to the operation of the Taft White

House for the first time. The politically astute Hilles also launched the renomination campaign for Will Taft as the two men looked ahead to 1912. Both Nellie and Will Taft wanted to achieve renomination to thwart any chance that Theodore Roosevelt might have of regaining the presidency. In her realistic moments, Mrs. Taft recognized that the chances for her to spend another four years in the White House were receding almost daily.

While the special session dragged on through July 1911, Will Taft kept assuring his wife that he would reach Beverly by mid-August, if not earlier. In his longhand letters, he told her of the obstacles the Democrats and dissident Republicans were putting in the way of his programs. She learned as well of his mounting disenchantment with Roosevelt, who attacked the president on conservation issues and foreign policy. "I am longing to be with you," he told her. "I am tired and I want quiet and rest. Hasten the day of adjournment." She did not write at the same length because of the lingering effects of her physical condition, but when he received a letter from her, his day was made. "I had a nice long letter from Nellie this morning," he wrote Mabel Boardman on 28 July. "I rejoice at it because it takes considerable effort for her to write."[42]

While her husband labored in steamy Washington, Nellie Taft relaxed at her new summer residence. The owners of the previous cottage where the Tafts had stayed decided that the constant noise and intrusion of the press was too much of a nuisance. Nellie Taft chose instead a home called Parramatta, which became the summer capital of America for these months. "The North Shore rest seems to help her," the president told his brother, Charles. She felt strong enough to say to the press "that the only thing necessary to make her comfort and happiness complete is the adjournment of Congress and the arrival of the President." For the most part, the first lady in these weeks kept to herself and did little in the way of public appearances.[43]

Even before Will Taft arrived in late August, his wife became a little more visible. Their close friend, Mabel Boardman, gave a bazaar to benefit the American Red Cross. Helen Taft "ably assisted" in the affair. Newspapers noted that "Mrs. Taft has appeared only at informal gatherings, and Miss Helen Taft has gone about but little." Accordingly, "the presence of the President household occasioned a turning out of the smart set such as the North Shore has not witnessed before this season."[44]

President Taft could only spend a few weeks with the first lady on the Massachusetts shore. As part of the reelection strategy that he and Hilles had crafted, he had scheduled a nationwide speaking tour on the model of what he had done during the autumn of 1909. He would be making nonpartisan speeches to push, among other things, his program of arbitration treaties with other nations to lessen the likelihood of war. He also hoped to have the benefits of the success of Canadian reciprocity on which voters in that country would be passing judgment at the polls in late September. While the president spoke to friendly audiences on these subjects, Hilles would meet with influential Republicans in each state to line up delegates for the president's renomination. With Roosevelt still on the sidelines as far as 1912 was concerned, the president's prospects for winning the GOP nomination seemed assured.

Nellie Taft would not be with her husband on this extended trip either. Her health would not stand the strain of such a lengthy journey. During the time when they were together at Beverly, she commented on the president's dislike of criticism of his policies. After dinner one evening, he asked Nellie if the afternoon New York newspapers had arrived. She gave him a copy of the New York *World*, a Democratic paper. "I don't want the *World*," he informed her. He had stopped reading it because "it only makes me angry." She reminded him that "you will never know what the other side is doing if you read only the [New York] *Sun* and the [New York] *Tribune*." However, Will Taft by now was so disillusioned with the press that nothing his wife said could change his pattern of shutting out journalistic criticism.[45]

Will Taft departed for his tour in mid-September. Nellie remained at Beverly and then returned to Washington in mid-October to await Will's arrival back from his swing around the country. As she told her daughter, she and her sister Eleanor "have led a very quiet life since you all departed." They read books by the rising young British politician, Winston Churchill, and drove around the countryside in the afternoons.[46] Her daughter wrote to President Taft's aunt that the summer had been "somewhat lonely" for the first lady "as she has not gone out at all and has so few intimate friends around here."[47]

During his long journey, Will Taft sent her regular telegrams about his doings and the reaction to his appearances, but there was only one letter of any length like the ones he had sent her in 1909. "I have been going at such a rate and working on speeches so much that I have had no opportunity to write," he informed her from San Francisco on 14 October. "Thus far," he continued, "I consider the trip to be a great success."[48] Other observers believed that although the president's crowds were friendly, he had done nothing to counteract the growing support for the Democrats in 1912.

During the autumn of 1911, Will Taft established a lead within the Republican Party for the 1912 nomination. The quiet work that he and Hilles did on the transcontinental trip would pay off in delegates in June 1912 at the GOP convention. In the court of public opinion, however, these months saw an erosion in Will Taft's popularity. Canadian voters rejected reciprocity in their September election. Most important, relations with Theodore Roosevelt worsened. By the end of the year, the former friends were no longer on speaking terms, and political pundits counted the time until Roosevelt would enter the race against the president.

The key event came while the president was still on his transcontinental speaking junket. In October 1911, the government filed an antitrust suit against United States Steel in which the formal indictment of the giant corporation contained explicit criticisms of Roosevelt's record as president. Will Taft had not seen the charges before they went in, but that made no difference in the mind of his one-time friend. An angry Roosevelt listened anew to suggestions that he should challenge Taft in 1912. If the people wanted him to run, the former president suggested, he would answer their call. Allies of Roosevelt mounted a public relations effort to demonstrate to him that Will Taft could not win the general election. Only Roosevelt could save the Republicans from defeat at the hands of the resurgent Democrats. The Republicans moved toward a bitter battle for the nomination in 1912.

In that contest, Nellie Taft would play only a minor role. During the nomination battle of 1912, the first lady would have to be on the sidelines. At Christmastime in 1911, the president told his former secretary, Charles D. Norton, that "though Mrs. Taft's speaking improves but slowly, her health and spirits are excellent and she enjoys life. She takes great pleasure in Bob's success at Harvard, in Charley's at Horace's, and in Helen's society stunts."[49] Summing up the possible first ladies from the impending presidential election, the *Washington Post* in December 1911 called her "an able politician and a farsighted critic. She knows politicians and their ways, and she knows the ways of their wives, which is sometimes almost as important."[50]

Additional public praise for the first lady came from an unlikely source as 1911 ended. The wife of Senator Robert La Follette wrote a column for the newspapers. In her comments on a White House reception for the Congressional Club, Belle Case La Follette noted that President Taft "had aged somewhat in the three years of his administration." Nellie Taft, however, "as she stood at his side, stately and calm, the pink of her brocaded gown bringing out the clearness of her complexion and the color of her dark eyes, looked unusually distinguished and showed no evidence of being worn." The social occasions of the Tafts were "in part free from restraint and truly enjoyable." Mrs. Taft was a "thoughtful, observant and reflective" first lady and her relationship with her husband reflected "equality, sympathy, and understanding, which is the basis of an ideal married comradeship."[51]

As she looked ahead to the election year of 1912, the first lady herself was realistic enough to know that her husband might well secure another nomination from his party. His chances for reelection against the resurgent Democrats were less positive. As she told him in November, "I think you will be renominated, but I don't see any chance for the election." Like Will, her major goal would be to see that Theodore Roosevelt did not win the GOP nomination or become president once again.[52]

For Mrs. Taft, the imminence of the Roosevelt candidacy fulfilled all the fears and suspicions she had harbored against the former president for the preceding decade. Despite her warnings to her husband, Will Taft had been too trusting, too much the believer that his onetime friend would not betray their relationship. Now the political nightmare she had anticipated was coming true in front of her. There was nothing she could do to stop the confrontation that would soon split the Republicans into two warring camps and assure that her husband would not gain a second term.

CHAPTER 7

GOOD FRIENDS
AND GOLDEN
OPINIONS

Nellie Taft experienced a painful year in 1912. Her husband's dreams of a second term vanished when Theodore Roosevelt split the Republican party. Archie Butt died in April when he went down on the *Titanic* in the North Atlantic. Finally, Mrs. Taft's father died during the summer. By the end of the year, she knew that her tenure in the White House would stop on 4 March 1913. Four years after she came to the role of first lady, her dreams were ending in frustration and defeat.

Throughout January 1912, the president and the first lady watched as their onetime friend and sponsor moved toward a challenge for the Republican nomination. Although he had told friends in late 1911 that he did not wish to run against Taft, Theodore Roosevelt decided during the first ten days of the new year to allow his name to be put forward as a candidate for the Republican nomination. Once he indicated such a willingness to run, it was not long before he came out in direct opposition to the president. "I am afraid I am in for a hard fight," Will Taft told a friend on 22 January.[1]

By early February, the race for the GOP nomination was on as both factions prepared for political battle. Roosevelt proclaimed his willingness to run in a public letter to seven progressive Republican governors in mid-February. Talking about the document at dinner on 25 February 1912, in the last conversation that Archie Butt recorded in his diary letters, Mrs. Taft said: "I told you so four years ago and you would not believe me." Her husband chuckled and replied: "I know you did, my dear, and I think you are perfectly happy now. You would have preferred the Colonel to come out against me than to have been wrong yourself."[2]

The extent to which the tension between Edith Roosevelt and Helen Taft influenced the breakup of the friendship of their husbands has never been measured. Because at bottom the split between Will Taft and Theodore Roosevelt turned on their contrasting views of regulatory power and the role of the president, greater harmony between their wives would probably not have mattered all that much. Yet there was an element in the fissure between the two men that grew out of the tension that their wives felt about each other. The private and the public tensions intermingled in ways that destroyed the Roosevelt–Taft friendship.

Edith Roosevelt regarded Will Taft as a second-rate successor to her husband. How much she influenced him against the former president after 4 March 1909 is difficult to determine. Like so many others around Theodore Roosevelt, she had little good to say about his successor and his performance in office. There were few pro-Taft voices close to him other than his son-in-law, Nicholas Longworth. In 1910, for example, James R. Garfield recorded that Mrs. Roosevelt "told us her experiences with the Tafts & her feelings about the present situation. It is astonishing that we ever should have been so mistaken in Taft."[3]

Nellie Taft, on the other hand, did nothing over the course of the presidency to conceal her sense that the former president was not to be trusted and was planning for another run for the Republican nomination in 1912. She persuaded herself for a brief moment in June 1910 that Roosevelt still held her husband in high regard. As she later wrote, "I was not destined to enjoy this faith and assurance for very long." For the most part, however, her suspicion of Roosevelt's intentions remained strong throughout the administration.[4]

To a degree, her skepticism about Roosevelt became a self-fulfilling prophecy. Anxious to demonstrate that she and her husband were not simply another term for Taft's predecessor, she went out of her way to emphasize the divergence between the two families. In the process, she committed petty acts that the Roosevelts interpreted as deliberate snubs. As Roosevelt saw it during the summer of 1911, Will Taft had "permitted his wife and brother, and a number of less disinterested advisors, to make him very jealous of me, and very anxious to emphasize the contrast between our administrations by sundering himself from my especial friends and followers, and appearing hereafter as the great wise conservative."[5]

Helen Taft had every right to run the White House as she saw fit. However, some explanations to Edith Roosevelt and the appearance of consultation during the transition might have tended to diminish misunderstanding between these two women. Reaching out to her predecessor would have made good sense from a human point of view. But that was not Nellie Taft's way. She had endured what she regarded as the slights toward a Cabinet wife from 1904 to 1908. When her time came, she was resolved to exercise her prerogatives to the full. The problem was that her insistence on these privileges conflicted with the political interests of her husband's presidency. From the election of 1908 through the onset of her stroke, Helen Taft behaved in a manner calculated to arouse animosity in the Roosevelt camp. Once her physical condition worsened, her opportunity to mend fences with the Roosevelt family disappeared.

The episode with Henry White in 1909 illustrated the limits of Nellie Taft's political insight. She had nursed a grudge against the diplomat for more than two decades and now claimed her revenge. She did not stop to consider the impact of her judgment on Theodore Roosevelt and his circle, where White was revered. In fact, she went out of her way in the small world of Washington politics to have people know why White had been relieved of the Paris embassy. White could have been eased out after a year or so without much fuss, but finesse was not part of how Nellie Taft handled those who were friendly with Theodore Roosevelt. In the end, she hurt her husband's administration more than she did Henry White.

Amid the partisan demands of the presidential election year, Nellie Taft also took account of the increasing publicity that now focused on the wife of the president. In December 1911, she responded to an inquiry from a New York newspaper to name the greatest women, alive or dead. Her list had some predictable choices—Queen Victoria, Joan of Arc, Florence Nightingale, and Susan B. Anthony. The French composer Cecile Chaminade reflected her musical interest, and observers noted the presence of Queen Louisa of Prussia (1767–1810), a staunch foe of Napoleon Bonaparte, and wondered whether Nellie was making an allusion to Theodore Roosevelt.[6]

During the late winter, Mrs. Taft agreed, along with the other former first ladies and families of the president, to donate her inaugural gown to the Smithsonian Museum as part of an effort "in preserving to future generations the costumes worn by notable women in the social and official life of the capital." Nellie Taft's dress became the foundation of the popular exhibit of first lady clothing that opened in 1914 and has been a fixture at the Smithsonian ever since.[7]

Another addition to the White House was a portrait of Dolley Madison that the Colonial Dames of Virginia donated to the mansion in May 1912. The first lady assured the patriotic organization in December 1911 that no formal action was needed for the generous donation to be made and accepted. In May, she and the president met with the Dames to receive the painting. "The portrait is exceedingly good," she told her eldest son, "and I want to put it by Madison's portrait in the Red Room. I don't know whether your father will allow it or not."[8]

In the political world of 1912, first ladies had little to do in a presidential campaign. Ellen Wilson might campaign with her husband as he sought the Democratic presidential nomination, but the wife of the president was expected to remain off the hustings. Accordingly, Mrs. Taft was not a large element in the race her husband ran against Roosevelt in the primaries during the winter and spring months. Her physical condition, while improved since the second attack of May 1911, would not have allowed her to travel with the president when he hit the campaign trail in April and May 1912. She had to remain at the White House as Will's fortunes fluctuated in the face of the Roosevelt challenge.

At first, the race seemed to go the president's way. Roosevelt's opening speech of the campaign, an address to the Ohio Constitutional Convention in February, came out for the recall of judicial decisions on economic and regulatory issues. Allowing the electorate to overturn judicial rulings on such matters aroused public dislike. Many conservative Republicans, otherwise sympathetic to the former president, returned to the Taft camp in opposition to what they regarded as dangerous radicalism. By mid-March, the conventional thinking in Washington was that the president would be renominated. His chances against the Democratic nominee in the fall were less positive.

Helen Taft continued her practice of attending sessions of Congress and committee hearings on controversial subjects. In Lawrence, Massachusetts, a bitter and violent strike between workers and clothing manufacturers had captured national attention. Congress held hearings on the labor unrest, and the first lady was there when the wives of strikers testified before a House committee. She heard their tales of beatings and police intimidation, and the desperate conditions under which they lived. Nellie Taft paid close attention, but the recitations did not shake her faith in the employers and their interests in the dispute.[9]

Her cooperation with the National Civic Federation and its women's welfare department produced tangible results two weeks later when President Taft issued an order calling for the inspection of all public buildings in the District of Columbia to provide for sanitary working conditions. The *Washington Post* reported that "she has endeavored to aid the women engaged in the active work of the organization, and has encouraged their efforts."[10]

The busy year became more hectic for the first lady when Katherine Letterman suffered an attack of appendicitis in mid-March. She had been in poor health for several weeks, partly because of her arduous duties "incident to the busy social season which preceded Lent." Laura Harlan, the daughter of the recently deceased Supreme Court justice John Marshall Harlan, stepped in to perform Letterman's duties until the social secretary recovered her health.[11]

At the end of the month, Nellie Taft's dream of seeing cherry trees in a more beautiful Washington, D.C., came true. After the disappointment of the diseased trees in early 1910, the Japanese decided to try again with another batch of six thousand trouble-free plants. The wife of the mayor of Tokyo wrote Nellie Taft in February 1911 to say that her husband had the second group of trees "grown in specially prepared and disinfected soil to prevent a like misfortune befalling them. We hope to hear of them blooming in the salubrious Washington climate reminding you all of Japan's faithful devotion and admiration for her old friend and tutor, America."[12]

With the precautions that the Japanese had taken to prevent in-

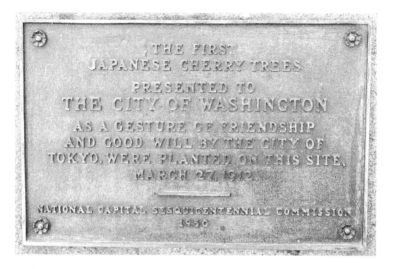

*The Japanese cherry trees. This plaque on the Tidal Basin in Washington marks
the spot where Helen Taft and the Japanese ambassador planted the first trees on
27 March 1912. (T. L. Hawkins)*

fection, a new batch of six thousand trees were readied for transmission to the United States in January 1912. On 6 March 1912, Colonel Spencer Cosby, the army officer in charge of the buildings and grounds for the White House, discussed with the first lady how the trees might be planted once they had arrived. Inspections revealed that the trees were disease free when they reached the United States on 13 March 1912. Two weeks later, in a small, unofficial ceremony that garnered minimal press coverage, Mrs. Taft "superintended the planting of a collection of rare Japanese cherry trees on the Speedway, which had been sent to her by the mayor of Tokio. One she planted herself." The ambassador of Japan, Viscount Chinada, and his wife were there. The ambassador's wife also planted a tree. Eliza Scidmore was present at the occasion; David Fairchild, the other sponsor of the cherry trees, was not.[13]

The efforts of subsequent first ladies, in particular Lady Bird Johnson, to beautify Washington have overshadowed Nellie Taft's original sponsorship of cherry trees. Nonetheless, she deserves credit for her efforts to make the Japanese gift in 1912 a permanent part of the landscape of the national capital. A dozen years later, Will Taft, now chief justice of the United States, wrote his daughter about the cherry trees in the spring. "The weather is beautiful. Your mother's cherry trees are now blushing out in full luxuriance and one loves to be in Washington at this time."[14]

In April, political events jolted the first lady as her husband's campaign faltered. On 9 April Theodore Roosevelt won the Illinois primary in a decisive victory over her husband. A week later came news of the sinking of the *Titanic* and the loss of so many prominent passengers. The trauma for Mrs. Taft was the death of Archie Butt, who had gone to Europe on a mission for the president and was returning to the United States. During his more than three years of service with the Tafts, Butt had become a fixture in the household. He was a confidant for Nellie, and his death wounded both the president and the first lady. During the weeks after the news of the tragedy came, official Washington went into mourning. Entertainment events and social occasions were reduced.

There were campaigns to memorialize the victims of the *Titanic* sinking. One narrative of the sad events focused on the willingness of men on the doomed ship to give women and children seats on the life boats at the sacrifice of their own lives. A campaign commenced to have donations from women fund a memorial to honor these men. Mrs. Taft contributed the first dollar to the fund. "I am very glad to do this in gratitude to the chivalry of American manhood, and I am sure that every woman will feel that the smallness of the contribution solicited will enable her to do the same."[15]

Money flowed into the fund, and $36,000 had accumulated by the time Mrs. Taft left the White House. The fund became controversial because it seemed to favor the memory of aristocratic men on the *Titanic* over men of middle and lower classes who had performed with equal bravery. It took nineteen years for the monument to become a reality. Helen Taft unveiled the statue on 26 May 1931 in a ceremony that President Herbert Hoover and Lou Henry Hoover attended with other dignitaries.[16]

The intense race against Theodore Roosevelt overshadowed the personal loss of Archie Butt for Will and Nellie Taft. The president had not responded to the strident attacks of Roosevelt on his character and record during the early stages of their campaign for the Republican nomination. By the end of April, however, Will Taft had decided that he could be silent no longer. He planned to make his rebuttal on 25 April in a speech at Boston. Nellie had gone to Charleston, South Carolina, to visit friends. She told her husband that "I feel very bad at your making that speech Thursday night, but there is no way out of it. I hope it may do some good, but don't know."[17]

Will Taft made the speech attacking Theodore Roosevelt and the race between the two men reached new levels of bitterness as the Republican National Convention approached in mid-June. For the first lady, this was a difficult period, but her health stood up to the strain of the preconvention battle. The president wrote his aunt in mid-May: "Except for the nervousness that Nellie feels from the present contest, and her reluctance to read Roosevelt's attacks on me, she is very well." Nellie followed the news of her husband's campaign through his aides. As she told her son on 26 May, "Hilles says Roosevelt put three hundred thousand dollars into Ohio" to defeat the president. She hoped it "will be better in New Jersey—but I don't know. Roosevelt seems to have captured the working man." Roosevelt won another victory in the New Jersey primary. Still, with her husband's control of the machinery of the Republican convention, his renomination seemed assured.[18]

The atmosphere for Nellie Taft as the GOP conclave neared was far different from the optimistic anticipation of 1908. The president and his allies in the Republican party had the votes to dominate the proceedings of the convention, but the prospect of a Roosevelt bolt cast a pall over the meeting. In any case, the prospects for the Grand Old Party and its nominee seemed dubious no matter how the nomination process turned out. The president and the first lady stayed in Washington, as was the custom in those days, and again waited at the end of the long-distance phone and telegraph wire for news about the struggle. The couple celebrated their twenty-sixth wedding anniversary on 19 June as telegrams flowed in from friends. Meanwhile, reports from the convention floor told of a Taft ascendancy in an ever more bitter Republican donnybrook.[19]

At the convention, Roosevelt withdrew once his defeat on the floor became inevitable. He promised to start a third party to sustain a presidential run and vindicate his opposition to Taft and the Republicans. Seeing that result, Nellie Taft "began to make plans for the future in which the White House played no part." She had, she recalled, stopped reading the opposition newspapers because they put her "in a state of constant rage which could do me no possible good."[20]

In the week after the Republicans had left Chicago, the Democrats held their nominating convention in nearby Baltimore. Helen joined the diplomatic corps and many other Washingtonians in visiting what proved to be a tumultuous gathering. Mrs. Taft came with Mrs. Norman Mack, whose husband headed the Democratic National Committee, and other Democratic spouses. William Jennings Bryan was proposing a resolution to the delegates that attacked the president as part of a general assault on Wall Street and its influence on American politics. Meeting the first lady in the hall, Bryan decided to leave out the language in his resolution assailing Will Taft. As he told the press, "I am not sorry that I spared the feelings of the President's wife."[21] The Democrats nominated Woodrow Wilson, the governor of New Jersey, and the consensus was that the president would not be able to defeat both of his rivals for the White House.

During the last summer of the presidency, Nellie Taft was once again in Massachusetts at their vacation residence while her husband dealt with the Democratic congress through another long session. He wrote her daily of his response to Theodore Roosevelt, his dislike of the Democratic lawmakers, and his skepticism about the presidential candidacy of Woodrow Wilson. She came down to the White House to be with her husband when he delivered his formal acceptance of the Republican nomination at a White House event on 1 August 1912. She then returned to Massachusetts to await the adjournment of Congress. On 5 August, Nellie learned that her eighty-five-year-old father, John W. Herron, had died after a protracted illness. The president and the first lady went out to Ohio for the funeral. She and the other children stayed in Cincinnati after the burial to settle what little remained of her father's estate.

Following the custom that incumbent presidents did not make an extensive personal campaign for reelection, Will Taft spent the months of August and September 1912 in New England at various events of a quasi-political nature. Nellie Taft accompanied him on these various junkets that did little to affect the outcome of the three-way contest. It had become evident by Labor Day in 1912 that

Mrs. Taft visits the Democrats. The first lady enjoyed attending political events in the Washington area. She went to the Democratic convention in Baltimore in late June 1912 with Mrs. Norman E. Mack, on her left, and Mrs. Hugh Wallace.
(*Library of Congress*)

the real race was between Woodrow Wilson, the Democratic nominee, and Theodore Roosevelt, running as a Progressive. Will Taft's chances of pulling out an upset victory were slim at best, and few pundits of the day thought such a result likely. Just before the election, Vice President James S. Sherman died of a heart attack. It was, Nellie wrote to Will, "very unfortunate, coming just at this time. You have the worst luck."[22]

In the end, President Taft came in a poor third among the major candidates, running behind Wilson, who was elected president, and Theodore Roosevelt for the Progressives. He and Nellie now knew that their time in the White House would end at noon on 4 March 1913. Friends lamented the election loss and kept Nellie busy dealing with their condolences. She professed to her son to be content with the outcome of the presidential race. "As your father would have had a democratic congress anyway, I was very glad that he was not elected—which is making the best of it."[23]

President Taft decided to make in late December one final inspection tour of the Panama Canal as it neared completion. For this trip, Nellie felt strong enough to accompany her husband and his official party on the voyage. They left the United States on 19 December for the short sail to the isthmus, and "the weather was fine and the sea smooth throughout the voyage." While the first lady cruised, in Washington all the talk was of the new order of things in the social sphere. As the *New York Herald* noted, "the roots of the present fashionable Washington society which are buried beneath sixteen consecutive years of Republican patronage, are about to be torn up and ruthlessly cast aside."[24]

President and Mrs. Taft determined to make the transition to Wilson and the Democrats as free of rancor and difficulty as possible. There would be no repetition of the strain of 1908–1909. Ellen Axson Wilson decided to retain the services of Elizabeth Jaffray as the housekeeper for the White House, a decision of which President Taft approved. The two first ladies did not communicate directly until just before the inauguration. There was no occasion when the two women toured the White House together, but on the whole, the shift from Helen Taft to Ellen Wilson was smooth and trouble-free.[25]

Three weeks after the inauguration, Ellen Wilson wrote to thank her predecessor for "the many courtesies" the Tafts had shown them during the transition to the presidency. In recognition of what Nellie Taft had accomplished during her four years, the new first lady expressed the hope that when the Wilsons left Washington they would "leave behind us as many good friends and as golden opinions" as Will and Helen Taft had achieved.[26]

As for the Tafts and their future, Will had decided that he could not practice law after the presidency because he had appointed so many federal judges. A happy solution was for him to become a professor of law at Yale University after a vacation to recuperate from the rigors of the White House years. For Nellie Taft, the decision involved a move to New Haven, Connecticut, and the shift from the presidential mansion to a rented house near the Yale campus. She spent some time shuttling between Washington and New Haven to supervise the move to their new home.

Washington society, which the Tafts had entertained with large receptions, parties, and musicales for four years, realized that a glamorous social era was coming to an end. The parties and large musicales of Will and Nellie would soon be a memory. The word was that the Wilsons emphasized small, intimate gatherings, often of just their immediate family. The cancellation of the inaugural ball was a signal of the new Democratic austerity. The playful, relaxed atmosphere that Will and Nellie Taft had cultivated was not the Wilson style. The abbreviated social season before the inauguration on 4 March 1913 would have to suffice for that part of Washington that liked a gala evening out with the city's upper crust. "President and Mrs. Taft will long be remembered for their many and pleasant entertainments, both formal and informal," wrote one society commentator. "There is an absence of self-consciousness and an interested attention in their greetings that make all social gatherings of which they are a part free from restraint and truly enjoyable."[27]

Nellie Taft poured her energies into the final months of her time as first lady, but she was still not entirely well. Senator Reed Smoot of Utah saw her at a White House function in December and concluded that although she had improved, her health was still not of the best. Despite this difficulty, she put on a series of cultural and musical occasions during January and February 1913 that kept the mansion filled with guests. On 4 February, at the reception for the army and navy at the White House, she danced the one-step with her military partner. The press reported that the first lady "threaded her way through the mazes of the dance which has taken the capital by storm."[28]

The first lady continued to seek out young new talent for these events. Although she later would become world famous for her monologues, Ruth Draper was still an amateur performer at age twenty-eight who appeared in private settings in the homes of the friends and the wealthy. Henry Adams was one of her backers. "She is a little genius," he wrote in 1911, "and quite fascinates me." Draper would not make her professional debut for another three years. When she gave her program at the White House on 7 January 1913, the audience anticipated a special occasion. Draper performed some of her monologues, such as "A French Dressmaker" and "A Southern Girl at a Dance," that would become part of her repertoire. Two others on "A Servian Scene" and "A French Actress at Home" did not gain inclusion in her subsequent professional career offerings.[29]

Four days after Ruth Draper appeared, Helen Taft welcomed two of her predecessors to the mansion in what newspapers called "the first time probably, in history, that the wives of three Presidents have ever gathered around the same table at the White House." The widow of Benjamin Harrison was visiting relatives in Washington while Mrs. Grover Cleveland was in town with her fiancé, Professor Thomas J. Preston. The president and the first lady had Mrs. Harrison and Mrs. Cleveland to dinner on 11 January. The next such assembly of first ladies would occur in 1929, when Mrs. Grace Coolidge, Mrs. Lou Hoover, and Mrs. Taft would be present at the inauguration of Herbert Hoover.[30]

Before they left the White House, the presidential couple took steps to provide for Mrs. Taft's secretary, Katherine Letterman. She had come over from the Department of State in 1910, and the president sought to return her to her former agency. He told the secretary of state, Philander Knox, that Letterman had been invaluable to the first lady. She had been "so efficient and of so much help to Mrs. Taft that I am more than usually anxious that she be well provided for before we go out of office." The best Knox could do was a position that would require Letterman to take a pay cut. Instead, she went out into private life and took a position with the American Woman's Club of Berlin in mid-1913. She did not find the work in Germany "congenial" and moved to France in 1914, where she remained throughout World War I.[31] In 1921 she wrote the former president to congratulate him on his nomination as chief justice of the United States.

The end of the Taft administration also saw Joseph Burr Tiffany leave the employment of Steinway & Sons as director of the art department. He joined the firm of Blakeslee and Company, prominent New York art dealers. In a farewell moment for his long service to the White House, he came to the Leo Slezak musicale on 7 February 1913 and dined with the Tafts and their other guests. Tiffany died in April 1917. His successor was Henry Junge, who stayed on until the administration of Franklin D. Roosevelt in the mid-1930s.[32]

To provide a suitable memento of Helen Taft's service as first lady, her friends, led by Mabel Boardman, took up a subscription to purchase a necklace for her. Sixty people contributed toward the acquisition of "a chain of pure white diamonds set in platinum with a pear-shaped stone forming a pendant." The group had some money left over, and they bought a scarf pin for President Taft to go along with the necklace. At the final musicale on 21 February, the gift was presented to the first lady. As she told her son Robert on the last day of the administration, "People seem so sorry to have us go, and many are coming to the station to see us go."[33] There was some realization among the Washington elite that Will and Nellie Taft had provided four productive years of musical events and cultural riches that had gone unnoticed during the political troubles of this presidency.

The president-elect and his wife came to the White House for the first time on 3 March 1913. The two wives had only a few moments to chat before the couples parted. The next day the Tafts rose a little later than usual, had breakfast, and then marked time until the inauguration commenced at noon. Helen Taft "went to the second floor where she spent her time walking around taking one last look as it were." She then wrote final White House letters to her two sons as time ran out on the presidency. The White House usher, Irwin "Ike" Hoover, prepared a lengthy memorandum about the events of that day. In it, he reported how the staff gave the first lady the register in which all the names of the White House guests were recorded. She smiled at the suggestion that she, like Mrs. Grover Cleveland in 1889, might return to the mansion for another term in four years.[34]

Hoover then noted that "the regrets were many for Mrs. Taft had just reveled in the life she had lived for the four years past and even with all the worries and trials she had passed through during that time, they seemed to have no effect on the entire satisfaction of the surroundings prevailing." Yet there were no formal goodbyes with the staff, and Hoover, who had not liked Mrs. Taft and her methods, commented that "there was not the same feeling prevalent between the household employes [*sic*], domestic and otherwise that has generally existed between the occupants and those around them."[35] Soon Mrs. Taft was in the car that would take her to the home of her sister, where she would wait until Will Taft joined her for the ride to the railroad station and their departure for a vacation in Augusta, Georgia.

The former president was delayed getting to Union Station because of traffic and the demands of the inauguration, but the party assembled in time to catch the 3:15 train to the South. Mrs. Taft, her daughter, and her sister came in "becoming black traveling dresses and carried bouquets of violets." As the Taft party moved toward the train, "the station crowd rushed to the ropes and cheered him with a vigor that bespoke sincerity." Soon the train had pulled out of the station and Will and Nellie were on their way from Washington, the presidency and its trials now passing into memory.[36]

Will and Nellie spent a month in Augusta, Georgia, before taking up their new home in New Haven. The former president told his doctor that "Mrs. Taft seems to have profited by her stay at Augusta quite as much as I did." He noted, "We have not found a home to our liking" because it involved "fitting a beer diet to a champagne appetite."[37] The couple did rent a house near the Yale campus and settled into what became a routine for the next five years. In addition to his well-received teaching duties, Will Taft emerged as a popular lecturer and was out on the lyceum circuit as often as possible.

Nellie Taft took to living in New Haven and became a great fan of the Yale athletic program. Her husband's absences on lecture tours gave her ample free time, which she put to use seeing the plays and concerts that she had enjoyed as first lady. Will Taft reported to a friend in July 1914 that his wife was "better now than she has been since her first attack in the White House." In April 1914, Nellie joined an anti–woman suffrage organization in New Haven, and a week later, her daughter Helen, now back at Bryn Mawr, enlisted with the Connecticut Woman Suffrage Association. Later that year, Nellie returned to Washington for the wedding of her son, Robert, to Martha Bowers. "It seems very nice to be here again," she informed reporters.[38]

During her first two years after the White House, Nellie Taft had embarked on a venture that provided her with another "first" among presidential wives. She became the first former first lady to have her memoirs published. The idea for her to prepare a series of magazine articles and eventually a book came from the offices of the *Delineator* magazine in New York City. Published by the Butterick Company, the periodical provided women with advice and information about the firm's sewing products and the latest styles in fashion. A friend of Will and Nellie Taft was Eleanor Franklin Egan, a journalist who had covered the Russo-Japanese War for *Leslie's Weekly*. Her husband, Martin F. Egan, was a press agent for the J. P. Morgan interests. Eleanor Egan's colleagues suggested the idea of a series of articles by Nellie Taft, and she conveyed the proposal to the former president and first lady during the spring of 1913.[39]

Helen Taft's initial reaction to the memoir proposal was negative. "She will not undertake" what the editors of the *Delineator* were proposing, reported her husband. The former first lady did suggest, however, "that our daughter Helen, who has been two years at Bryn Mawr, and expects to spend two years more there, has some literary taste and ambition." Because she had spent three years in the White House, "she might undertake something of the kind." Egan laid out her proposal in a lengthy letter of 24 May 1913. In it she proposed that she and the younger Helen Taft "go to work along experimental lines." After further talks at the end of May, Egan and Helen Taft went to work.[40]

The two women consulted a journal that Archie Butt had assembled about the first lady's activities and reviewed other family papers. Collaborating with Nellie Taft, they put her recollections into the first person and constructed a narrative by the process. With chapters in hand, they approached Dodd, Mead, & Co. about a book-length publication. A substantial portion of that narrative appeared in the *Delineator* with revisions and some passages that were not included in the finished book.[41]

By the spring of 1914, the manuscript was ready. Then the project hit a snag. The agreed-upon title was "Recollections of Full Years," but executives at Dodd, Mead, & Co. balked. They preferred "Recollections of a President's Wife," which, in their opinion, told "the whole story in the best way and is far better than anything that has been suggested from the selling." As they informed the Tafts, they were "awfully keen to make a great killing with Mrs. Taft's book, and we feel that just the right title is a very important point."[42]

At this point, Will and Nellie Taft drew back. They informed their daughter that they would prefer not to publish at all because they regarded the Dodd, Mead, & Co. title as something that sounded "foolish or cheap." However, these objections were resolved, probably because the Tafts, as their daughter indicated, had gone too far to withdraw from the commitment to Dodd, Mead, & Co. On 20 April 1914, Helen Taft and her husband signed a contract with the publishers that provided for a $2,000 advance against future royalties. Profits would be divided equally between author and publisher.[43]

Because of the time when her recollections were assembled, Nellie Taft decided not to do more than allude in a guarded manner to the split between Theodore Roosevelt and her husband. Most of the volume focused on the years in the Philippines and her experiences there. The section on the presidency concentrated on the ceremonial aspects of the position of first lady, with discussions of the social season, the operation of the White House, and her thoughts about her time in Washington.

She mentioned her stroke only in passing, and she said almost nothing about the musicales and the musicians who performed for her. Whether that was the decision of her daughter and Eleanor Egan cannot be determined. The failure to discuss her musical program left out a large part of her important contribution as first lady. The book has a sense of a missed opportunity to be more candid about what she went through between 1909 and 1913, but in parts her narrative is interesting and informative.

Recollections of Full Years appeared during the autumn of 1914, just as World War I and American neutrality were having their effects on the United States. The *New York Times* devoted a full page of coverage to what the former first lady had said about her tenure. "Some of her revelations of affairs of international importance, as they appeared to her, are of startling interest." Most of the story summarized the high points of the narrative but to have such extensive attention devoted to her book in a major newspaper was a plus for the new first lady author. The brief notice in *Current Opinion* said that "men as well as women will read with pleasure the new book by the former mistress of the White House." Dodd, Mead, & Co. priced the book at $3.50 and advertised it widely. In the first two years of publication, it sold about 2,300 copies and earned back two-thirds of her advance. However, as late as 1921, there still remained almost $400 of the advance still unearned from sales.[44]

The book itself soon faded from memory. The next first lady to write memoirs was Edith Bolling Wilson, whose recollections came out in 1939 under the title *My Memoir*. Historian Henry Steele Commager, reviewing her book in March 1939 for the *New York Times*, said of Wilson's volume: "Curiously enough, this is the first volume of memoirs which has ever been written by the wife of an American President."[45]

Helen Taft's life after the White House fell into three distinct periods. From 1913 to the summer of 1921, she and her husband lived in New Haven during the years when Will Taft taught at Yale. In 1918 they returned to Washington when the former president served on the War Labor Board during 1919–1920. They were back in New Haven through the election of 1920. The following year, President Warren G. Harding nominated Taft to be the chief justice of the United States. He took up his duties during the autumn of 1921 and remained on the court until shortly before his death in 1930. For the last thirteen years of her life, until her death in 1943, Nellie Taft lived in Washington, D.C. By the time she died in the midst of World War II, her time as first lady seemed a fading memory to most Washingtonians.

She enjoyed her years in New Haven with its relative proximity to the theaters and concerts of New York City. If she took an early train, she could "do her shopping" in the city and be back home for dinner. A trip later in the morning would allow her to take in a matinee and still return to New Haven for dinner. She continued her regular attendance at plays and recitals in Manhattan. To a large extent, their busy schedules kept the couple on separate courses during this period. In January 1914, she reported to the president's aunt that "Will is busy lecturing, and attending dinners in New York and elsewhere that I don't have a chance to see him more than half a hour at a time."[46]

After five years in New Haven, she resumed life in Washington in April 1918 when President Woodrow Wilson named Will Taft to the War Labor Board. With her son, Charles, in France during World War I, she worried about his fate at the front. In 1920 her daughter Helen married Frederick Manning, a history teacher first at Yale and then at Swarthmore, even though her parents fretted that her decision meant a delay in the completion of her doctoral thesis at Yale. Both Will and Nellie followed the political scene as Woodrow Wilson's presidency faltered and the Republicans, with Warren G. Harding as their nominee, swept to a landslide victory in the 1920 presidential contest. Suddenly, the prospect seemed real that Will Taft might achieve his cherished dream of becoming chief justice of the United States.

President Harding nominated Will Taft for this position in July

1921, and he was quickly confirmed as chief justice of the United States. For the next eight years, Will and Nellie settled into a routine in Washington. The new chief justice devoted long hours to deciding cases and holding conferences with his brethren on the court. Nellie Taft resumed her round of concerts, theatergoing, and social occasions. "Your mother and I are in my study like Darby and Joan. She reads and I write," Will Taft informed their daughter in 1928. "She has the satisfaction of looking back on theaters, bridge parties, dinners and luncheons galore."[47]

Will and Nellie Taft had one of their few strong disagreements over Prohibition during the 1920s. "The truth is," he wrote in 1929, "that Nellie and I differ on prohibition. We might as well face that, because I am utterly out of sympathy with her and she with me."[48] When the family vacationed at Murray Bay in the summers, the chief justice insisted that the family observe the American restrictions on liquor even in a foreign country. Otherwise, critics might say that he and his relatives simply went to Canada to drink and flout American laws. Nellie Taft concurred in words, but her deeds were something else. She was once asked at a social gathering what she would like to drink. Her husband replied: "Anything, as long as it's alcohol."[49]

So while the Tafts paid lip service to Will's ban on liquor, his wife arranged to have a screen placed in the room where guests gathered. Behind the screen was a small bar with a selection of alcoholic beverages. Visitors would simply disappear behind the barrier and emerge with their refreshment. Their daughter recalled that the comings and goings often partook of the atmosphere of a French farce.

Chief Justice Taft also insisted that the family observe the treaties between the United States and Canada that governed the taking of game birds from one country to the other. When he and Nellie visited their daughter and her husband in New Haven during the 1920s, Will Taft told them that he had to prevent Nellie from bringing partridges with them from Canada. As he related what had happened, Helen Manning noted that her mother was smiling. After the chief justice left the room, Nellie took partridges out of her ample purse and said that her daughter should clean and serve them for that evening's meal.

During the years when her husband was chief justice, Nellie Taft appeared at many ceremonial events. When Woodrow Wilson died in February 1924, she attended the funeral when an illness kept Will Taft at home. Of the proceedings, she told her son, Charles, "I thought it was a pretty poor funeral." The Tafts noted the way that the officials at the National Cathedral asserted themselves and excluded one of Wilson's clergymen from Princeton from any role in the last rites. Will Taft told his family that when it came time for his funeral, "don't let those body snatchers at the Cathedral get me." Nellie Taft made sure that did not happen. When Will Taft died in 1930, he was buried at Arlington Cemetery.[50]

As was customary for presidential widows, Nellie Taft enjoyed the franking privilege for her mail. Her exercise of the privilege, however, transcended national boundaries. When she vacationed at Murray Bay during the summer in the 1930s, she wrote "Helen Taft Free" on her envelopes as she did in the United States and mailed them through the Canadian mail system. The local postmaster asked the government in Ottawa what should be done with the former first lady's letters. The decision was to allow Nellie Taft to continue to send her mail with the same freedom she enjoyed in the United States.[51]

In the thirteen years after Will Taft's death, his widow lived on her own in their home in Washington, D.C. She traveled until failing health prevented further journeys. A reporter caught up with her in 1933 and noted that "she reads much, listens to good music, plays contract [bridge] a little, motors a little, and occasionally appears at social affairs."[52] She died on 22 May 1943, with her son Charles at her bedside. Her estate of $143,000 was divided among her three children. She was buried next to her husband in Arlington Cemetery, and remained the only first lady so honored until 1993, when Jacqueline Kennedy Onassis was buried beside President John F. Kennedy.[53]

Helen Herron Taft's death, coming as it did during the midst of World War II, did not prompt much of a review of her life and times. In fact, as Taft scholarship languished for the next two decades, very little attention was given to her role in the family or as first lady. The Washington reporter Marianne Means included a chapter on Mrs. Taft in her 1963 survey of first ladies, *The Woman in*

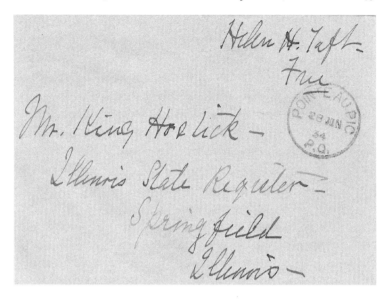

Mrs. Taft and her free frank. This envelope from Mrs. Taft was sent from Canada and illustrates her use of the franking privilege even in a foreign country during the years after she was first lady. (Penn State University, Harrisburg Library)

the White House. Ishbel Ross, *An American Family: The Tafts, 1678 to 1964* (1964) examined Helen Taft within the context of her family's history. It is a valuable and useful volume, but rarely gets beneath the surface of her role as first lady.

Paolo Coletta's *The Presidency of William Howard Taft* (1973) summed up Nellie Taft's accomplishments in a single page. The most extended treatment of her role in the presidency occurred in Judith Icke Anderson's *William Howard Taft: An Intimate Biography* (1981) with a chapter devoted to her White House role. Unfortunately, Anderson did not delve in any depth into Mrs. Taft's musical interests or her general cultural campaign to elevate Washington.

The only biography appeared in 2005 by Carl Sferrazza Anthony, an independent chronicler of first ladies. Based on thorough research, *Nellie Taft: The Unconventional First Lady of the Ragtime Era* (2005) dealt with Mrs. Taft's life and times from the familiar perspective of William Howard Taft as a presidential failure. Anthony provided an excellent survey of Nellie Taft's work with the Cincinnati Symphony in the 1890s. A notable absence, however, was any sustained discussion of Helen Taft's musical emphasis in the White House. The political setting of such issues as Roosevelt's role in Taft's presidential campaign, the ouster of Henry White, or the impact of the Payne-Aldrich Tariff on the administration was also absent. It is unlikely that another biography of Helen Taft will be written, but she deserves more scrutiny than she has received to date.

· Among the twentieth-century presidential wives, Helen Taft is in many respects the most poignant. She brought substantial gifts to the institution: a command of music, a knowledge of high culture, and talent as a hostess. Given four years of good health and sustained hard work, she might have reshaped the role of the first lady decades earlier than Eleanor Roosevelt or Lady Bird Johnson did. Her stroke in May 1909 rendered much of her tenure anticlimactic and incomplete. When she left Washington, memories of her charm and ability as the mistress of the White House soon disappeared.

Yet in those four years she presented Washington society with an array of musical artists that can stand comparison with any similar roster of performers in the twentieth century. From Fritz Kreisler to Loraine Wyman, from Olga Samaroff to Efrem Zimbalist, she enticed the best available practitioners of serious music to come to the White House and share their art with her guests. In so doing, she provided recognition to these talented individuals and offered them a patronage that boosted careers and stimulated creativity. In the process, the cultural life of Washington itself was enriched. If for those accomplishments alone, Helen Taft's record as a musical first lady should earn her a greater respect than has been accorded her during the century since she departed the nation's capital on 4 March 1913.

WHITE HOUSE
MUSICAL
PERFORMANCES
FOR HELEN TAFT,
1909–1913

All the programs for the musicales and recitals that Mrs. Taft sponsored are in the William Howard Taft Papers at the Library of Congress, unless otherwise indicated. I have provided the full names and dates for the composers whose works were played at these performances. I found this information through on-line sources where other biographical data on their compositions can be easily located. Because classical music is not an area where I have any expertise beyond the research I did for this book, it seemed the wisest course not to try to assess the significance of these musicians on my own.

PHILIPPINE CONSTABULARY BAND

6 APRIL 1909

1. Overture "William Tell"..................................Rossini[1]

2. Excerpt from "La Giocanda"—"Dance of the Hours".........Ponchielli[2]

3. Potpourri of Filipino Airs..............................Escamilla[3]

4. American Sketch "By the Suwanee River"..................Lyddleton[4]

5. Minuet No. 1 ....Paderewski[5]

6. Overture "Poet and Peasant" ....Suppe[6]

7. Sextette from "Lucia di Lammermoor" ....Donizetti[7]

8. Salon piece "First Heart Throbs" ....Eilenberg[8]

9. Moonlight Sonata.......................................Beethoven[9]

10. Entre Act "Rouse Mousse" ....Bosc[10]

11. Valse Lente "Amoureusse" . . . . Berger[11]

12. Suite de Valses "Espana". . . . . Hernandez[12]

NOTES

1. Gioachino Rossini (1792–1868)

2. Amilcare Ponchielli (1834–1886)

3. Antonio Escamilla

4. W. H. Myddleton (1858–1917)

5. Ignace Paderewski (1860–1941)

6. Franz von Suppe (1819–1895)

7. Domenico Gaetano Maria Donizetti (1797–1848)

8. Richard Eilenberg (1848–1925)

9. Ludwig van Beethoven (1770–1827)

10. Auguste Bosc (1868–1945)

11. Rodolphe Berger (1864–1916)

12. Juan de S. Hernandez

LEILA LIVINGSTON MORSE, MEZZO SOPRANO
12 APRIL 1909
MISS MARY HARRISON, AT THE PIANO

PROGRAM
I

1. Des Glockenthürmers Tochterlein . . . . Loewe[1]

2. Zueignung . . . . Strauss[2]

3. Fruhlingnacht. . . . . Schumann[3]

4. Summer and Winter. . . . . Atkinson[4]

5. Alone upon the Housetops . . . . Galloway[5]

6. There's no Spring but You. . . . . "A. L."[6]

II

1. La Nuit . . . . Hahn[7]

2. La coeur de ma mie . . . . Dalcroze[8]

3. Aime Moi. . . . . Bemberg[9]

4. Expectancy . . . . La Forge[10]

5. When Spring Comes Laughing . . . . Galloway

6. Fruhlingszeit . . . . Becker[11]

NOTES

1. Johann Carl Gottfried Loewe (1796–1869)
2. Richard Strauss (1864–1949)
3. Robert Schumann (1810–1856)
4. Holway Atkinson
5. Tod B. Galloway (1863–1935)
6. Mrs. R. Lehmann
7. Reynaldo Hahn (1874–1947)
8. E. Jacques Dalcroze (1865–1950)
9. Herman Bemberg (1859–1931)
10. Frank La Forge (1879–1953)
11. Reinhold Becker (1847–1924)

MISS ESTELLA NEUHAUS, PIANIST

22 APRIL 1909

PROGRAM

First movement Concerto in A Minor . . . . Schumann

Russian

Mazourka . . . . Rebikoff[1]
Arabesque . . . . Wrangell[2]
Spinning Song. . . . . Yonferoff[3]

French

Arabesque. . . . . Debussy[4]
Ballet Music . . . . Massenet[5]

Andante Spianato and Grande Polonaise . . . . Chopin[6]

NOTES

1. Wladmir Rebikoff (1866–1920)
2. Vasily Wrangell (1864–1901)
3. I have not been able to identify this composer
4. Claude Debussy (1862–1918)
5. Jules Massenet (1842–1912)
6. Frederic Chopin (1810–1849)

OLGA SAMAROFF, PIANIST

F. VER TREESE POLLOCK, TENOR

11 FEBRUARY 1910

PROGRAMME

Una Furtiva Lagrima (L'Elisir D' Amore)...................... Donizetti[1]
Mr. Pollock

Etude, C Minor (Revolutionary)............................... Chopin
Nocturne, F Sharp Major..................................... Chopin
Nymphs and Satyrs....................................... Paul Juon[2]
Rhapsodie No. 12 .... Liszt[3]
Mme Olga Samaroff

I'll Sing Thee Songs of Araby........................... Frederick Clay[4]
Nocturne... George Chadwick[5]
The Year's at the Spring.......................... Mrs. H. H. A. Beach[6]
Mr. Pollock

Prelude, G Minor..................................... Rachmaninoff[7]
Nocturne, for the left hand only............................. Scriabin[8]
The Ride of the Valkyries........................ Wagner-Hutcheson[9]
Mme Olga Samaroff

Arioso (Pagliacci)..................................... Leoncavallo[10]
Mr. Pollock
Mr. Harold O. Smith at the piano

NOTES

1. Domenico Gaetano Maria Donizetti (1797–1848)
2. Paul Juon (1872–1940)
3. Franz Liszt (1811–1886)
4. Frederick Clay (1838–1899)
5. George Chadwick (1854–1931)
6. Mrs. H. H. A. "Amy" Beach (1867–1944)
7. Sergei Rachmaninoff (1873–1943)
8. Aleksandr Scriabin (1872–1915)
9. Richard Wagner (1813–1883)
10. Ruggero Leoncavallo (1857–1919)

THE HESS-SCHROEDER QUARTET

21 FEBRUARY 1910

Willy Hess	First Violin
Julius von Theodorowicz	Second Violin
Emile Ferir	Viola
Alwin Schroeder	Violoncello
Assisted by *Ernest Hutcheson*	Pianist

PROGRAMME

1. Grieg: Two movements from Quartet for two violins, viola, and violoncello, in G Minor, Opus 27

   (a) un poco andante; Allegro molto ed agitato

   (b) Romance; Andantino; Allegro agitato; Tempo I[1]

2. Arthur Foote: Tema con Variazioni for two violins, viola, and violoncello, in A minor, Opus 32[2]

3. Debussy: Two movements from Quartet for two violins, viola, and violoncello, in G Minor, Opus 10

   (a) Andantino doucement expressif

   (b) Assez vif et bien rythme

4. Schumann: Quintet for pianoforte, two violins, viola, and violoncello, in E flat major, Opus 44

   (a) Allegro brillante

   (b) In modo d'una Marcia

   (c) Scherzo

   (d) Allegro ma no troppo

NOTES

1. Edvard Grieg (1843–1907)

2. Arthur Foote (1853–1937)

YOLANDA MÉRO, PIANIST

CARL JÖRN, TENOR

11 MARCH 1910

PROGRAMME

Prize Song from Die Meistersinger . . . . Wagner

Aria from Pagliacci . . . . Leoncavallo

Mr. Carl Jörn

Tolle Gesellschaft. . . . . Dohnanyi[1]
Impromptu, G major . . . . Schubert[2]
Scherzo, C sharp minor . . . . Chopin
Mme Yolanda Mero

Cavatina from Faust . . . . Gounod[3]
I am Thine . . . . Max Liebling[4]
Mr. Carl Jörn

Serenade. . . . . Rachmaninoff
Valse. . . . . Merkler[5]
Liebestraum . . . . Liszt
Rhapsodie, No. 2 . . . . Liszt
Mme Yolanda Mero

Paradiso, from l'Africaine . . . . Meyerbeer[6]
Mr. Carl Jörn
Mr. Max Liebling, at the Piano

NOTES

1. Erno Dohnanyi (1877–1960)
2. Franz Schubert (1797–1828)
3. Charles-Francis Gounod (1818–1893)
4. Max Liebling (1845–1927)
5. Andor Merkler (1862–1922)
6. Giacomo Meyerbeer (1791–1864)

FANNIE BLOOMFIELD-ZEISLER

FRITZ KREISLER

15 APRIL 1910

PROGRAMME

Variations . . . . Tartini[1]
Spanish Serenade . . . . Chaminade[2]
Caprice Viennois . . . . Kreisler
Fritz Kreisler

Turkish March from "The Ruins of Athens"................... Beethoven
Transcribed for Piano by Rubinstein
Chorus of Dancing Dervishes from "The Ruins of Athens"....... Beethoven
Transcribed for Piano by Saint Saens[3]
Valse, Op. 64, No. 1.. Chopin
Etude, Op. 25, no. 3.. Chopin
Polonaise Op. 53... Chopin
Fannie Bloomfield-Zeisler

Sarabande... Sulzer[4]
Humoresque .... Dvorak[5]
Scene de Czardas... Hubay[6]
Fritz Kreisler

Song without Words, Op. 62, No. 6 .... Mendelssohn[7]
The Juggleress, No. 4, from Six Fantasies Op. 52.............. Moszkowski[8]
Liebestraum, Nocturne, No. 3..................................... Liszt
Passepied, No. 6, from Scenes du Bal........................... Delibes[9]
   Six Dances in the old Style
March Militaire, No. 1, from three Piano Duets.................. Schubert
   Op. 51...
Transcribed for Piano by Tausig[10]
Fannie Bloomfield-Zeisler
Mr. Bidkar Leete at the piano

NOTES

1. Giuseppe Tartini (1692–1770)
2. Cecile Chaminade (1857–1944)
3. Camille Saint-Saens (1835–1921)
4. Joseph Sulzer (1850–1926)
5. Antonin Dvorak (1841–1904)
6. Jeno Hubay (1858–1937)
7. Felix Mendelssohn-Bartholdy (1809–1847)
8. Moritz Moszkowski (1854–1925)
9. Leo Delibes (1836–1891)
10. Carl Tausig (1841–1871)

LIEDERKRANZ SOCIETY

XAVER SCHARWENKA

7 DECEMBER 1910

There was no program for this musicale. The *Washington Herald* reported the occasion on 8 December 1910:

> An important feature of the programme was the appearance of the celebrated Polish pianist and composer, Xaver Scharwenka, who is in the country for a few months. He played the Chopin fantasie and a number of his own Polish dances, known to most of the piano players and students in this country. Mr. Scharwenka made a great triumph before the distinguished group of music lovers. The male choruses were Schubert's "Du bist du Ruh," Wengert's "Die Irene," Haydn's "Serenade," Jungst's "Der Scheerenschleiter," Spicker's "Im Gruse Thants," Schuman's "Ritornelle," Zoellner's "Enkehr," and Foster's "My Old Kentucky Home."[1]

NOTE

1. In addition to the composers previously identified, those mentioned in this paragraph are: Julius Wengert (1871–1925), Franz Joseph Haydn (1732–1809), Hugo Jungst (1853–1923), Max Spicker (1858–1912), Carl Friedrich Zollner (1800–1860), Stephen Foster (1826–1864).

H. EVAN WILLIAMS, TENOR

MRS. F. A. SEIBERLING, SOPRANO

15 DECEMBER 1910

PROGRAMME

Sound an Alarm . . . . Handel[1]

All Through the Night . . . . Old Welsh

Little Boy Blue . . . . Nevin[2]

Prize Song . . . . Wagner

Mr. Williams

Hindoo Song . . . . Bemberg

Po' L'il Lamb . . . . C. J. Bond[3]

Charity . . . . McDermid[4]

Mrs. Seiberling

Ah, Love, but a Day....................................... Protheroe[5]

Murmuring Zephyrs... Jensen[6]

Spirit Song .... Haydn

Drink to me Only .... Old English

A Dream... Bartlett[7]

Lend Me Your Aid .... Gounod

Mr. Williams

Duet, Passage Bird's Farewell................................ Hildach[8]

Mrs. Seiberling and Mr. Williams

Mrs. Katherine Bruot at the piano

NOTES

1. George Friedrich Handel (1685–1759)

2. Ethelbert Nevin (1862–1901)

3. Carrie Jacobs Bond (1868–1946)

4. James G. McDermid (1875–1960)

5. Daniel Protheroe (1866–1934)

6. Adolf Jensen (1837–1879)

7. James Campbell Bartlett (1850–1929)

8. Eugen Hildach (1849–1924)

KNEISEL QUARTET
ARTHUR FRIEDHEIM
10 MARCH 1911

PROGRAMME

Beethoven	Sonata appassionata, Op. 57
Chopin	Seven preludes: C minor, C major, G major, B minor,
	B flat minor, G minor, D minor
Arthur Friedheim	
Grieg	Quartet in G minor, Op. 27
	Un poco Andante-Allegro molto ed agitato
	Romanza Andantino
	Intermezzo, Allegro molto marcato
Kneisel Quartet	

Liszt   Polonaise in A flat

Mephisto Waltz

Le Carnaval de Paris

Arthur Friedheim

Bach[1]   Sonata in D major, for Violoncello alone

Taniew[2]   Theme and Variations from the Quartet in D minor, Op. 7

Kneisel Quartet

NOTES

1. Johann Sebastian Bach (1685–1750)

2. Serge Taniew (1856–1915)

ALEXANDER HEINEMANN, GERMAN LIEDER SINGER

MR. JOHN MANDERBROD, AT THE PIANO

LILLA ORMOND, MEZZO SOPRANO

MISS DAISY GREEN, AT THE PIANO

ALMA STENZEL, PIANIST

24 MARCH 1911

PROGRAMME

Es blinkt der Tau; Der Asra . . . . Rubinstein[1]

Prologue from "Pagliacci" . . . . Leoncavallo

Mr. Heinemann

Ballade, G Minor. . . . . Chopin

Miss Stenzel

Chant Bindour . . . . Bemberg

Envoi des fleurs . . . . Gounod

Fetes Galantes. . . . . Hahn

Miss Ormond

Auf Flugeln des Gesanges . . . . Mendelssohn-Liszt

Valse Caprice . . . . Strauss Tausig

Miss Stenzel

From the Land of Sky Blue Water . . . . Cadman[2]

Leezie Lindsay . . . . Old Scotch

May, the Maiden . . . . Carpenter[3]
Spring's Singing . . . . McFayden[4]
Miss Ormond

Erlkonig, Wohin . . . . Schubert
Die beiden Grenadiere . . . . Schumann
Mr. Heinemann

NOTES

1. Anton Rubinstein (1829–1891)
2. Charles Wakefield Cadman (1881–1946)
3. John Alden Carpenter (1876–1951)
4. Alexander Macfayden (1879–1936)

JOSEF HOFMANN, PIANIST
7 APRIL 1911

PROGRAMME

Andante Spianato et Grande Polonaise
Nocturne, E flat major
Valse, A flat major . . . . Chopin
Polonaise, A flat major

Poeme . . . . Scriabin
Prelude, G minor . . . . Rachmaninoff
Tabatiere a Musique . . . . Liadow[1]
Rhapsodie, No. 2 . . . . Liszt

NOTE

1. Anatol Liadow (1855–1911)

FRANCES ALDA, SOPRANO
ALICE SOVEREIGN, CONTRALTO
MR. KURT SCHINDLER, AT THE PIANO
21 APRIL 1911

PROGRAMME

Lungi del caro bene . . . . Secchi[1]
When the Roses Bloom . . . . Reichardt[2]

Sapphische Ode; Botschaft. . . . . Brahms[3]
Miss Sovereign

Chanson triste . . . . Duparc[4]
Chant juif . . . . Mussorgsky[5]
Romance . . . . Debussy
Si les fleurs avaient des yeux . . . . Massenet
Chant Venitien . . . . Bemberg
Madame Alda

Irish Folk Song . . . . Foote
But lately in Dance . . . . Arensky[6]
Floods of Spring . . . . Rachmaninoff
Miss Sovereign

Life, the Rosebud
Expectancy. . . . . La Forge
Dissonance . . . . Borodin[7]
From the Land of Sky Blue Water . . . . Cadman
Abendstandchen . . . . Schindler[8]
Madame Alda

NOTES

1. Antonio Secchi (1761–1833)

2. Luise Reichardt (1779–1826)

3. Johannes Brahms (1833–1897)

4. Henri Duparc (1848–1933)

5. Modest Moussorgsky (1839–1881)

6. Anton Arensky (1861–1906)

7. Alexandr Borodin (1833–1887)

8. Kurt Schindler (1882–1935)

SALT LAKE TABERNACLE CHOIR

15 NOVEMBER 1911

EVAN STEPHENS, CONDUCTOR

J. J. MCCLELLAND, ACCOMPANIST

EDWARD P. KIMBALL, ASSISTANT

PROGRAM

Soldier's Chorus from "Faust" . . . . Gounod
Salt Lake Tabernacle Choir

The Kiss Waltz . . . . Arditi[1]
Mrs. Lizzie Thomas-Edward

Finale to "Death of Minnehaha" . . . . Taylor[2]
Salt Lake Tabernacle Choir

The Irrigated Region (From Prize Ode) . . . . McClellan[3]
Miss Evans, Mr. Graham and Choir

Harp Solo, Autumn . . . . Thomas[4]
Miss Lydia White

Aria from "La Boheme" . . . . Puccini[5]
Mr. David Reese

My Gipsy Sweetheart . . . . Herbert[6]
Mr. Horace S. Ensign and Choir

Violin Solo, Cradle Song . . . . Sourett[7]

Sextette from "Lucia" . . . . Donizetti
Fifty Soloists and Choir

THE STAR SPANGLED BANNER

NOTES

1. Luigi Arditi (1822–1903)

2. Samuel Coleridge-Taylor (1875–1912)

3. John J. McClellan (1874–1925)

4. John Thomas (1826–1913)

5. Giacomo Puccini (1858–1924)

6. Victor Herbert (1859–1924)

7. I have not been able to identify this composer

ELOISE BAYLOR, SOPRANO

ALICE BURRAGE, AT THE PIANO

16 JANUARY 1912

PROGRAMME

Melodie des Baisers . . . . Massenet
Printemps Noveau . . . . Vidal[1]
Green . . . . Debussy
Chanson Espagnole. . . . . Delibes
Pastoral . . . . Carey[2]
My Wee Bird . . . . Roy Smith[3]
Love Song . . . . Harsche[4]
Primavera . . . . J. Strauss[5]

NOTES

1. Paul Vidal (1863–1931)
2. Henry Rao Carey (1690–1743)
3. Carey Roy Smith
4. Ada Koppitz Harsche
5. Johann Strauss (1825–1899)

ALICE NIELSEN, SOPRANO

17 FEBRUARY 1912

MRS. E. ROMAYNE SIMMONS, AT THE PIANO

PROGRAMME

Voi che sapete "Nozze di Figaro" . . . . Mozart[1]
Im Kahne. . . . . Grieg
Du bist wie eine Blume . . . . Schumann
Solvejgs Lied . . . . Grieg

Far off I hear a lover's flute. . . . . Cadman
Love has wings . . . . Rogers[2]
Down in the forest . . . . Ronald[3]
Miss Nielsen

Polonaise . . . . Chopin
Mrs. E. Romayne Simmons

Mandoline . . . . Debussy

Fileuse "Gwendoline" . . . . Chabrier[4]

Si mes vers avaient des ailes . . . . Hahn

Vissi d'arte "Tosca" . . . . Puccini

Miss Nielsen

NOTES

1. Wolfgang Amadeus Mozart (1756–1791)
2. James H. Rogers (1857–1940)
3. Landon Ronald (1873–1938)
4. Alexis-Emmanuel Chabrier (1841–1894)

FRANCES ALDA, SOPRANO

1 MARCH 1912

ANDRES DE SEGUROLA, BARITONE

A. RANDEGGER, PIANO

There is no program for this musicale. The *Washington Post*, 3 March 1912, reported the selections as follows:

PROGRAM

"Notte e giorno" . . . . Mozart

"La jeune Princesse" . . . . Grieg

"Flurette" . . . . McGeoch[1]

"Margoton" . . . . Fifteenth century

Mr. De Segurola

"Je ne suis qu'une Bergere" . . . . Philidor[2]

"Apaisement" . . . . Chausson[3]

"Berceuse" and "Petits Oiseaux" . . . . Gretchaninow[4]

"Chant Veniten" . . . . Bemberg

Mme Alda

"Offrande" . . . . Hahn

"Le The" . . . . Koechlin[5]

"Sais-tu?" . . . . Fontenailles[6]

"Voisinage" . . . . Chaminade

Mr. De Segurola

"Jean" . . . . Spross[7]

"Expectancy" . . . . LaForge

"My Heart" . . . . Randegger[8]

"The Birth of Morn" . . . . Leoni[9]

"Cuckoo" . . . . Lehman[10]

Mme Alda

"Plaisir d'Amour" . . . . Martini[11]

Mme Alda and Mr. De Segurola

NOTES

1. Daisy McGeoch. I have not been able to locate the dates for this Australian composer

2. Ander Danican Philidor (1681–1731)

3. Ernest Chausson (1855–1899)

4. Alexander Gretchaninow (1864–1956)

5. Charles Koechlin (1867–1950)

6. Henri de Fontenailles (1858–1923)

7. Charles Gilbert Spross (1874–1961)

8. Alberto Randegger (1832–1911)

9. Frano Leoni (1864–1949)

10. Liza Lehman (1862–1918)

11. Jean Paul Martini (1741–1816)

JOHANNA GADSKI, SOPRANO

ARTHUR SHATTUCK, PIANIST

15 MARCH 1912

PROGRAMME

Zueignung . . . . R. Strauss

In the Time of Roses . . . . Reichardt

The Little Gray Dove . . . . L. V. Saar[1]

Madame Gadski

Suite in D minor . . . . d'Albert[2]

    Allemande

    Gavotte

    Musette

Mr. Shattuck

Widmung; Wean ich fruh in den Garten geh . . . . Schumann

Das Madchen Spricht; Auf dem Kirchof . . . . Brahms

Der Erlkonig . . . . Schubert
Madame Gadski

Magic Fire Music . . . . Wagner-Brassin[3]

Tabatiere a Musique (Music Box) . . . . Friedmann[4]

Legend: St Franciscus de Paulus Walking on the Waves . . . . Liszt
Mr. Shattuck

The Swan Bent Low . . . . MacDowell[5]

The Maiden and the Butterfly . . . . D'Albert

Three Children's Songs . . . . Homer[6]

Love is the Wind . . . . Macfayden[7]
Mr. Richard Hagemann, at the piano Madame Gadski

NOTES

1. Louis Victor Saar (1868–1937)

2. Eugen Francis Charles d'Albert (1864–1932)

3. Louis Brassin (1840–1884)

4. Ignaz Friedmann (1882–1918)

5. Edward McDowell (1860–1948)

6. Sidney Homer (1865–1953)

7. Alexander Macfayden (1879–1936)

ELLEN BALLON, PIANIST

ANNA CASE, SOPRANO

MR. WILLIAM STICKLES, AT THE PIANO

MR. EFREM ZIMBALIST, VIOLINIST

MR. S. CHATZINOFF, AT THE PIANO

12 APRIL 1912

PROGRAMME

Impromptu (Rosamunde) . . . . Schubert

Scherzo Op. 16, E minor . . . . Mendelssohn

Etude (Si Oiseau j'etais) . . . . Hensell[1]
Miss Ballon

Ich mochte schweben uber Thai un Hugel . . . . Emil Sjogren[2]

In April . . . . Chas. Gilbert Spross

The Silver Ring . . . . Chaminade

Spring . . . . Henschel[3]

Miss Case

Preislied . . . . Wagner

Humoresque . . . . Dvorak

Hungarian Dance, E minor . . . . Brahms

Mr. Zimbalist

Impromptu A flat major

Etude F. Major Op. 15 No. 3 . . . . Chopin

Valse E minor

Rhapsodie Hongroise No. XI . . . . Liszt

Miss Ballon

Sans Amour . . . . Chaminade

E tanto ce pericol ch'io ti lasci . . . . E. Wolf-Ferrari[4]

Un verde practicello sensa piante . . . . E. Wolf-Ferrari

Ah, Love, but a day! . . . . Mrs. H. H. A. Beach

Miss Case

Oriental . . . . C. Cui[5]

Zephyrs . . . . Hubay

Liebesfreud . . . . Kreisler

Mr. Zimbalist

NOTES

1. Fanny Hensell (1805–1847)

2. Emil Sjogren (1853–1918)

3. George Henschel (1850–1934)

4. Ermanno Wolf-Ferrari (1876–1948)

5. Cesar Cui (1835–1918)

ANNE ATKINSON BURMEISTER, PIANIST

LOUISE ALICE WILLIAMS, NEGRO FOLKS SONGS AND STORIES

20 APRIL 1912

PROGRAMME

Sonnette del Petrarca, No. 123 . . . . Liszt

Mrs. Burmeister

A Darkey Ghost Story
  Originally taken from life in Dixie
Log Cabin Anecdotes of Old Negro Humor
    (a) How Uncle Ned Found and Lost a Fortune
    (b) Mandy's Bridegroom
    (c) A Debate Among the Deacons
Miss Williams

Arabesques. . . . . Debussy
Spring Song. . . . . Van der Stucken-Burmeister[1]
Mrs. Burmeister

A Monologue Sketch, "Lookin' for Marse Willie" . . . . Martha S. Gielow[2]
  With introduction of old Negro spiritual
"Swing Low, Sweet Chariot"
Walkin' Egypt
  Originally taken from life in the South
Miss Williams

Senta's Ballade . . . . Wagner-Liszt
Mrs. Burmeister

NOTES

1. Frank Van der Stucken (1858–1929) and Richard Burmeister (1860–1944)
2. Martha S. Gielow (1854–1933)

JULIA CULP
11 JANUARY 1913
COENRAAD VOS, AT THE PIANO

PROGRAMME

Ave Maria . . . . Schubert
Rastlose Liebe
Standchen
Du bist die Ruh

Widmung. . . . . Schumann
Du bist wie eine Blume
Mondnacht
Fruhlingsnacht

Immer leiser wird mein Schlummer............................ Brahms
Feldeinsamkeit
Wiegenlied

LORAINE WYMAN

21 JANUARY 1913

MRS. LOUIS H. SMITH, AT THE PIANO

PROGRAMME

English Ballads
 William Taylor
 Keys of Heaven
 The Outlandish Knight
 The Next Market Day
Old French Songs
 Les Cloches de Nantes
 Ma Fille veux-tu un Bouquet
Old French Songs
 Corbleu Mation
 Petit Tambour
Old English Songs
 Lord Lovell
 I Know Where I'm Goin'
 A Welsh Song
 A Bargain

LUDOVIC BREITNER, PIANIST

ASDRIK KAVOOKDJI, PIANIST

PAUL REIMERS, TENOR

THEODORE FLINT, AT THE PIANO

25 JANUARY 1913

PROGRAMME

Variations and Fugue .... Saint Saens
 (Theme of Beethoven)
Professor Breitner and *Miss Kavookdji*

Auf Flugeln des Gesanges. . . . . Mendelssohn

Wohin? . . . . Schubert

Le coeur de ma mie. . . . . Dalcroze

Mr. Reimers

Romance . . . . Rubinstein

Etude . . . . Chopin

March Turque. . . . . Beethoven

Professor Breitner

Apres un reve . . . . Faure[1]

Songs My Mother Taught Me. . . . . Dvorak

Der Jager . . . . Grieg

Mr. Reimers

Man lebt sur einmal . . . . Strauss-Tausig

Professor Breitner and *Miss Kavookdji*

NOTES

1. Gabriel Faure (1864–1924)

BEATRICE BOWMAN

31 JANUARY 1913

MARK ANDREWS AT THE PIANO

PROGRAMME

Polonaise "Je suis Titania" (Mignon) . . . . Thomas

Mandolin . . . . Debussy

My Laddie. . . . . Thayer[1]

Will o' the Wisp . . . . Gilbert Spross

When Roses Blow . . . . Mark Andrews[2]

Caro Nome (Rigoletto). . . . . Verdi[3]

Waltz Song (Romeo and Juliette). . . . . Gounod

NOTES

1. W. A. Thayer

2. Mark Andrews (1875–1939)

3. Giuseppe Verdi (1813–1901)

LEO SLEZAK, TENOR

ERNEST SCHELLING

7 FEBRUARY 1913

PROGRAMME

Aria from La Africaine . . . . Meyerbeer
Mr. Slezak

Fantasy and Fugue . . . . Bach-Liszt
Two Songs without Words . . . . Mendelssohn
Mr. Schelling

O komm im Traum . . . . Franz Liszt
Wiegenlied . . . . Humperdinck[1]
Ich frage meine Minne . . . . Richard Strauss
Caecilia . . . . Richard Strauss
Mr. Slezak

Nocturne, F sharp
Two Etudes, A flat, Op. 15, G flat, Op. 10 . . . . Chopin
Mazourka
Polonaise, A flat
Mr. Schelling

Aria from La Gionconda . . . . Ponchielli
Mr. Slezak
Miss Florence McMillan, at the piano

NOTE

1. Englebert Humperdinck (1854–1921)

ERNESTINE SCHUMANN-HEINK, CONTRALTO

21 FEBRUARY 1913

OTTO GORITZ, BARITONE

PAUL KEFER, CELLIST

JOSEPHINE HARTMAN VOLLER, AT THE PIANO

KATHERINE HOFFMAN, AT THE ORGAN

PROGRAMME

Aria from Der fliegende Hollander . . . . Wagner
Mr. Goritz

Chants Russes . . . . Lalo[1]

Hungarian Rhapsody. . . . . Popper[2]

Mr. Kefer

Spring Aria from Samson et Dalila. . . . . Saint-Saens

Agnus Dei. . . . . Bizet[3]

Cello-Organ-Piano Accompaniment

Madame Schumann-Heink

Ich grolle nicht. . . . . Schumann

Der Wanderer . . . . Schubert

Wohl auf noch getrunken. . . . . Schumann

Spielmannslied . . . . Hoffman[4]

Mr. Goritz

Tod and das Madchen . . . . Schubert

Die Forelle. . . . . Schubert

Spinnerlied (17th century) . . . . Reimann[5]

When the Roses Bloom (17th Century) . . . . Reichardt

Down in the Forest . . . . Landon Ronald

Cry of Rachel . . . . Mary Turner Salter[6]

Kerry Dance . . . . Malloy[7]

Madame Schumann-Heink

NOTES

1. Edouard Lalo (1823–1892)

2. David Popper (1843–1913)

3. Georges Bizet (1838–1875)

4. August Heinrich Hoffmann von Fallersleben (1798–1874)

5. Hugo Riemann (1849–1919)

6. Mary Turner Salter (1856–1938)

7. James L. Molloy (1837–1909)

NOTES

CHAPTER 1: FROM CINCINNATI TO WASHINGTON

1. Helen Herron Taft, *Recollections of Full Years* (New York: Dodd, Mead, & Co., 1914), 2.

2. Ibid., 5 (both quotations).

3. Grenville L. Howe, *A Hundred Years of Music in America* (n.p.: Willard Smythe Babcock Matthews, 1899), 635; "Music Teachers," *Chicago Daily Inter Ocean,* 8 July 1882; for Moscheles, see Harold C. Schonberg, *The Great Pianists from Mozart to the Present* (New York: Simon & Schuster Paperbacks, 1987), 121–126.

4. Taft, *Recollections*, 5. Craig Roell, *The Piano in America, 1890–1940* (Chapel Hill: University of North Carolina Press, 1989), 8–9, for the quotation and the analysis of piano teaching during the period when Helen Herron was a young girl.

5. "Music Room Plays Large Part in White House Life," *New York Times,* 8 May 1910 (first quotation); "Mrs. Taft's Musicales," *Idaho Daily Statesman,* 28 May 1911 (second quotation). After her stroke in 1909, Mrs. Taft played the piano less often. Her granddaughter does not recall her playing at all during the 1920s and 1930s. Telephone interview with Helen Manning Hunter, 9 June 2008, hereafter Hunter interview.

6. "Mrs. Taft Alert and Posted," *Washington Post,* 8 June 1908. Rutherford B. Hayes Diary, 28 December 1878, 516, online version (http://www.ohiohistory .org/onlinedoc/hayes/index.cfm), Hayes Library, Fremont, Ohio.

7. Taft, *Recollections,* 10. Henry F. Pringle, *The Life and Times of William Howard Taft,* 2 vols. (New York: Farrar and Rinehart, 1939), 1:71.

8. Ishbel Ross, *An American Family: The Tafts, 1678 to 1964* (Cleveland, Ohio: World Publishing, 1964), 83.

9. Ibid., 85; Pringle, *Life and Times,* 1:76.

10. Ross, *American Family,* 88.

11. Pringle, *Life and Times,* 1:79.

12. Margaret B. Downing, "Mrs. William Howard Taft," *Washington Post,* 5 May 1907.

13. The wedding is described in "The Tafts to Celebrate Their Silver Wedding June 19," *New York Times*, 11 June 1911; Charles Hardinge to James Bryce, 26 March 1909, Bryce Embassy Papers, Box 29, Bodleian Library, Oxford. Allan Nevins, *Henry White: Thirty Years of American Diplomacy* (New York: Harper & Bros., 1930), 299.

14. Ross, *American Family*, 116.

15. Pringle, *Life and Times*, 1:82.

16. *Taft and Roosevelt: The Intimate Letters of Archie Butt, Military Aide*, 2 vols. (Garden City, N.Y.: Doubleday, Doran & Co., 1930), 1:22.

17. Taft, *Recollections*, 24.

18. Ibid., 27.

19. Helen Taft to Taft, 5 October 1908, William Howard Taft Papers, Manuscript Division, Library of Congress.

20. Taft, *Recollections*, 30. Louis Russell Thomas, "A History of the Cincinnati Symphony Orchestra to 1931" (Ph.D. diss., University of Cincinnati, 1972), 101–107. Carl Sferrazza Anthony, *Nellie Taft: The Unconventional First Lady of the Ragtime Era* (New York: William Morrow, 2005), 110–126, has an informative chapter on Mrs. Taft's tenure with the orchestra.

21. Thomas, "History," 129–134, 212.

22. "Current Notes and News," *Cincinnati Musical Visitor*, November 1897, 304. William Osborne, *Music in Ohio* (Kent, Ohio: Kent State University Press, 2004), 213–214.

23. Joseph Horowitz, *Classical Music in America: A History of Its Rise and Fall* (New York: W. W. Norton, 2005), 175–176.

24. Theodore Roosevelt to Anna Roosevelt, 7 January 1894, in *The Letters of Theodore Roosevelt*, ed. Elting E. Morison et al., 8 vols. (Cambridge: Harvard University Press, 1952), 1:345; Henry Cabot Lodge to Theodore Roosevelt, 8 March 1897, in *Selections from the Correspondence of Theodore Roosevelt and Henry Cabot Lodge*, ed. Henry Cabot Lodge, 2 vols. (New York: Charles Scribner's Sons, 1925), 1:253; Helen Taft to William Howard Taft, 22 August 1891, Taft Papers.

25. Taft, *Recollections*, 33, 35.

26. Rene R. Escalante, *The Bearer of Pax Americana: The Philippine Career of William H. Taft, 1900–1903* (Quezon City: New Day Publishers, 2007), 71, 74, 136.

27. Taft, *Recollections*, 361.

28. Escalante, *Bearer*, 136.

29. Claiborne T. Richardson, "The Filipino-American Phenomenon: The Loving Touch," *Black Perspectives in Music* 10 (Spring 1982): 3–28.

30. Ross, *American Family*, 150.

31. Taft, *Recollections,* 269.

32. Ibid., 280.

33. Helen Taft to Will Taft, 1 February 1902, Taft Papers.

34. Will Taft to Helen Taft, 12 October 1904, Taft Papers.

35. Anthony, *Nellie Taft,* 402.

36. Stacy A. Cordery, *Alice: Alice Roosevelt Longworth from White House Princess to Washington Power Broker* (New York: Viking, 2007), 116–123.

37. Taft, *Recollections,* 292–294.

38. Helen Taft to Will Taft, 6 July 1902, 29 October 1904, 31 October 1906, Taft Papers. The October 29 letter is dated 1908 by the Library of Congress, but the only concert that the Kneisel Quartet gave in Washington during these years was in October 1904. August Trenkler (1836–1910) directed the Dresden Orchestra from 1890 to 1903.

39. "The Strenuous Side of Social Life at Our National Capital," *New York Times,* 17 December 1905.

40. "Fads of Washington Women," *Kansas City Star,* 23 April 1907 (first and second quotations); "Merry Week for Capital Society," *Philadelphia Inquirer,* 7 April 1907 (bridge); "Personality of Wives of Candidates for Presidency," *Macon Daily Telegraph,* 20 July 1907 (last quotation).

41. Pringle, *Life and Times,* 1:315.

42. Roosevelt to Taft, 15 March 1906, Morison et al., *Letters,* 6:183, 186.

43. Entry for 4 April 1906, James R. Garfield Diary, Garfield Papers, Manuscript Division, Library of Congress.

44. Helen Taft to Taft, 27 October 1906, Taft Papers.

45. Taft to Roosevelt, 31 October 1906, Roosevelt to Taft, 8 November 1906, Taft Papers.

46. "Mrs. Taft on Divorce," *Washington Post,* 24 June 1908.

CHAPTER 2: "I LOVE PUBLIC LIFE"

1. Helen Herron Taft, *Recollections of Full Years* (New York: Dodd, Mead, & Co., 1914), 302.

2. Helen Taft to William Howard Taft, 29 October 1906, Will Taft to Helen Taft, 1 November 1906, William Howard Taft Papers, Manuscript Division, Library of Congress, hereafter Taft Papers.

3. Taft to Mabel Boardman, 11 September 1907, Mabel Boardman Papers, Manuscript Division, Library of Congress.

4. Margaret B. Downing, "Mrs. William Howard Taft," *Washington Post,* 5 May 1907.

5. "The Family and Home Life of Mrs. Taft," *New York Times*, 21 June 1908; Downing, "Mrs. William Howard Taft."

6. Downing, "Mrs. William Howard Taft."

7. Everett Walters, *Joseph Benson Foraker: An Uncompromising Republican* (Columbus: Ohio History Press, 1948), 260.

8. Helen Taft to Will Taft, 1 April 1907, Taft Papers.

9. Helen Taft to Will Taft, 1 April 1907, Taft Papers.

10. Helen Taft to Will Taft, 3 April 1907, Taft Papers.

11. Taft to Mabel Boardman, 11 September 1907, Boardman Papers.

12. Entry for 11 September 1907, Helen Taft Diary, Taft Papers. "Seattle Symphony Orchestra," Answers.com.

13. Entry for 11 September 1907, Nellie Taft Diary, Taft Papers. Helen Taft to Taft, 3 April 1907, Taft Papers; Taft, *Recollections*, 311.

14. "Mrs. Taft at Card Party," *New York Times*, 24 October 1907.

15. Taft, *Recollections*, 321.

16. H. H. Kohlsaat, *From McKinley to Harding: Personal Recollections of Our Presidents* (New York: Charles Scribner's Sons, 1923), 161–162.

17. Henry F. Pringle, *The Life and Times of William Howard Taft*, 2 vols. (New York: Farrar & Rinehart, 1939), 1:313; Carl Sferrazza Anthony, *Nellie Taft: The Unconventional First Lady of the Ragtime Era* (New York: William Morrow, 2005), 185–186; "Ex-President Taft Succeeds White as Chief Justice," *New York Times*, 1 July 1921, quotes Taft. Kohlsaat places the tale during "early January, 1908," but he was not listed as a White House visitor in the newspapers at that time. Moreover, Roosevelt wrote him on 15 January 1908 and at the end of the letter wished him "many happy new years to you and yours." If he had been a guest at the White House early in the month, there would have been no need to make such a statement. Roosevelt to Kohlsaat 15 January 1908 in *The Letters of Theodore Roosevelt*, ed. Elting E. Morison et al., 8 vols. (Cambridge, Mass.: Harvard University Press, 1951–1954), 908.

18. Helen Taft to William Howard Taft, 15 February 1908, Memorandum for Mrs. Taft, 30 March 1908, enclosing C. W. Raymond to A. I. Vorys, 26 March 1908, Taft Papers.

19. "Mrs. Taft Happy; Eager For News," *Washington Times*, 18 June 1908.

20. Ibid.

21. Henry L. Stoddard, *As I Knew Them: Presidents and Politics from Grant to Coolidge* (New York: Harper & Bros., 1927), 339–340.

22. "Glorious, Says Mrs. Taft," *New York Times*, 29 July 1908.

23. Ibid.

24. "Glorious, Says Mrs. Taft," *New York Times,* 29 July 1908; Helen Taft to Robert A. Taft, 20 September 1908, in Anthony, *Nellie Taft,* 457, n. 7.

25. Helen Taft to Taft, 26 September 1908, Taft Papers.

26. Helen Taft to Taft, 25 September 1908, 27 September 1908, Taft Papers.

27. Taft to Helen Taft, 3 October 1908, Helen Taft to Taft, 14 October 1908, Taft Papers.

28. Taft, *Recollections,* 347. On one occasion, Mrs. Taft did work with Theodore Roosevelt's sister in making the household arrangements for the mansion. See Elizabeth Jaffray, *Secrets of the White House* (New York: Cosmopolitan Book Corp., 1927), 6.

29. Nicholas Longworth to Theodore Roosevelt, 27 April 1910, Theodore Roosevelt Papers, Manuscript Division, Library of Congress.

30. *The Letters of Archie Butt: Personal Aide to President Roosevelt,* ed. Lawrence F. Abbott (Garden City, N.Y.: Doubleday, Page & Co., 1924), 53.

31. "Mrs. Taft's New Secretary—Miss Mary D. Spiers," *New York Times,* 13 March 1910. The accounts of Mrs. Taft in the White House tend to be thin and general. See, for example, Edna M. Colman, *White House Gossip from Andrew Johnson to Calvin Coolidge* (Garden City, N.Y.: Doubleday, Page & Co., 1927), 319–339, and Irwin Hood (Ike) Hoover, *Forty-Two Years in the White House* (Boston: Houghton Mifflin, 1934), 40–48. Hoover is an unreliable source on Helen Taft.

32. "Changes at White House," *New York Times,* 4 March 1909; Abbott, *Letters of Archie Butt,* 205–206.

33. Abbott, *Letters of Archie Butt,* 234.

34. Ibid.

35. Entry of 4 January 1909, George von Lengerke Meyer Diary, Manuscript Division, Library of Congress.

36. "Wife to Ride with Taft," *New York Times,* 1 March 1909.

37. Abbott, *Letters of Archie Butt,* 362.

38. Taft, *Recollections,* 325.

39. Charles Selden, "Six White House Wives and Widows," *Ladies Home Journal,* June 1927, 109.

40. Taft, *Recollections,* 327.

41. Ibid., 327.

42. Ibid., 332.

43. "Mrs. Taft to Make White House a Home," *New York Times,* 7 March 1909.

44. For information on Alice Blech, see "Will Wed Naval Officer," *Washing-*

ton Post, 28 November 1909, and "Miss Alice Blech to Wed," *New York Times,* 29 November 1909.

45. Fred W. Carpenter to Alice Blech, 1909, in Series 5, Case File 2999, Temperance, Taft Papers. Blech to Carpenter, 1909, Series 5, Case File 3560, Taft Papers. Helen Herron Taft to Helen Taft, dated 1912 in the Taft papers, but clearly 1909 or 1910 because of the reference to Alice Blech.

46. "Mrs Taft's Ambition: Hopes to Make the Capital Nation's Social Center," *Washington Post,* 14 November 1908.

47. "The New Regime within the White House," *New York Times,* 14 March 1909.

48. "Society at Variance," *Washington Post,* 14 March 1909.

49. Roosevelt to Kermit Roosevelt, 27 January 1908, in Morison et al., *Letters of Theodore Roosevelt,* 6:916; Taft, *Recollections,* 353–354.

50. "Mrs. Taft Drives New Auto," *New York Times,* 25 April 1909; "Mrs. Taft to Have an Auto," *Washington Post,* 5 March 1909; "Mrs. Taft Drives Her Car," *New York Times,* 25 April 1909.

51. Memorandum for Mrs. Taft, 25 March 1909, Taft Papers.

52. Allan Nevins, *Henry White: Thirty Years of American Diplomacy* (New York: Harper & Bros., 1930), provides a record of White's diplomatic career.

53. Pringle, *Life and Times,* 1:540.

54. A. Mitchell Innes to Edward Grey, 12 November 1908, FO 371/562, British National Archives, Kew; Taft to Henry White, 11 January 1909, Taft Papers; Henry Cabot Lodge to White, 12 January 1909, Henry Cabot Lodge Papers, Massachusetts Historical Society. Emily Bax, *Miss Bax of the Embassy* (Boston: Houghton Mifflin, 1939), 23.

55. White to Lodge, 4 May 1909, Lodge Papers. Charles Hardinge to James Bryce, 26 March 1909, Bryce Embassy Papers, BL 29, Bodleian Library, Oxford.

56. Entry of 11 March 1909, George von Lengerke Meyer Diary, Manuscript Division, Library of Congress.

57. Henry White to Joseph Hodges Choate, 22 July 1909, Joseph Hodges Choate Papers, Manuscript Division, Library of Congress.

58. "Mrs. Taft to Preside," *Washington Post,* 4 April 1909; "To Aid Women's Work," *Washington Post,* 9 April 1909. Christopher J. Cyphers, *The National Civic Federation and the Making of a New Liberalism, 1900–1915* (Westport, Conn.: Praeger, 2002), 84, 85.

59. "Mrs. Taft Entertains Box Party at Concert," *Washington Post,* 17 March 1909 (first quotation); "Mrs. Taft Gives a Song Recital at White House," *Wash-*

ington Post, 13 April 1909; "Mrs. Taft to Give Dance at the White House," *Washington Post,* 9 April 1909; "Music Room Plays Large Part in White House Life," *New York Times,* 8 May 1910 (second quotation).

60. Lucien Wulsin to Helen Taft, 2 February 1909, Lucien Wulsin Papers, Cincinnati Historical Society.

61. Helen Taft to Wulsin, 7 March 1909, 7 February 1910, Wulsin Papers.

62. Roberta V. Bradshaw, "Mrs. Taft Sets New Fashions in Washington," (*San Francisco*) *Call,* 4 April 1909.

63. *Washington Wife: Journal of Ellen Maury Slayden from 1897–1919,* ed. Walter Prescott Webb and Terrell Webb (New York: Harper & Row, 1962, 1963), 126.

64. Helen Taft to Eliza Scidmore, 7 April 1909 and the memorandum of the landscape gardener are quoted in Ann McClellan, *The Cherry Blossom Festival: Sakura Celebration* (Boston, Mass.: Bunker Hill Publishing, 2005), 27, 31; "Bring on the Cherry Trees," *Washington Post,* 29 August 1909. David Fairchild, *The World Was My Garden: Travels of a Plant Explorer* (New York: Scribner's, 1944), 410–414, discusses his role in the first lady's campaign. Yukio Ozaki, *The Autobiography of Ozaki Ukio: The Struggle for Constitutional Government in Japan* (Princeton, N.J.: Princeton University Press, 2001), 231–232, provides a Japanese perspective on these events.

65. *Taft and Roosevelt: The Intimate Letters of Archie Butt, Military Aide,* 2 vols. (Garden City, N.Y.: Doubleday, Doran & Co., 1930), 1:39. "Busy with Esplanade," *Washington Post,* 4 April 1909.

66. *Taft and Roosevelt,* 1:56; "Mrs. Taft's Plan a Success," *Washington Post,* 29 April 1909; Marietta Minnigerode Andrews, *My Studio Window: Sketches of the Pageant of Washington Life* (New York: E. P. Dutton, 1928), 323.

67. "Interesting Women of the Capital," *Harper's Bazaar* 43 (May 1909): 484.

68. *Taft and Roosevelt,* 1:85–86.

CHAPTER 3: "MRS. TAFT TAKEN ILL"

1. "Mrs. Taft's Social Crown," *Kansas City Star,* 16 May 1909.

2. Thomas F. Logan, "Behind the Scenes at the Nation's Capital," *Philadelphia Inquirer,* 17 May 1909. Helen Taft Diary, 26 April 1909, William Howard Taft Papers, Manuscript Division, Library of Congress. The "diary" was a daybook in which the White House staff kept a record of Mrs. Taft's activities.

3. Elizabeth Jaffray, *Secrets of the White House* (New York: Cosmopolitan Book Corp., 1926), 10.

4. Taft to Robert A. Taft, 18 May 1909, Taft Papers. Henry Adams to Elizabeth

Cameron, 22 June 1909, in *The Letters of Henry Adams, Volume 6: 1906–1918,* ed. J. C. Levenson et al. (Cambridge: Belknap Press of Harvard University Press, 1988), 6:250.

5. Helen Taft to Will Taft, 5 February 1902, Taft Papers.

6. *Taft and Roosevelt: The Intimate Letters of Archie Butt, Military Aide,* 2 vols. (Garden City, N.Y.: Doubleday, Doran, 1930), 1:87.

7. *Taft and Roosevelt,* 1:32–33, described the events of that afternoon. Taft to Robert A. Taft, 18 May 1909, Taft Papers, gave the perspective of the president on what had happened to his wife.

8. "Specialist in Surgery," *New York Times,* 3 November 1936, profiled Delaney's career.

9. "Wife of President Seized with Illness," *Lexington (Ky.) Herald,* 18 May 1909. Taft to Horace Lurton, 22 May 1909, Taft Papers.

10. Letters, *Time Magazine,* 11 September 1964, http://www.time.com/time/magazine/article/0,9171,830626,00.html.

11. Edith Roosevelt to Kermit Roosevelt, 19 May 1909, Kermit Roosevelt Papers, Box 11, Manuscript Division, Library of Congress.

12. Dennis C. Tanner, *The Family Guide to Surviving Stroke and Communication Disorders,* 2nd ed. (Sudbury, Mass.: Jones and Bartlett, 2008), 44.

13. J. C. Rosenbek, R. D. Kent, and L. L. LaPointe, "Apraxia of Speech: An Overview and Some Perspectives," in *Apraxia of Speech: Physiology, Acoustics, Linguistics, Management,* ed. John C. Rosenbek, Malcolm R. McNeil, and Arnold E. Aronson (San Diego: College-Hill Press, 1984), 13.

14. Henry Adams to Elizabeth Cameron, 22 June 1909, in Levenson et al., *Letters of Henry Adams,* 6:252–253. Taft to Frances Edwards, 25 June 1909, Taft Papers. Edith Roosevelt to Kermit Roosevelt, 16 June 1909, Box 11, Kermit Roosevelt Papers.

15. "Mrs. Taft's Health Better," *New York Times,* 9 July 1909; "Mrs. Taft's Health Better," *Washington Post,* 4 August 1909.

16. Taft to Frances Edwards, 25 June 1909, Taft Papers; Henry Adams to Elizabeth Cameron, 22 June 1909, Levenson et al., *Letters of Henry Adams,* 6:253.

17. Taft to Mabel Boardman, 27 June 1909, Mabel Boardman Papers, Manuscript Division, Library of Congress.

18. Jaffray, *Secrets,* 27.

19. Taft to Frances Edwards, 25 June 1909, Taft Papers.

20. Helen Taft to Robert A. Taft, June 1909, in Carl Sferrazza Anthony, *Nellie Taft: The Unconventional First Lady of the Ragtime Era* (New York: William Morrow, 2005), 266; Taft to Frances Edwards, 25 June 1909, Taft Papers.

21. *Taft and Roosevelt*, 1:108, 113.

22. Spencer Cosby to Fred W. Carpenter, 25 June 1909, Taft Papers.

23. Mabel Boardman, "The Summer Capital," *Outlook*, 25 September 1909, 172.

24. John Hays Hammond to Helen Taft, 13 April 1909, Helen Taft to Hammond, 13 April 1909, R. D. Evans to Hammond, 13 April 1909, Taft Papers; "Tafts Start Realty Boom," *New York Times*, 19 April 1909.

25. Taft to Helen Taft, 9 July 1909, 14 July 1909, Taft Papers.

26. Helen Taft to Taft, 17 July 1909, Taft Papers.

27. "Guarding Mrs. Taft," *New York Times*, 7 July 1909.

28. "Mrs. Taft's Health Better," *Washington Post*, 9 July 1909; Taft to Lebbeus Wilfley, 25 August 1909, Taft Papers.

29. "Essex Links for Taft," *Washington Post*, 15 August 1909.

30. Taft to Horace Taft, 11 August 1909, Taft Papers.

31. Taft to Helen Taft, 24 October 1909, Taft Papers.

32. Helen Taft to Taft, 28 October 1909, 5 November 1909, Charles P. Taft to Taft, 15 November 1909, Taft Papers.

33. Matthew Delaney to Taft, 26 October 1909, Taft Papers. This letter is listed in the index to the Taft Papers as if the physician spelled his name as De Laney.

34. Ibid.

35. "Will Wed Naval Officer," *Washington Post*, 28 November 1909.

36. "Destroy Tokio Gift Trees," *New York Times*, 29 January 1910; "Trees to Be Destroyed," *Washington Post*, 29 January 1910.

37. *Taft and Roosevelt*, 1:228.

38. Will Taft to Helen Taft, 14 July 1909, Taft Papers; "Crane Takes Post as Envoy to China," *New York Times*, 17 July 1909.

39. *Taft and Roosevelt*, 1:147.

40. Ibid., 1:228. "Crane, Forced Out, Calls Knox Unfair," *New York Times*, 13 October 1909.

41. "Calhoun Has China Post," *New York Times*, 7 December 1909.

42. "Mrs. Taft the White House Hostess," *Kansas City Times*, 1 January 1910.

43. "Tafts Held First Levee," *Grand Forks Daily Herald*, 2 January 1910. "Group of Four Herron Sisters," *Columbus (Ga.) Enquirer-Sun*, 10 February 1910.

44. Constance Carruthers, "Social Gossip of the National Capital," *Idaho Daily Statesman*, 23 January 1910.

45. "And No 'Blue Room Circle.' Mrs. Taft Opens the Season with a New Re-

ception Plan," *Kansas City Times,* 5 January 1910; Constance Carruthers, "Social Gossip of Washington," *Idaho Daily Statesman,* 2 January 1910 (last quotation).

46. "Taft Tosses Ball," *Washington Post,* 15 April 1910; "Commend Mr. and Mrs. Taft," *Washington Post,* 20 April 1910; "Garden Fete Popular," *Washington Post,* 25 April 1910. "To Aid Orphans in Japan," *Washington Post,* 18 April 1910.

47. Charles D. Hilles to Nathaniel McKay, 20 May 1912, Taft Papers; "Garden Fete Popular," *Washington Post,* 25 April 1910.

48. Will Taft to Charles W. Fairbanks, 5 April 1910, Taft Papers; "Guests Received by Mrs. Taft on the White House Lawn," *Washington Times,* 7 May 1910.

49. For the Coburn Players, see "Coburn Players at Columbia," *New York Times,* 26 July 1910, and "Mrs. C. D. Coburn, Actress, Is Dead," *New York Times,* 28 April 1937. The quotation comes from the program of the Coburn Players for *As You Like It* and *Twelfth Night* in the Charles Coburn Papers, Manuscript 1186, Box 208, Hargrett Library, University of Georgia, Athens.

50. "Play on White House Lawn," *New York Times,* 18 June 1910; "Shakespeare Heard in Miniature Arden," *Washington Times,* 18 June 1910; Charles Coburn to Mary Fanton Roberts, 20 June 1910, Mary Fanton Roberts Papers, Smithsonian Institution, Reel D 163, Frame 527. The Roberts Papers have been digitized and are available online.

51. Taft to Horace Taft, 5 March 1910, Taft Papers.

52. "Laughlin a Suicide," *Washington Post,* 13 March 1910; "Mrs. Taft's Father Sinking," *Washington Post,* 30 May 1910.

53. "Mrs. Taft's New Secretary—Miss Mary D. Spiers," *New York Times,* 13 March 1910; "Position Is Exacting," *Washington Post,* 14 February 1910.

54. Mary Dandridge Spiers to William Howard Taft, 15 April 1910, Taft Papers. Huntington Wilson to Fred W. Carpenter, 15 April 1910, discusses the assignment of Letterman to the White House. William Howard Taft to Philander Knox, 21 February 1913, mentions her successful performance of her duties for the first lady; Taft Papers.

55. Nicholas Longworth to Roosevelt, 27 April 1910, Roosevelt Papers.

56. Ibid.

57. Taft to Theodore Roosevelt, 26 May 1910, Taft Papers.

58. Taft to Roosevelt, 14 June 1910, Taft Papers.

59. *Taft and Roosevelt,* 1:392.

60. Helen Taft to Edith Roosevelt, 16 June 1910, in Sylvia Jukes Morris, *Edith Kermit Roosevelt: Portrait of a First Lady* (New York: Coward, McCann & Geoghegan, 1980), 362.

61. *Taft and Roosevelt,* 1:423; Helen Herron Taft, *Recollections of Full Years* (New York: Dodd, Mead, & Co., 1914), 383, 384.

62. Henry White to Margaret White, 15 April 1910, Henry White Papers, Manuscript Division, Library of Congress.

CHAPTER 4: MUSIC FOR NELLIE TAFT, 1909–1910

1. Carl Sferrazza Anthony, *Nellie Taft: The Unconventional First Lady of the Ragtime Era* (New York: William Morrow, 2005), 301–302; Elise Kirk, *Music at the White House: A History of the American Spirit* (Urbana: University of Illinois Press, 1986), 188–192; Beth M. Waggenspack, "Helen Herron Taft: Opportunity and Ambition," in *Inventing a Voice: The Rhetoric of American First Ladies of the Twentieth Century,* ed. Molly Meijer Wertheimer (Lanham, Md.: Rowman & Littlefield, 2004), 70, 75, makes only passing references to Mrs. Taft's musical interests. Judith Icke Anderson, *William Howard Taft: An Intimate History* (New York: W.W. Norton, 1981), 158, 165, mentions the musicales but does not discuss their cultural significance in detail.

2. Helen Herron Taft, *Recollections of Full Years* (New York: Dodd, Mead, & Co., 1914), 361. Taft to Helen Taft, 16 July 1909, William Howard Taft Papers, Manuscript Division, Library of Congress, mentions hearing "the opera singing down below, under the guidance of Captain Butt."

3. Helen Taft to Robert A. Taft, 21 January 1912, Robert A. Taft Papers, Manuscript Division, Library of Congress; "Reception for Irish Actor," *Washington Post,* 21 January 1912; "Olcott in New Heroic Role," *New York Times,* 6 February 1912.

4. "Compliment to President," *Washington Post,* 1 January 1911.

5. "Opera for Capitol," *Washington Post,* 16 December 1909. "Mr. Taft Accepts Hammerstein Box," *New York Times,* 21 December 1909. Vincent Sheean, *Oscar Hammerstein I: The Life and Exploits of an Impresario* (New York: Simon & Schuster, 1956), 295.

6. "First Night of Opera a Brilliant Success." *Washington Post,* 11 January 1910.

7. Luisa Tetrazzini, *My Life of Song* (London: Cassell and Co., 1921), 37–38.

8. For this event, see "President Aids Press Agent Feat," *Washington Times,* 12 January 1910. Mary Garden and Louis Biancolli, *Mary Garden's Story* (New York: Simon & Schuster, 1951), 283; Michael T. R. B. Turnbull, *Mary Garden* (Portland, Ore.: Amadeus Press, 1997), 76; Gordon T. Ledbetter, *The Great Irish Tenor: John McCormack* (Dublin, Ireland: Town House, 2003), 112; *Taft and Roosevelt: The Intimate Letters of Archie Butt, Military Aide,* 2 vols. (Garden City, N.Y.: Doubleday, Doran & Co., 1930), 1:258–259.

9. "Taft Praises Tetrazzini," *New York Sun,* 15 January 1910. McCormack's wife mentioned the visit to the White House in Lily McCormack, *I Hear You Calling Me* (Milwaukee: Bruce Publishing Co., 1949), 60.

10. Tetrazzini, *My Life of Song,* 272–273. Tetrazzini's career is assessed in Nigel Douglas, *The Joy of Opera* (London: Andre Deutsch, 1996, 2000), 63–68.

11. *Kansas City Times,* 11 January 1910; "Tetrazzini Likes Taft," *Kansas City Times,* 30 January 1910; *San Jose Mercury News,* 27 January 1910. Luisa Tetrazzini to Taft, 2 January 1911, Taft Papers. "President Sends Message of Thanks to Cantrice," *San Francisco Call,* 27 December 1910.

12. J. B. Tiffany to Fannie Bloomfield-Zeisler, 22 December 1903 (quotation), 7 January 1904, 16 January 1904, Fannie Bloomfield-Zeisler Papers, American Jewish Archives, Cincinnati, Ohio.

13. Constance McLaughlin Green, *Washington: Capital City, 1879–1950* (Princeton, N.J.: Princeton University Press, 1963), 198–199.

14. John Dizikes, *Opera in America: A Cultural History* (New Haven, Conn.: Yale University Press, 1993), 330–334, 370–381. Richard Trabuner, *Operetta: A Theatrical History* (Garden City, N.Y.: Doubleday, 1983), 366–374.

15. Philip Furia, *Irving Berlin: A Life in Song* (New York: Schirmer Books, 1998), 39–45, examines the impact of "Alexander's Ragtime Band" on popular culture in 1911.

16. Helen Taft to Robert A. Taft, 22 November 1910, Robert A. Taft Papers, Box 2, Folder 2, Manuscript Division, Library of Congress. "Offerings at the Local Theaters: Belasco-Fritzi Scheff in 'The Mikado,'" *Washington Post,* 22 November 1910, echoed the first lady's opinion.

17. "Mrs. Taft to See 'Elektra' To-day," *New York Times,* 12 February 1910. For examples of her theater and concertgoing, see "Mrs. Taft Entertains Box Party at Concert," *Washington Post,* 17 March 1909; "Mrs. Taft and Sister Occupy Box at Theater," *Washington Post,* 19 October 1909; "Mrs. Taft and Guests Occupy Box at Theater," *Washington Post,* 12 March 1912; "Mrs Taft Occupies a Box at Miss Rubner's Recital," *Washington Post,* 23 March 1912.

18. *Taft and Roosevelt,* 2:616–617. "'Herodiade' Not Naughty," *Washington Post,* 21 April 1911, noted the presence of the president and Mrs. Taft in "the stage box."

19. These programs are located in the records of Mrs. Taft's daily schedule in the Taft Papers, Series 11, Vol. 23, March–December 1909.

20. "Hearty Cheers for Philippine Band," *New York Times,* 6 March 1909. For a complete listing of all the selections played at Mrs. Taft's musical events at the White House, see Appendix.

21. "Informal Musical Tea at White House Is Given by Miss Morse and Miss Harrison," *Washington Times,* 13 April 1909. Mary Harrison was the accompanist for the event. "Mrs. Taft Gives a Song Recital at White House," *Washington Post,* 13 April 1909. For Morse's appearance during the Roosevelt presidency, see "Society in Washington," *New York Times,* 5 March 1902. "Society," *Washington Herald,* 18 April 1909.

22. "Song Recital," 12 April 1909 and "Piano Recital," 22 April 1909, Taft Papers. "Mrs. Taft Entertains," *Washington Times,* 23 April 1909 (second quotation). "At the White House," *New-York Tribune,* 23 April 1909 (first quotation). "Estella Neuhaus in Recital," *New York Times,* 12 April 1916, has a critical review of one of her other recitals.

23. Donna Staley Kline, *An American Virtuoso on the World Stage: Olga Samaroff Stokowski* (College Station: Texas A&M University Press, 1996), 60–61, on the discrimination against female artists at this time.

24. "Our Washington Letter," *Town and Country,* 15 April 1911, 3387 (quotation); "Fashionable Fasting May Come to $100 a Plate," *Washington Post,* 21 March 1909; "Lent Here Wednesday," *Washington Post,* 27 February 1911 (quotation).

25. Helen Taft to J. Burr Tiffany, 15 February 1912, Taft Papers; "White House Musicales Noteworthy," *Washington Post,* 5 November 1911. "Joseph Burr Tiffany," *New York Times,* 4 April 1917. Joseph Burr Tiffany, "Artistic Piano Decoration—Old and New," *International Studio* 36 (November 1980): xxvii. There is a biographical sketch of Tiffany in George Willoughby, "Typical Americans: Joseph Burry Tiffany," *National Magazine,* July 1912, 367–370. Tiffany's work for Steinway is not mentioned in the history of the company. See, for example, Richard K. Lieberman, *Steinway & Sons* (New Haven, Conn.: Yale University Press, 1995). "Joseph Burr Tiffany Dead," *Washington Post,* 8 April 1917 (quotation).

26. "World's Artists to Appear Here," *Washington Times,* 12 September 1909.

27. "White House Musicales Noteworthy," *Washington Post,* 5 November 1911, is the most detailed description of the Taft musicales.

28. For Pollock, see "Theatrical Gossip," *New York Times,* 17 November 1897; "The Rose of Algeria," *New-York Tribune,* 21 September 1909; "Frank Pollock's Holiday," *New York Times,* 4 August 1912 (quotation). Programs for all the musicales can be found on reels 599–600 of the Taft Papers in the chronological list of receptions held between 1909 and 1913.

29. Dixie Hines and Harry Prescott Hanaford, eds., *Who's Who in Music and Drama, 1914* (New York: H. P. Hanaford Publishers, 1914), has a brief sketch of

Pollock. Adrienne Fried Block, *Amy Beach, Passionate Victorian: The Life and Work of an American Composer, 1867–1944* (New York: Oxford University Press, 1998), 150–151.

30. Olga Samaroff Stokowski, *An American Musician's Story* (New York: W. W. Norton, 1935), provided her own account of her career.

31. "Mrs. Taft Gives Musicale at the White House," *Washington Post*, 12 February 1910; "White House Musicales Noteworthy," *Washington Post*, 5 November 1911 (first quotation); Kline, *American Virtuoso*, 77, 138.

32. "Hess-Schroeder Quartet," *New York Times*, 15 January 1909. "Hess-Schroeder Quartet," *New York Times*, 8 April 1909.

33. "At the White House," *New-York Tribune*, 22 February 1910.

34. For the program of the quartet, see *Washington Times*, 22 February 1910; "At the White House," *New-York Tribune*, 22 February 1910; "Hess Schroeder Quartet," *New York Times*, 15 January 1909.

35. "Music," *New-York Tribune*, 21 November 1909; "Karl Jorn to Sing at White House," *New York Times*, 25 December 1909; "Jorn to be Naturalized," *New York Times*, 2 January 1910; "Karl Jorn," *New York Times*, 20 December 1947; Anthony Boucher, "Complete into a Horn," *New York Times*, 18 November 1962.

36. "White House Musicale Attended by Society," *Washington Times*, 12 March 1910.

37. "The World of Music, Abroad," *Etude*, October 1909, 713 (first quotation); "Mrs. Yolanda Mero-Irion Dead; Organized Musicians' Aid Fund," *New York Times*, 19 October 1963.

38. "White House Musicale Attended by Society," *Washington Times*, 22 February 1910.

39. Helen Taft to Mrs. Robert Shaw Oliver, 12 April 1910, copy at "Custodians of History," 2004, http://www.custodiansofhistory.com.

40. Musicale Program, 15 April 1910, Taft Papers; "Men and Women of Interest," *Harper's Bazaar* 44 (January 1910): 38. "The World of Music," *Etude*, December 1909, 857; Louis P. Lochner, *Fritz Kreisler* (New York: Macmillan, 1951), does not mention Kreisler's appearance at the Taft White House. Amy Biancolli, *Fritz Kreisler: Love's Sorrow, Love's Joy* (Portland, Ore.: Amadeus Press, 1998), is also silent on Kreisler's performance for Mrs. Taft and her guests.

41. "Bloomfield-Zeisler's Recital," *New-York Tribune*, 6 February 1910.

42. "White House Musicales Noteworthy," *Washington Post*, 5 November 1911. For Longworth's abilities as a musician, see Clara Longworth de Chambrun, *The Making of Nicholas Longworth: Annals of an American Family* (New York: Ray Long & Richard Smith, 1933), 209–224.

43. Helen Taft to Robert A. Taft, 11 December 1910, Robert A. Taft Papers.

44. *Washington Herald,* 8 December 1910.

45. Ibid.; "Scharwenka Reappears," *New York Times,* 28 November 1910.

46. J. Penfield Seiberling to Mrs. Dewitt, 17 March 1976, reviewed the background for the December 1910 occasion. He was the son of Gertrude Seiberling and had asked relatives and members of the Dick family about the circumstances that led to his mother's appearance at the White House. The letter is held by the Stan Hywet Museum in Akron, Ohio, and I am grateful to them for furnishing me with a copy.

47. "Evan Williams Dies," *New York Times,* 25 May 1918; "Evan Williams Recital," *New York Times,* 3 November 1906.

48. Musicale Program, 15 December 1910, Taft Papers; *Taft and Roosevelt,* 2:567. "President and Mrs. Taft Give Dinner for Cabinet," *Washington Post,* 16 December 1910. On Seiberling, see Annasue McCleave Wilson, "English Manor in the Heartland," *New York Times,* 20 September 1998, which mentions that the collection at Stan Hywet Hall in Akron contains the dress that she wore when she sang at the White House.

49. "In the Social World," *Washington Herald,* 16 December 1910.

50. "The Week in Society," *Town and Country,* 13 April 1912, 3349.

CHAPTER 5: MUSICALES AND MEDALS, 1911–1913

1. Charles D. Norton to Tiffany and Company, 4 April 1911, William Howard Taft Papers, Manuscript Division, Library of Congress; Mary Randolph, *Presidents and First Ladies* (New York: D. Appleton, 1936), 219.

2. "Musicians Fete for Paderewski," *New York Times,* 4 May 1913, quotes Schelling. For other references to these medals, see "A Singer Honored by President Taft," *Town and Country,* 20 May 1911, 3392, mentioning Lilla Ormond, and Gdal Saleski, *Famous Musicians of a Wandering Race* (New York: Bloch, 1927), 306, about Arthur Friedheim, who performed for the Tafts in 1911.

3. "The Passing of the Kneisel Quartet—Some Facts in a Notable Organization's History," *New York Times,* 1 April 1917, gives a brief history of the quartet. For the 1907 White House appearance, see the program at the Kneisel Hall Archives, Julliard School, New York City.

4. Helen Taft to Will Taft, 29 October 1904, Taft Papers. The letter is dated with a question mark as 1908? in the Taft Papers, but the only time the Kneisel Quartet performed in October during these years was in 1904. "Kneisel Quartet Concert," *Washington Post,* 29 October 1904. For the quartet's Washington activities during the Taft presidency, see "Kneisel Quartet," *Washington Times,* 11

April 1909; "At the White House," *New-York Tribune,* 1 December 1910. The program for the event at the Netherland Legation, 29 November 1910, is in the Kneisel Hall Archives.

5. "Mr. Friedheim's Recital," *New York Times,* 18 December 1910. "Arthur Friedheim, Pianist, Dies at 72," *New York Times,* 20 October 1932.

6. Arthur Friedheim, *Life and Liszt: The Recollections of a Concert Pianist* (New York: Taplinger, 1961), 241, 242.

7. *Washington Post,* 11 March 1911. *New York Herald,* 11 March 1911, clipping in Kneisel Hall Archives. For more commentary on the occasion, see "In the World of Society," *Washington Star,* 11 March 1911, "Washington Society," *Philadelphia Public Ledger,* 11 March 1911, and *Brooklyn Daily Eagle,* 11 March 1911, Kneisel Hall Archives.

8. "Mr. Heinemann's Recital," *New York Times,* 4 November 1910 (first quotation); "Heinemann's Style Pleases Audience," *New York Times,* 24 January 1911 (second and third quotations).

9. Passport application of Lilla Ormond, 3 May 1909, Ancestry.com; "Saengerbund Concert," *New York Times,* 21 March 1910; "A Singer Honored by President Taft," *Town and Country,* 20 May 1911, 3392.

10. Biographical information on Alma Stenzel was found in "Music and Musicians," *Washington Post,* 26 February 1911.

11. Musicale program, 24 March 1911, Taft Papers. Helen Taft to Robert A. Taft, 26 March 1911, Robert A. Taft Papers, Manuscript Division, Library of Congress, Box 2, Folder 2.

12. "In the Social World," *Washington Herald,* 8 April 1911; "Hofmann Recital," *New York Times,* 9 April 1911; Joseph Horowitz, *Classical Music in America: A History of Its Rise and Fall* (New York: W. W. Norton, 2005), 334; Nell S. Graydon and Margaret D. Sizemore, *The Amazing Marriage of Marie Eustis and Josef Hofmann* (Columbia: University of South Carolina Press, 1965), is silent on Hofmann's White House appearance.

13. "Society," *Washington Post,* 16 April 1911; *Taft and Roosevelt* 2:667–668. Butt misdates the event to 30 May 1905 (p. 264); *The Cambrian* 26 (1906): 359. The programs in the Taft Papers do not include a listing of the selections that Gunter performed.

14. "Alice Sovereign's Recital," *New York Times,* 15 November 1917.

15. "Opera House Astir over an Alda Talk," *New York Times,* 18 December 1908. Alda's memoir, *Men, Women and Tenors* (Boston: Houghton Mifflin, 1937), does not mention either of her appearances at the Taft White House.

16. Musicale Program, 21 April 1911, Taft Papers.

17. For Rogovoy, see "Music and Musicians," *Washington Post*, 30 April 1911, and "Musician Loses Czar's Medal," *New York Times*, 7 March 1918; "Mrs. Taft's Garden Musicale," *New York Times*, 13 May 1911.

18. "Sings at White House," *Washington Post*, 16 November 1911.

19. Augusta Gregory, *A Chapter of Autobiography* (New York: G. P. Putnam's Sons, 1914), 196. Mary Lou Kohfeldt, *Lady Gregory: The Woman behind the Irish Renaissance* (New York: Atheneum, 1985), 229. Gregory did not mention her encounter with Taft in *Seventy Years, Being the Autobiography of Lady Gregory*, ed. Colin Smythe (New York: Macmillan, 1974).

20. "Our Washington Letter," *Town and Country*, 25 November 1911, 32.

21. "Sings for the President," *New York Times*, 17 January 1912; "Hotel Men Profit by a German Tour," *New York Times*, 10 May 1914; Helen Taft to Robert A. Taft, 21 January 1912, Robert A. Taft Papers.

22. Dall Wilson, *Alice Nielsen and the Gayety of Nations* (New York: published by author, 2008), 617.

23. Alda, *Men, Women and Tenors*, 98.

24. Andres de Segurola, *Through My Monocle* (Steubenville, Ohio: Crestville Publishing, 1990), 351–352.

25. Ibid., 352–353; "Mr. and Mrs. Taft Hosts at White House Dinner," *Washington Post*, 2 March 1912; "Music and Musicians," *Washington Post*, 3 March 1912, gives the program for the evening. "Mrs. Taft Heads Throng of Society at Concert," *Washington Post*, 25 January 1911, and "Debut of Philharmonic," *Washington Post*, 25 January 1911, describe Gadski's earlier singing in Washington.

26. Helen Taft to Will Taft, 31 October 1906, Taft Papers; "Music and Musicians," *Washington Post*, 17 March 1912.

27. "Arthur Shattuck Plays," *New York Times*, 19 January 1921; "Arthur Shattuck, Pianist, 70, Is Dead," *New York Times*, 17 October 1951. Helen Taft to Robert A. Taft, 17 March 1912, Robert A. Taft Papers, mentions Johanna Gadski's appearance but confuses Arthur Friedheim and Arthur Shattuck.

28. Wilfred Laurier to Ellen Ballon, 5 August 1912, copy in author's files of the original that was sold on eBay during the late spring of 2009. Will Taft and Laurier had negotiated a Canadian–American trade agreement in 1911 that the United States Congress approved. Canadian voters turned it down in September 1911 and turned Laurier out of office. The former prime minister still had friendly feelings for his trading partner.

29. Eric McLean, "Ellen Ballon," *Canadian Encyclopedia*, http://www.the canadianencyclopedia.com/. "Music Here and There," *New York Times*, 18 February 1912.

30. "Miss Anna Case's Recital," *New York Times,* 12 October 1916; Philip Furia, *Irving Berlin: A Life in Song* (New York: Schirmer Books, 1998), 139–140; Richard Guy Wilson, *Harbor Hill: Portrait of a House* (New York: W. W. Norton, 2008), 153–154.

31. Susan Heller Anderson and Maurice Carroll, "New York Day by Day," *New York Times,* 11 October 1984.

32. "Mr. Zimbalist's Recital," *New York Times,* 11 November 1911; Roy Malan, *Efrem Zimbalist: A Life* (Portland, Ore.: Amadeus Press, 2004), 118–119, mentions Zimbalist's recordings but not his White House appearance. Helen Taft to Robert A. Taft, 17 March 1912, Robert A. Taft Papers. There is an indication that the Tafts later got to know the Zimbalists. See Alma Gluck Zimbalist to William Howard Taft, 23 December 1916, Taft Papers.

33. "Atkinson–Burmeister," *Charlotte Daily Observer,* 29 June 1899; "Frau Burmeister Is Coming," *Columbia (S.C.) State,* 13 October 1907; "Social Affairs at the Capital," *Columbia (S.C.) State,* 10 March 1912; "Atkinson–Chamberlayne Wedding," *New York Times,* 3 October 1915.

34. "Louise Alice Williams in Spirituals," *New York Times,* 13 May 1927 (quotation); "Miss Williams's Lenten Recital," *New York Times,* 14 March 1915; "Entertains Fort Hamilton Soldiers," *New York Times,* 12 July 1917; "To Sing Southern Songs," *New York Times,* 23 October 1935.

35. Charles D. Hilles to Ralph M. Easley, 19 April 1912, 20 April 1912, Taft Papers; "Miss Easley Sings at Musicale," *New York Times,* 30 April 1912; "Donna Easley Appears," *New York Times,* 10 December 1912. "Donna Easley," Vertical File Biographies," Kansas Historical Society, http://www.kshs.org./genealogists/individuals/vertical./bios/easleydonna.htm.

36. "Mme. Julia Culp Appears," *New York Times,* 11 January 1913; "Mme. Culp in Recital," *Washington Post,* 5 February 1913; "Society Flocks to Recital by European Singer," *Washington Post,* 5 February 1913. Malan, *Efrem Zimbalist,* 79.

37. Helen Taft to Robert A. Taft, 26 January 1913, Robert A. Taft Papers. Henry L. Minton, *Departing from Deviance: A History of Homosexual Rights and Emancipatory Science in America* (Chicago: University of Chicago Press, 2002), 124, mentions Wyman as having an affair with Henry Painter.

38. "Loraine Wyman: Old French and English Songs in Costume," promotional brochure, circa 1914, found on "Traveling Culture: Circuit Chautauqua in the Twentieth Century," University of Iowa Libraries; Loraine Wyman, *Lonesome Tunes: Folk Songs from the Kentucky Mountains* (New York: H. W. Gray, 1916); Loraine Wyman, *Twenty Kentucky Mountain Songs* (Boston: O. Ditson Co., 1920); there is a sketch of Wyman in Ralph Lee Smith and Madeline Mc-

Neil, *Folks Songs of Old Kentucky: Two Song Catchers in the Kentucky Mountains* (Pacific, Mo.: Mel Bay Publishers, 2004), 18–30.

39. On Breitner, see "Notes of Musical Doings," *New York Times,* 9 February 1902, and "The News of Newport," *New York Times,* 30 August 1902.

40. "Paul Reimers's Recital," *New York Times,* 11 February 1913; "Paul H. Reimers, 65, of Julliard School," *New York Times,* 15 April 1942.

41. Helen Taft to Robert A. Taft, 26 January 1913, Robert A. Taft Papers.

42. Edmund Dwight to Charles D. Hilles, 15 January 1913, Series 6, Case File 4322, "Bowman," William Howard Taft Papers.

43. Hilles to Helen Herron Taft, 16 January 1913, Bowman File, Taft Papers.

44. "Charles Spross Dead," *New York Times,* 25 December 1961; Dwight to Hilles, 15 January 1913, Hilles to Helen Taft, 16 January 1913, Katherine Letterman to Hilles, 21 January 1913, Bowman File, and Musicale Program, Reel 610, all in Taft Papers.

45. "Mr. and Mrs. Taft Hosts at Dinner and Musicale," *Washington Post,* 8 February 1913; "Recital by Schelling," *Washington Post,* 13 February 1913.

46. Walter Slezak, *What Time's the Next Swan?* (Garden City, N.Y.: Doubleday & Co., 1962), 210; Martin Mayer, *The Met: One Hundred Years of Grand Opera* (New York: Simon & Schuster, 1983), 146.

47. Helen Taft to Robert A. Taft, 9 February 1913, Robert A. Taft Papers, Box 2, Folder 2.

48. "Otto Goritz's Home Looted by Thieves," *New York Times,* 1 September 1919; "Mr. and Mrs. Taft Host Dinner and Musicale," *Washington Post,* 22 February 1913.

49. "Otto Goritz, Honor Guest," *New York Times,* 10 May 1910; "Paul A. Kefer," *New York Times,* 23 February 1941; Nancy Toff, *Monarch of the Flute: The Life of Georges Barrere* (New York: Oxford University Press, 2005), 127–128.

50. Mary Lawton, *Schumann-Heink, the Last of the Titans* (New York: Macmillan, 1928), 284. See also "Madame Ernestine Schumann-Heink: World Famous Contralto," promotional brochure, Redpath Musical Bureau Collection, University of Iowa, Iowa City.

51. Randolph, *Presidents and First Ladies,* 219; Mayer, *The Met,* 78.

52. Helen Taft to Robert A. Taft, 4 March 1913, Robert A. Taft Papers, Box 2, Folder 3.

CHAPTER 6: "I DON'T SEE ANY CHANCE
FOR THE ELECTION"

1. Constance Carruthers, "She May Give Up School for the Social Whirl," Boise, *Idaho Daily Statesman,* 3 July 1910; "Miss Taft Will Help Receive at the White House," *Columbus (Ga.) Daily Enquirer,* 21 September 1910.

2. Lewis L. Gould, *Reform and Regulation: American Politics from Roosevelt to Wilson* (Prospect Heights, Ill.: Waveland Press, 1996), 127.

3. *Taft and Roosevelt: The Intimate Letters of Archie Butt, Military Aide,* 2 vols. (Garden City, N.Y.: Doubleday, Doran & Co., 1930), 1:461–462.

4. Ibid., 462.

5. Ibid., 493.

6. Taft to Helen Taft, 24 September 1910, William Howard Taft Papers, Manuscript Division, Library of Congress.

7. "Mrs. Taft's Car Hits Boy," *Washington Post,* 12 October 1910.

8. Taft to Mabel Boardman, 5 November 1910, Mabel Boardman Papers, Manuscript Division, Library of Congress.

9. "Mrs. Taft Hears Returns," *Washington Post,* 9 November 1910.

10. Sylvia Jukes Morris, *Edith Kermit Roosevelt: Portrait of a First Lady* (New York: Coward, McCann & Geoghegan, 1980), 337.

11. Ibid., Taft to Edith Roosevelt, 31 December 1910, 337–338.

12. *Taft and Roosevelt,* 2:370–371. Roosevelt to Taft, 7 January 1911, in *The Letters of Theodore Roosevelt,* ed. Elting E. Morison et al., 8 vols. (Cambridge, Mass.: Harvard University Press, 1951–1954), 7:204.

13. Helen Taft to Robert A. Taft, 6 November 1910, Robert A. Taft Papers, Manuscript Division, Library of Congress; Taft to Mrs. Aaron F. Perry, 3 November 1910, Taft Papers. On her expectations to be on the Panama trip, see Helen Taft to Lilian Grosvenor, 29 October 1910, Grosvenor Family Papers, Manuscript Division, Library of Congress.

14. Henry Adams to Elizabeth Cameron, 30 January 1911, *The Letters of Henry Adams,* ed. J. C. Levenson et al., 6 vols. (Cambridge, Mass.: Belknap Press of Harvard University Press, 1988), 6:409.

15. "Helen Taft Manning, Ex-Dean of Bryn Mawr," *New York Times,* 23 February 1987.

16. There was some press coverage of Helen Taft at Bryn Mawr. When she played the role of Theseus in a production of *A Midsummer's Night's Dream,* the *New-York Tribune* wrote about the "May Revel at Bryn Mawr," 8 May 1910.

17. "Helen Pink the Color Now," *Kansas City Star,* 1 February 1911; "Miss Taft's Characteristics," *Charlotte Observer,* 20 April 1911. Waldon Fawcett, "Miss Helen Taft," *Harper's Bazaar,* February 1911, 68.

18. "President Trips Light Fantastic," *Philadelphia Inquirer,* 2 February 1911. *Taft and Roosevelt,* 2:585.

19. "Mrs. Taft Heard Trusts Plead," *Kansas City Star,* 19 January 1911.

20. *Taft and Roosevelt*, 2:595. "Mr. and Mrs. Taft Hosts to Mr. and Miss Cannon," *Washington Post*, 15 February 1911.

21. *Taft and Roosevelt*, 2:595.

22. *Taft and Roosevelt*, 2:613.

23. "A Lesson in Politeness," *Washington Post*, 28 May 1911.

24. "Mrs. Taft's Epigram," *Washington Post*, 10 September 1911.

25. *Taft and Roosevelt*, 2:638.

26. "Women Delegates Arrive," *Washington Post*, 5 May 1911; "Urge Closer Union," *Washington Post*, May 1911; *Taft and Roosevelt*, 2:642.

27. *Taft and Roosevelt*, 2:651.

28. "Mrs. Taft Improved," *Washington Post*, 15 May 1911; "Mrs. Taft to Return," *Washington Post*, 16 May 1911. *Taft and Roosevelt*, 2:651–652. Taft to Charles Warren Fairbanks, 15 May 1911, Taft Papers.

29. Henry L. Stimson, Recollections, "First Meeting with the President," May–June 1911, Henry L. Stimson Papers, Sterling Memorial Library, Yale University, New Haven, Conn.

30. Taft to Helen Taft, 11 May 1911, 17 May 1911, Taft Papers.

31. Taft to Mabel Boardman, 25 May 1911, Mabel Boardman Papers; Taft to Horace Taft, 25 May 1911, Taft Papers; "Mrs. Taft Will Rest," *New York Times*, 22 May 1911.

32. Mabel Boardman to F. B. Tracy, 18 September 1911, copy in James T. Williams Jr. Papers, Duke University Library, Durham, N.C.

33. Helen Herron Taft, *Recollections of Full Years* (New York: Dodd, Mead, & Co., 1914), 391 (both quotations).

34. "Tafts to Ask 4,000 to Silver Wedding," *New York Times*, 13 June 1911. Taft to Robert A. Taft, 7 June 1911, Taft Papers.

35. "How Taft Won Bride," *Washington Post*, 19 June 1911.

36. Taft, *Recollections*, 391.

37. *Taft and Roosevelt*, 2:679; *Washington Wife: Journal of Ellen Maury Slayden from 1897 to 1919*, ed. Walter Prescott Webb and Terrell Webb (New York: Harper & Row, 1963), 156. For examples of responses to the gifts they received, see Taft to Helen Taft, 26 July 1911, Taft Papers.

38. "Tafts Welcome 5,000 on White House Lawn," *Washington Post*, 20 June 1911.

39. Ibid.; "Washington Talks of Silver Wedding," *Philadelphia Inquirer*, 25 June 1911.

40. Taft to Charles Phelps Taft, 20 June 1911, Taft Papers.

41. Taft, *Recollections*, 392.

42. Taft to Helen Taft, 3 August 1911, Taft Papers. Taft to Mabel Boardman, 28 July 1911, Mabel Boardman Papers.

43. Taft to Charles P. Taft, 8 August 1911, Taft Papers.

44. "Mrs. Taft Assists Miss Boardman at Red Cross Benefit," *New York Times,* 20 August 1911.

45. *Taft and Roosevelt,* 2:749.

46. Helen Herron Taft to Helen Taft, 1 October 1911, Taft Papers.

47. Helen Taft to Delia Torrey, 10 October 1911, Taft Papers.

48. Taft to Helen Taft, 14 October 1911, Taft Papers. For example of his telegrams, see Taft to Helen Taft, 16 September 1911, 30 September 1911, Taft Papers.

49. Taft to Charles D. Norton, 26 December 1911, Taft Papers.

50. "Silent Partners of Presidential Candidates," *Washington Post,* 24 December 1911.

51. Mrs. Robert M. La Follette, "Thought for Today: The President and Mrs. Taft," *Washington Post,* 16 January 1912.

52. *Taft and Roosevelt,* 2:768.

CHAPTER 7: GOOD FRIENDS AND GOLDEN OPINIONS

1. Taft to Otto Bannard, 22 January 1912, William Howard Taft Papers, Manuscript Division, Library of Congress.

2. *Taft and Roosevelt: The Intimate Letters of Archie Butt, Military Aide,* 2 vols. (Garden City, N.Y.: Doubleday, Doran & Co., 1930), 2:850.

3. Entry for 16 January 1910, James R. Garfield Diary, Box 9, James R. Garfield Papers, Manuscript Division, Library of Congress.

4. Helen Herron Taft, *Recollections of Full Years* (New York: Dodd, Mead, & Co., 1914), 384.

5. Theodore Roosevelt to Cecil Spring Rice, 22 August 1911, in *The Letters of Theodore Roosevelt,* ed. Elting E. Morison et al., 8 vols. (Cambridge: Harvard University Press, 1951–1954), 7:333.

6. "Mrs. Taft's List of Greatest Women," *New York Times,* 14 December 1911.

7. "Notable Women Donate Gowns to Museum," *Philadelphia Inquirer,* 11 March 1912.

8. Helen Taft to Robert A. Taft, 5 May 1912, Robert A. Taft Papers, Manuscript Division, Library of Congress, Box 2, Folder 2. Helen Taft to Mrs. William Ruffin Cox, 13 December 1911, reproduced on eBay, Catherine Barnes Autographs, 2003–2008.

9. "Tots in Jail Cells," *Washington Post,* March 1912; "Mrs. Taft Listens to Strike Charges," *New York Times,* 6 March 1912.

10. "Aided by Mrs. Taft," *Washington Post,* 17 March 1912.

11. "Mrs. Taft's Aid Ill," *Washington Post,* 13 March 1912; "Miss Harlan Mrs. Taft's Aid," *Washington Post,* 15 March 1912.

12. Yei Theodora Ozaki to Helen Taft, 25 February 1911, Taft Papers. Ann Mc-Clellan, *The Cherry Blossom Festival: Sakura Celebration* (Boston, Mass.: Bunker Hill Publishing, 2005), 34–37.

13. "Mrs. Taft Plants a Tree," *Washington Post,* 28 March 1912.

14. William Howard Taft to Helen Taft Manning, 13 April 1924, Taft Papers. Eleanor Roosevelt paid tribute to Helen Taft's campaign for the cherry trees in "Cherry Blossom Time in Washington," *Reader's Digest* 32 (April 1938): 55–56.

15. "Mrs. Taft Heads the List for Men Lost on Titanic," *Los Angeles Times,* 29 April 1912.

16. "President and First Lady Hear Men of Marine Disaster Lauded," *Washington Post,* 27 May 1931.

17. Helen Taft to Will Taft, 23 April 1912, Taft Papers.

18. Will Taft to Delia Torrey, 12 May 1912, Taft Papers; Helen Taft to Robert A. Taft, 26 May 1912, Robert A. Taft Papers, Box 2, Folder 2.

19. "Tafts Wed 26 Years," *Washington Post,* 20 June 1912.

20. Taft, *Recollections,* 392.

21. *New York Times,* 26 July 1912.

22. Helen Taft to Will Taft, 2 November 1912, Taft Papers. The Republicans replaced Sherman on the ticket with Nicholas Murray Butler, the president of Columbia University.

23. Helen Taft to Robert A. Taft, 26 November 1912, Robert A. Taft Papers, Box 2, Folder 2.

24. "Social Upheaval Anticipated in Washington with the New Administration," *Washington Post,* 22 December 1912, reprinted the article from the *New York Herald*; "Taft Inspects Gatun Dam," *Washington Post,* 25 December 1912.

25. Woodrow Wilson to William Howard Taft, 2 January 1913, William Howard Taft to Ellen Axson Wilson, 3 January 1913, William Howard Taft to Woodrow Wilson, 6 January 1913, Wilson to William Howard Taft, 8 January 1913, Ellen Axson Wilson to William Howard Taft, 10 January 1913, Ellen Axson Wilson to William Howard Taft, 23 January 1913, in *The Papers of Woodrow Wilson, Volume 27—1913,* ed. Arthur S. Link et al. (Princeton, N.J.: Princeton University Press, 1978), 5, 12–13, 16–19, 28–29, 69, cover this series of discussions.

26. Ellen Axson Wilson to Helen Taft, 26 March 1913, Taft Papers. Ellen Wilson would die the following year of kidney disease.

27. "Social Season at Capital Ends: Mrs. Taft as an Entertainer Will Probably Long Be Missed," *Philadelphia Inquirer,* 9 February 1913.

28. "Mrs. Taft Dance 1-Step," *Kansas City Star,* 5 February 1913. *In the World: The Diaries of Reed Smoot,* ed. Harvard Heath, 12 December 1912 (Salt Lake City: Signature Books, 1997).

29. "Original Monologues by Miss Ruth Draper," Taft Papers; *The Letters of Ruth Draper: A Self-Portrait of a Great Actress,* ed. Neilla Warren (New York: Charles Scribner's Sons, 1979), 349–358; Henry Adams to Elizabeth Cameron, 30 January 1911, *The Letters of Henry Adams, Volume 6: 1906–1918,* ed. J. C. Levenson et al., 6 vols. (Cambridge: Belknap Press of Harvard University Press, 1988), 409.

30. "Three First Ladies Will Grace the White House," *Washington Post,* 10 January 1913. Virginia T. Peacock, "Here with Fiancé," *Washington Post,* 9 January 1913.

31. Taft to Philander Knox, 22 February 1913, Knox to Taft, 24 February 1913, Taft Papers; "Place for Mrs. Taft's Secretary," *New York Times,* 12 July 1913; "Record Contingent on Cuxhaven Train," *New York Times,* 5 October 1913, mentions Letterman leaving the club. Her passport application, available on Ancestry.com, indicates that she returned to the United States in 1921. Letterman to Will Taft, 14 July 1921, Taft Papers.

32. Henry Junge to Joseph P. Tumulty, 4 January 1913, Woodrow Wilson Papers, Manuscript Division, Library of Congress.

33. "Give Necklace to Mrs. Taft," *New York Times,* 22 February 1913; Helen Taft to Robert A. Taft, 4 March 1913, Robert A. Taft Papers, Box 2, Folder 3.

34. Memoir of Irwin H. Hoover, 4 March 1913, Irwin H. Hoover Papers, Manuscript Division, Library of Congress, available through the "American Memory" Web site, Library of Congress, in "I Do Solemnly Swear . . .: Presidential Inaugurations." Irwin Hood (Ike) Hoover, *Forty-Two Years in the White House* (Boston: Houghton Mifflin, 1934), 49–59, bases his chapter on this memoir, albeit with a tilt against Helen Taft.

35. Memoir of Irwin H. Hoover.

36. "Crowds Cheer Taft as He Leaves City," *New York Times,* 5 March 1913.

37. Will Taft to Mabel Boardman, 13 April 1913, Mabel Boardman Papers. Taft to Frederick Forchheimer, 2 April 1913, Taft Papers.

38. Taft to Mrs. Eugene Stafford, 9 July 1914, Taft Papers. "Mrs. Taft among the Antis," *New York Times,* 11 April 1914; "Miss Taft is a Suffragist," *New York Times,* 18 April 1914; "Mrs. Taft, on First Visit since Leaving White House, Happy to Be in National Capital Again," *Washington Post,* 17 October 1914.

39. Eleanor Franklin Egan to William Howard Taft, 24 May 1913, Taft Papers.

40. William Howard Taft to Eleanor Egan, 9 April 1913, 13 April 1913, 24 May 1913, Egan to Taft, 11 May 1913, 20 May 1913, 24 May 1913, all in Taft Papers.

41. See, for example, Helen Taft, "Parties We Gave at the White House," *Delineator* 85 (October 1914): 18–19, 47, and Taft, *Recollections,* 365–381.

42. Edward H. Dodd to Eleanor Egan, 9 April 1914, Taft Papers.

43. Helen Taft to "Dear Papa," circa 12 April 1914, Taft Papers; "Memorandum of Agreement," 20 April 1914, Dodd, Mead, & Co., MSS, Manuscripts Department, Lilly Library, Indiana University, Bloomington.

44. Dodd, Mead, & Co. to Helen Taft, 6 November 1914, Royalty report, 1 February 1916, Royalty report, 1 September 1920, Taft Papers; "Mrs. Taft's New Book Deals with Big Events," *New York Times,* 8 November 1914; *Current Opinion* 57 (December 1914), IV; "Outlook," 2 June 1915, 284. For advertising, see *Dial* 57 (1 November 1914): 318; *Los Angeles Times,* 6 December 1914, AB5.

45. Henry Steel Commager, "The Memoirs of Mrs Wilson," *New York Times,* 12 March 1939, 93.

46. Helen Taft to Delia Torrey, 7 January 1914, Taft Papers. The Library of Congress dates the letter to 1913, but it is on the stationery for 387 Prospect Street in New Haven, where the Tafts lived during the Yale years.

47. William Howard Taft to Helen Taft Manning, undated but 1928, Taft Papers. The letter refers to the campaign of Herbert Hoover for president.

48. Taft to Horace Taft, 3 October 1929, Taft Papers.

49. Helen Manning Hunter related this story to me in February 2009.

50. Helen Taft to Charles Phelps Taft, February 1924, Box 22, Charles P. Taft Papers, Manuscript Division, Library of Congress; Helen Manning Hunter interview (second quotation).

51. "Granting a Franking Privilege to Helen H. Taft," U.S. House of Representatives, 71 Cong., 2nd Sess., No. 1037; "Vote Franking Right for Mrs. Taft," *New York Times,* 7 June 1930.

52. "Presidents' Widows," *New York Times,* 15 January 1933.

53. "Mrs. W. H. Taft Dies, President's Widow," *New York Times,* 23 May 1943; "$143,000 Estate Left by Mrs. Taft to Three Children," *Washington Post,* 9 June 1943.

BIBLIOGRAPHIC ESSAY

The essential source for a study of Helen Taft as first lady are the William Howard Taft Papers at the Library of Congress (LC). However, this large, well-indexed collection also presents serious gaps for scholarly work on her White House years. On the positive side, the Taft Papers contain the correspondence that Helen Taft exchanged with her husband when they were separated, as often happened from 1909 to 1913. Correspondence with Taft family members is also useful, especially for tracing the progress of Mrs. Taft's recovery from the stroke she experienced in May 1909. The various case files for the presidential years document the ways in which the public reached out to the first lady.

Notably absent, however, from the Taft Papers are documents detailing her musical interests. The file on the singer Beatrice Bowman (Series 6, Case File 4322) is the only exception to the relative dearth of letters and memoranda about the recruitment of artists to perform at the White House. There are, for example, only two brief telegrams from Mrs. Taft to Joseph Burr Tiffany of the Steinway Piano Company about musicians. At one time, there likely were many more documents of this kind. The Taft Papers do contain a complete collection of the programs of the musicales and other related events that reflected Mrs. Taft's musical interests. These programs are available on Reels 609 and 610 of the Taft Papers. The bulk of the Taft Papers were at the Library of Congress in 1933, and Helen Taft died a decade later. What happened to any papers she might have retained for herself is not clear.

Mrs. Taft corresponded with her oldest son, Robert, on a regular basis, and her letters to him in the Robert A. Taft Papers (LC) provide the richest source for her comments about the various musicians who played for her and her guests. The Helen Taft Manning Papers (LC) are useful for her life after the White House. The Charles Phelps Taft Papers (LC) are very enlightening for her life during the 1920s. The Grosvenor Family Papers (LC) have a few important letters about her musicians and her work with Tiffany written to members of the Grosvenor family. The Lucien Wulsin Papers at the Cincinnati Historical Society document her acquisition of the Baldwin piano for the White House and her musical interests.

Many manuscript collections provide the perspectives of individuals close to the Tafts and also of their political opponents. At the Library of Congress, the Mabel Boardman Papers, the James R. Garfield Papers, the George von Lengerke Meyer Diaries, the Theodore Roosevelt Papers, and the Henry White Papers were very helpful. I found pertinent information in the Henry Cabot Lodge Papers at the Massachusetts Historical Society. The James Bryce Embassy Papers at the Bodleian Library at Oxford University proved important in understanding the Henry White controversy and Mrs. Taft's role.

In tracking down the musicians who appeared at the White House, the results were generally not encouraging. The Fannie Bloomfield-Zeisler Papers at the American Jewish Archives yielded three useful letters from Joseph Tiffany about musicales during the Roosevelt White House. The Charles Coburn Papers at the Hargrett Library, University of Georgia, contained some programs and photographs from the staging of Shakespeare on the White House grounds in 1910 that were invaluable for understanding that episode. The Mary Fanton Roberts Papers, Smithsonian Institution, which are available online, have a significant Charles Coburn letter with his reaction to his White House appearance. The Stan Hywet Hall & Gardens in Akron, Ohio, generously shared a copy of a letter about the appearance of Evan Williams and Mrs F. A. Seiberling at the White House in December 1910.

The record for other musicians and performers is more discouraging. The Steinway Archives at LaGuardia Community College in New York had virtually nothing on Joseph Tiffany. The Julliard Library has some pertinent programs and clippings about the appearance of the Kneisel Quartet at the White House. The Ernestine Schumann-Heink papers at the Honnold-Mudd Libraries do not contain anything about her White House performance. The same is true for the Josef Hofmann Papers at the International Piano Archives at the University of Maryland. The Loraine Wyman Collection at Brown University does not have anything on Wyman's engagement at the White House in early 1913. Several interesting letters from Mrs. Taft did appear on eBay while I was doing research for this book. A letter about pianist Ellen Ballon's White House engagement also came up on eBay. The Redpath Musical Bureau Collection at the University of Iowa showed how artists such as Loraine Wyman and Ernestine Schumann-Heink mentioned their White House engagements in their professional advertising.

Newspapers were invaluable for tracing Mrs. Taft's activities. In addition to the *New York Times* and the *Washington Post,* I found the indexed copies of the *New-York Tribune,* the *Washington Herald,* and the *Washington Times* that are now available through the "Chronicling America" Web site through 1910 of even greater help for Mrs. Taft's musicales. The online project of "America's Historical Newspapers" enabled me to survey a wide array of regional reporting about Mrs. Taft as first lady. Important newspaper articles about Mrs. Taft include "White House Musicales Noteworthy," *Washington Post*, 5 November 1911, "Music Room Plays Large Part in White House Life," *New York Times*, 8 May 1910, "The Tafts to Celebrate Their Silver Wedding June 19," *New York Times*, 11 June 1911, and "Mrs. Taft's New Book Deals with Big Events," *New York Times*, 8 November 1914.

Elting E. Morison et al., eds., *The Letters of Theodore Roosevelt*, 8 vols. (Cambridge: Harvard University Press, 1951–1954), document the strained relations between President Roosevelt and Helen Taft. Arthur S. Link et al., eds., *The Papers of Woodrow Wilson, Volume 27—1913* (Princeton: Princeton University Press, 1978), has important letters about the transition from the Tafts to the Wilsons. J. C. Levenson et al., eds., *The Letters of Henry Adams, Volume 6: 1906–1918* (Cambridge: Belknap Press of Harvard University Press, 1988), have some characteristically acidic and insightful comments from Adams about Helen Taft and her situation. Clarence E. Wunderlin Jr. et al., eds., *The Papers of Robert A. Taft, Volume 1, 1889–1939* (Kent, Ohio: Kent State University Press, 1997), print several letters from Mrs. Taft's oldest son during the post–White House years.

The most important book about Helen Taft is her own memoir, *Recollections of Full Years* (New York: Dodd, Mead, & Co., 1914), written by her daughter, Helen, and the journalist Eleanor Egan. Although there is much that is interesting and valuable in the book, the narrative says little about her musicales or the musicians that she brought to the White House. The book is essential but often frustrating because of what the two ghostwriters for the first lady chose to include or not include. Excerpts from the book appeared in the women's fashion magazine *The Delineator* during 1914. Helen Taft, "Parties We Gave at the White House," *Delineator* 85 (October 1914): 18–19, 47.

Carl Sferrazza Anthony, *Nellie Taft: The Unconventional First Lady of the Ragtime Era* (New York: William Morrow, 2005) is the only biography of Mrs. Taft. Anthony's research is thorough and his comments about his subject often of value. He devoted only two pages to her musicales and thus missed the main area of her interest while she was in the White House. As I explain in the introduction, I also have reservations about his handling of politics, the evaluation of how Mrs. Taft dealt with her stroke, and the cursory discussion of how her memoirs were written. Because it is unlikely that there will be another biography of Helen Taft, the strengths and weaknesses of Anthony's book make it both important and a work to be read with care.

The biographies of William Howard Taft examine his courtship and marriage from varying perspectives. Henry F. Pringle, *The Life and Times of William Howard Taft*, 2 vols. (New York: Farrar & Rinehart, 1939), is good on the way these two people met and fell in love. After that, Helen Taft appears in greatest detail as her husband contemplates becoming a presidential candidate in 1905–1908. Pringle has little on Nellie Taft's years in the White House and her musical interests. Ishbel Ross, *An American Family: The Tafts, 1678 to 1964* (Cleveland, Ohio: World Publishing, 1964), is more sensitive to Helen Taft's personality and cultural interests, but a survey of the entire family could not get much beneath the surface of events. Judith Icke Anderson, *William Howard Taft: An Intimate History* (New York: W. W. Norton, 1981), devotes a chapter to Helen Taft's time in the White House, but she is limited on such matters as the occasion of the May 1909 stroke, the range of the first lady's musical endeavors, and the political setting in which the Tafts operated. Paolo Coletta, *The Presidency of William Howard Taft* (Lawrence: University Press of Kansas, 1973), allocated very little space to Helen Taft in the White House. Michael L. Bromley, *William Howard Taft and the First Motoring Presidency* (Jefferson, N.C.: McFarland & Co., 2003), has much interesting information about Helen Taft in the context of the author's overall interpretation about the impact of automobiles on the presidential couple.

Helen Taft's contributions have been assessed in a number of biographical chapters. That process began with Marianne Means, *The Woman in the White House: The Lives, Times and Influence of Twelve Notable First Ladies* (New York: Random House, 1963), 116–134. Stacy Cordery, "Helen Herron Nellie Taft," in *American First Ladies: Their Lives and Their Legacy*, edited by Lewis L. Gould (New York: Garland, 1996), 321–339, and Lewis L. Gould, *American First Ladies: Their Lives and Their Legacy*, 2nd ed. (New York: Routledge, 2001), 212–225, are well-informed and shrewd essays. Beth M. Waggenspack, "Helen Herron Taft: Opportunity and Ambition," in *Inventing a Voice: The Rhetoric of American First Ladies of the Twentieth Century*, edited by Molly Meijer Wertheimer (Lanham, Md.: Rowman & Littlefield, 2004), 59–78, synthesizes well the existing sources on Helen Taft as first lady.

Articles about Mrs. Taft that appeared during the White House years were Mabel Boardman, "The President and Mrs. Taft at Their Summer Home, Beverly Massachusetts," *Outlook*, 25 September 1909, 172–179; George Griswold Hill, "The Wife of the New President," *Ladies Home Journal*, March 1909, 6; Katherine Graves Busbey, "Mrs. Taft's Homemaking," *Good Housekeeping*, September 1911, 290–298; and "Interesting Women of the Capital: Mrs. William H. Taft," *Harper's Bazaar* 43 (May 1909): 484–485. Charles A. Selden, "Six White House Wives and Widows," *Ladies Home Journal*, June 1927, 18–19, 109–110, 112–113, 115, looks back at Edith Roosevelt and Helen Taft among others.

The most important firsthand account of the Tafts during the presidency is *Taft and Roosevelt: The Intimate Letters of Archie Butt, Military Aide,* 2 vols. (Garden City, N.Y.: Doubleday, Doran, 1930). Butt has a riveting description of Mrs. Taft's stroke and other key events in the lives of Helen and Will Taft. He recounts some of the important musical events involving Helen Taft and is silent on many others. Butt gives the best contemporary treatment of Mrs. Taft's personality. When he quotes her, however, there is little evidence of any effects from the impact of the stroke on her speech.

Other memoirs that dealt with Helen Taft in the White House include Isabel Anderson, *Presidents and Pies: Life in Washington, 1897–1919* (Boston: Houghton Mifflin, 1920), Marietta Minnigerode Andrews, *My Studio Window: Sketches of the Pageant of Washington Life* (New York: E. P. Dutton, 1928), David Fairchild, *The World Was My Garden: Travels of a Plant Explorer* (New York: Scribner's, 1944), Augusta Gregory, *A Chapter of Autobiography* (New York: G. P. Putnam's Sons, 1914), Elizabeth Jaffray, *Secrets of the White House* (New York: Cosmopolitan Book Corp., 1927), Mary Randolph, *Presidents and First Ladies* (New York: D. Appleton, 1936), Walter Prescott Webb and Terrell Webb, eds., *Washington Wife: Journal of Ellen Maury Slayden from 1897–1919* (New York: Harper & Row, 1963). Irwin Hood (Ike) Hoover, *Forty-Two Years in the White House* (Boston: Houghton Mifflin, 1934), is very negative about Mrs. Taft and should be judged from that perspective. H. H. Kohlsaat, *From McKinley to Harding: Personal Recollections of Our Presidents* (New York: Charles Scribner's Sons, 1923), has one famous anecdote about Helen Taft and her ambitions for her husband to be president that never occurred. Alice Roosevelt Longworth, *Crowded Hours* (New York: Scribner's, 1933), details the tensions between Mrs. Taft and the former president's daughter.

Helen Taft's role in the collapse of her husband's friendship with Theodore Roosevelt is discussed, usually in critical terms, in Mark Sullivan, *Our Times: The United States, 1900–1925, IV, The War Begins, 1909–1914* (New York: Scribner's, 1932), William Manners, *TR & Will: A Friendship that Split the Republican Party* (New York: Harcourt, Brace and World, 1969), Sylvia Jukes Morris, *Edith Kermit Roosevelt: Portrait of a First Lady* (New York: Coward, McCann & Geoghegan, 1980), and Patricia O' Toole, *When Trumpets Call: Theodore Roo-*

sevelt after the White House (New York: Simon & Schuster, 2005). Stacy A. Cordery, *Alice: Alice Roosevelt Longworth from White House Princess to Washington Power Broker* (New York: Viking, 2007), has much of interest on the tension between her subject and Helen Taft.

For general information on the musicians who played for Helen Taft, I found relevant material in Joseph Horowitz, *Classical Music in America: A History of Its Rise and Fall* (New York: W. W. Norton, 2005), Gdal Saleski, *Famous Musicians of a Wandering Race* (New York: Bloch, 1927), Martin Mayer, *The Met: One Hundred Years of Grand Opera* (New York: Simon & Schuster, 1983), and Nancy Toff, *Monarch of the Flute: The Life of Georges Barrere* (New York: Oxford University Press, 2005). Vincent Sheean, *Oscar Hammerstein I: The Life and Exploits of an Impresario* (New York: Simon & Schuster, 1956), provided valuable information on the rivalry between Hammerstein and the Metropolitan Opera as the Taft years began. Elise Kirk, *Music at the White House: A History of the American Spirit* (Urbana: University of Illinois Press, 1986), has a brief but well-researched and well-informed account of the musical contributions of Helen Taft. Constance McLaughlin Green, *Washington: Capital City, 1879–1950* (Princeton, N.J.: Princeton University Press, 1963), was helpful for background on Washington's cultural setting when the Tafts occupied the White House. Louis Russell Thomas, "A History of the Cincinnati Symphony Orchestra to 1931" (Ph.D diss., University of Cincinnati, 1972), is informative on Mrs. Taft's contributions to the creation of the orchestra. William Osborne, *Music in Ohio* (Kent, Ohio: Kent State University Press, 2004), mentions Helen Taft briefly.

Memoirs of the musicians themselves were of varying assistance. Frances Alda, *Men, Women and Tenors* (Boston: Houghton Mifflin, 1937), does not say anything about her White House appearances but is excellent for recreating the world in which musicians moved in this period. Mary Garden and Louis Biancolli, *Mary Garden's Story* (New York: Simon & Schuster, 1951), mentions her visit to the Taft White House. Lily McCormack, *I Hear You Calling Me* (Milwaukee: Bruce Publishing Co., 1949), describes her husband's encounter with the president in 1910. Mary Lawton, *Schumann-Heink, the Last of the Titans* (New York: Macmillan, 1928), has a good anecdote about her White House engagement. Dall Wilson, *Alice Nielsen and the Gayety of Nations* (New York: published by author, 2008), has a characteristic story of President Taft as a listener. Olga Samaroff Stokowski, *An American Musician's Story* (New York: W. W. Norton, 1935), discussed her playing for Taft and the press reaction to her appearance. Donna Staley Kline, *An American Virtuoso on the World Stage: Olga Samaroff Stokowski* (College Station: Texas A & M University Press, 1996), provides more information about the meeting of president and pianist. Luisa Tetrazzini, *My Life of Song* (London: Cassell and Co., 1921), was ghostwritten and stretches the truth in places, but the recollections of her 1910 performance for the Tafts in a Washington opera house track with contemporary press accounts. Charles Neilson Gattey, *Luisa Tetrazzini: The Florentine Nightingale* (Portland, Ore.: Amadeus Press, 1995), does not add anything to Tetrazzini's own account. Andres de Segurola, *Through My Monocle* (Steubenville, Ohio: Crestville Publishing, 1990), has a lively retelling of Segurola's singing for the Tafts in 1912. Arthur Friedheim, *Life and Liszt: The Recollections of a Concert Pianist* (New York: Taplinger, 1961), has some brief but useful comments on his 1911 appearance at the White House.

Joseph Burr Tiffany remained an elusive figure in Mrs. Taft's story. Joseph Burr Tiffany, "Artistic Piano Decoration—Old and New," *International Studio* 36 (November 1908): xxvi, George Willoughby, "Typical Americans: Joseph Burr Tiffany," *National Magazine*, July 1912, 367–370, and "Joseph Burr Tiffany," *New York Times*, 4 April 1917. Tiffany's connection with Steinway is not mentioned in Richard K. Lieberman, *Steinway & Sons* (New Haven, Conn.: Yale University Press, 1995), and is only alluded to in brief in Ronald V. Ratcliff, *Steinway* (Los Angeles: Perpetua Press, 2002).

Although it does not mention Helen Taft, I found useful the memoir of Efrem Zimbalist's pianist for the atmosphere of the time. See Samuel Chotzinoff, *Days at the Morn* (New York: Harper & Row, 1964). Amy Biancolli, *Fritz Kreisler: Love's Sorrow, Love's Joy* (Portland, Ore.: Amadeus Press, 1998), is excellent on the life of the charismatic violinist. Roy Malan, *Efrem Zimbalist: A Life* (Portland, Ore.: Amadeus Press, 2004), is also good on one of Kreisler's distinguished contemporaries. Walter Slezak, *What Time's the Next Swan?* (Garden City, N.Y.: Doubleday & Co., 1962), helped me understand the impact of his father on the opera world during the Taft years.

For her nonmusical contributions as William Howard Taft's wife and as first lady, see Ann McClellan, *The Cherry Blossom Festival: Sakura Celebration* (Boston: Bunker Hill Publishing, 2005), Christopher J. Cyphers, *The National Civic Federation and the Making of a New Liberalism, 1900–1915* (Westport, Conn.: Praeger, 2002), and Rene Escalante, *The Bearer of Pax Americana: The Philippine Career of William H. Taft, 1900–1903* (Quezon City: New Day Publishers, 2007).

INDEX